THE
REALITY
OF
ETHNOMETHODOLOGY

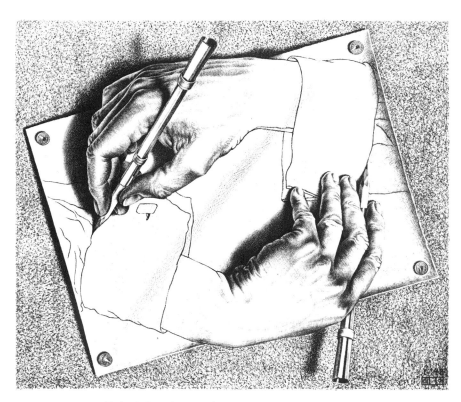

Escher's *Drawing Hands:* a visual display of reflexivity

THE
REALITY
OF
ETHNOMETHODOLOGY

HUGH MEHAN　　　　**HOUSTON WOOD**

A WILEY-INTERSCIENCE PUBLICATION

JOHN WILEY & SONS, New York • London • Sydney • Toronto

Library of Congress Cataloging in Publication Data:

Mehan, Hugh, 1941-
    The reality of ethnomethodology.

    "A Wiley-Interscience publication."
    Bibliography: p.
    Includes index.
    1. Sociology—Methodology. I. Wood, Houston,
1944-   joint author. II. Title.

HM24.M446   301'.01'8   75-1190
ISBN 0-471-59060-6

Printed in the United States of America

10 9 8 7 6 5 4 3 2 1

For
Aaron,
who first served us the sweet poison

Preface

The vision of ethnomethodology presented in this book is not universally shared by ethnomethodologists. These chapters should be read as a prospectus, not as an authoritative text.

The first person singular has been adopted throughout to emphasize that this book is the voice of a union and not of particular individuals. Although this book is the result of collaboration among particular persons at particular times, it now exists independent of them. Whoever enters the form of life this book embodies becomes the "I" who speaks here.

Ethnomethodology has many quarreling factions. I neither wish to quarrel nor create another faction. My vision of ethnomethodology sees diversity as a sign of strength.

Most of these factions are unconcerned with why a person should live ethnomethodology. But the terror of that question led to the vision of ethnomethodology displayed in this book.

To paraphrase the coda of a book far more important than this one, my words are a ladder. Those who climb the ladder must go on, leaving the scaffolding behind.

The following friends, colleagues, and strangers have assisted in the composition of this book: Egon Bittner, Cotton Broede, Lindsay Churchill, Aaron Cicourel, Sam Edward Combs, Robert Emerson, Harold Garfinkel, Erving Goffman, Alvin Gouldner, Bill Helbing, Dell Hymes, Sybillyn Jennings, Bennetta Jules-Rosette, Peter McHugh, Harvey Molotch, Melvin Pollner, Margaret Riel, Marshall Shumsky, Tom Wallace, D. Lawrence Wieder, Thomas P. Wilson, and Don H. Zimmerman.

The following scholars graciously allowed us access to unpublished works: Carlos Castaneda, Lindsay Churchill, Aaron Cicourel, Robert Emerson, Trent Eglin, Paul Filmer, Daniel C. Foss, Bennetta Jules-Rosette, Gail Jefferson, Ron Kaiman, Michael Phillipson, Stanley Rafael, Reyes Ramos, Howard B. Schwartz, Harvey Sacks, Emmanuel Schegloff, David Silverman, Tom Wallace, David Walsh, Susan Wedow, D. Lawrence Wieder, Thomas P. Wilson, and Don H. Zimmerman.

Anonymous referees of an earlier draft, Susan Osborn Montrose, and our editor Eric Valentine combined to convince us that we had not written English. We rewrote the manuscript on the basis of their complaints, and are grateful for their candor.

Susan Osborn Montrose typed and retyped early drafts and refused to be impressed with anything. Colleen Carpenter typed the final manuscript expertly. Carol Loomis provided us with a home and comforts. With love, she expressed a strong skepticism, continually inquiring when we were going to begin "some real work." Mel and Judy Pollmen and Christa Backson provided a home for the work as well. Compelling kept compelling. We rely on Harold Garfinkel's work more than references can reveal.

HUGH MEHAN
HOUSTON WOOD

LaJolla, California
Honokaa, Hawaii
February 1975

Acknowledgments

We are grateful to the following for permission to reproduce material: Collection Haags Gemeentemuseum, The Hague, for M. C. Escher's "Drawing Hands," which belongs to Escher Foundation—Haags Gemeentemuseum, The Hague. Carlos Castaneda for quotes from *A Separate Reality,* © 1971, Simon & Schuster. Clarendon Press for quotes from E. E. Evans-Pritchard's *Witchcraft, Oracles, and Magic Among the Azande,* 1937. By permission of the Clarendon Press, Oxford. Educational Testing Services for illustrations from the Cooperative Primary Reading Test (Form 12A). From *Cooperative Primary Tests.* Copyright © 1965 by Educational Testing Service. All rights reserved. The University of Chicago Press for quotes from Thomas S. Kuhn's *The Structure of Scientific Revolutions.* Copyright © 1970 by University of Chicago Press, Grove Press and the Harold Matson Company, Inc., for quotes from Tobias Schneebaum's *Keep the River on Your Right.* Reprinted by permission of Grove Press, Inc., and the Harold Matson Company, Inc., Copyright © 1969 by Tobias Schneebaum. Don H. Zimmerman and Thomas P. Wilson for quotes from "Prospects for Experimental Studies of Meaning Structures." Thomas P. Wilson for quotes from "The Regress Problem and the Problem of Evidence in Ethnomethodology." Don H. Zimmerman and D. Lawrence Wieder for quotes from "The Social Bases for Illegal Behavior in the Student Community." Prentice-Hall, for quotes from Harold Garfinkel's *Studies in Ethnomethodology,* © 1967, and Walter Buckley's *Sociology and Modern Systems Theory,* © 1967. By permission of Prentice-Hall, Inc., Englewood Cliffs, New Jersey. John Wiley & Sons, Inc., for quotes from Aaron V. Cicourel, *Theory and Method in a Study of Argentine Fertility,* 1973, Academic Press for quotes from Aaron V.

Cicourel et al., *Language Use and School Performance,* 1974. P. W. Anderson, for quotes from "More Is Different," *Science* **177**:393–396. Copyright 1972 by the American Association for the Advancement of Science. Dwarf Music, for lyrics by Bob Dylan, *Just Like a Woman,* Copyright © 1966, Dwarf Music. Used by permission of Dwarf Music. Peter McHugh, Stanley Raffel, Daniel C. Foss, and Alan F. Blum, and Routledge & Kegan Paul Ltd., for quotes from *On the Beginning of Social Inquiry,* 1974. Edicom N. V., for quotes from D. Lawrence Wieder's *Language and Social Reality,* © 1973, Mouton, The Hague. Harold Garfinkel, for quotes from "A Conception of, and Experiments with, 'Trust' as a Condition of Stable Concerted Actions" in *Motivation and Social Interaction,* edited by O. J. Harvey. Copyright © 1963, The Ronald Press Company, New York. R. C. Hill for quotes from R. C. Hill and K. S. Crittenden, *The Purdue Symposium on Ethnomethodology,* Monograph 1, Institute for the Study of Social Change, Purdue University.

H.M.
H.W.

Contents

THE
REALITY
OF
ETHNOMETHODOLOGY

PART ONE

A
DISPLAY
OF
ETHNOMETHODOLOGY

CHAPTER ONE

Ethnomethodology as Science

Ethnomethodology is sometimes identified with a methodological style, sometimes with a body of findings, sometimes with a theory, and sometimes with a world view. None of these alone or together captures my vision of ethnomethodology. For me, ethnomethodology is not *a* body of findings, nor *a* method, nor *a* theory, nor *a* world view. I view ethnomethodology as a form of life (cf. Wittgenstein, 1953; see Chapter 2 below). It is a way of working which creates findings, methods, theories; it enables its practitioners to enter other realities (e.g., Castaneda, 1968, 1971, 1972), there to experience the assembly of world views.

I cannot reproduce enthnomethodology here for your inspection, as no form of life can be captured by symbols. My strategy is to treat ethnomethodology in several ways. These treatments should not be viewed as pictures of ethnomethodology, but rather as fingers pointing toward ethnomethodology. My first treatment is a description of ethnomethodology as a science.

THE SCIENCE OF UNKNOWABLES

General systems theory differentiates among the sciences according to the complexity of the phenomenon that each studies. These varying complexities are called "systems." A system is composed of its parts. Systems theory relates sciences to one another by the way each treats the parts. In this way the sciences are understood to study different

Table 1   An Organization of the Sciences (after Anderson, 1972:393)

X	Y
solid state or many-body physics	elementary particles physics
chemistry	many-body physics
molecular biology	chemistry
cell biology	molecular biology
.	.
.	.
.	.
psychology	physiology
social sciences	psychology
(ethnomethodology)	social sciences

phenomena, even though they may sometimes examine comparable "facts."

Anderson (1972) summarizes this perspective by claiming each science seeks symmetries (see Table 1). A symmetry is an internal order of explanation. For example, the laws of elementary particles establish symmetries.

At the next level of organization, these symmetries become problematic. The task of the solid state physicist is to examine the "broken" symmetries of elementary particle physics and seek new symmetries. The symmetries of solid state physics will be "more complex" than symmetries of elementary particle physics. Similar relations obtain among the contiguous x-y links in the chain of the sciences.

This formulation leads to the conclusion that sociology's phenomenon, what Buckley (1968:383) calls the "socio-cultural system," is "a natural system that has evolved from and is continuous with the other levels of natural systems that are studied by the major sciences: a hierarchy of levels including the atom, molecules, cells, organs, organisms, and various stages of social organization of numbers of organisms."

For social scientists who employ the systems metaphor, the socio-cultural system is accepted as the "most complex" system science encounters. One possible description of ethnomethodology is as a scientific discipline that studies yet more complex systems. Ethnomethodology can be seen as the study of the broken symmetries that appear when sociology's symmetries are placed within a broader organizational arrangement.

Ethnomethodology is an attempt to display the reality of a level which exists beyond the sociological level.

Sociological theories assume there is a meaningful external world independent of social interaction. This assumption is an implicit resource when such concepts as "norms," "rules," "structures," and "exchange" are used. Ethnomethodology investigates the interactional work that sustains this assumption. It differs from sociology much as sociology differs from psychology.

This difference is often obscured, since ethnomethodology and sociology both speak of "social interaction." This common term has separate meanings within the two disciplines. Sociologists define "social interaction" as a process in which people communicate using symbols with common meanings (e.g., Weber, 1947; Mead, 1934). Or to use Buckley's (1967:40-41) terminology, sociology sees interaction as an "open, complex adaptive system of information exchanges with positive and negative feedback loops." Such definitions view meaning as a stable thing. They assume that interaction occurs within a world that is independent of interaction, and that interaction exchanges information (or symbols) *about* that external world. Ethnomethodologists treat sociology's implicit resource of an external world independent of interaction as a phenomenon (Garfinkel, 1964, in 1967a:75; cf. Sacks, 1963; Zimmerman and Pollner, 1970). For them, interaction is activity that accomplishes a sense of an external world. Meaning is viewed as ceaseless sensuous activity.

That I view ethnomethodology at one extreme of Anderson's hierarchy of the science does not mean that ethnomethodology is the "queen of the sciences," as Comte hailed sociology to be. Ethnomethodology studies the most complex system. Physics studies the most basic system. The other sciences treat phenomena with differing degrees of complexity. No single discipline has a total view of reality. In fact, I argue in the following chapters that, even joined together, the various sciences do not possess the true view. Scientists live but one of innumerable forms of life. They know no more, no less than is known within any other form (cf. Blum, 1970b).

Systems theory is only one of many ways to describe the sciences. I am pushing this metaphor to its limits here because sociologists have often feared that ethnomethodology was seeking to bury them (e.g., Coleman, 1968). The systems metaphor allows us to assuage this fear. Ethnomethodology is not seeking to replace sociology any more than sociology seeks to supplant psychology, or psychology to replace biology.

Sociology and ethnomethodology are separate enterprises, engaging different phenomena.

Understood as a scientific activity, ethnomethodology fits neatly within the general systems approach. However, because alone among the sciences it treats meaning itself as a phenomenon, ethnomethodology exhibits several novel characteristics as well. Boulding (1956; in Buckley, 1968) was among the first systems theorists to anticipate the appearance of a science that would examine phenomena beyond the sociocultural system. Boulding (1968:8) said such a discipline would employ the methods of the sciences but ask "questions that do not have answers." The phenomena of this discipline would thus be the "ultimates and absolutes and the inescapable unknowables" (Ibid.). Boulding's description presages the vision of ethnomethodology I offer in this book.

THE PLAN OF THE BOOK

In the following chapters I provide various other descriptions of ethnomethodology which have no apparent kinship with general systems theory. The variety of these descriptions displays my belief that ethnomethodology cannot be captured by description. It is a form of life to be lived.

Chapter 2 describes ethnomethodology as a reality that investigates the common features of all realities. I claim that ethnomethodology understands itself and other realities to be phenomena dependent upon ceaseless (1) reflexive use of (2) bodies of social knowledge in (3) interaction. As this reflexive interactional work assembles the reality, without it, the reality could not be sustained. Hence, each reality (4) is fragile. Insofar as people may experience more than one reality, realities are said to be (5) permeable.

In Part 2 (Chapters 3 through 8), I display some of the work ethnomethodologists have done. Whenever feasible, I have presented the researcher's own materials along with my interpretations. Readers are encouraged to create their own interpretations and to contrast these with mine and with those of the researchers discussed.

In Part 3 (Chapters 9 through 12), I offer my vision of ethnomethodology as a form of life. In Chapter 9, I sketch a general theory of social ordering. In Chapter 10, I discuss some philosophical grounds for ethnomethodology, detailing an ethnomethodological image of man.

In Chapter 11, I review the moral implications of entering the reality of ethnomethodology. In Chapter 12, I summarize my conception of science and offer a manual that enables readers to immediately begin pursuing ethnomethodological studies of their own.

CHAPTER TWO

Five
Features
of
Reality

REALITY AS A REFLEXIVE ACTIVITY

When the Azande of Africa are faced with important decisions, decisions about where to build their houses, or whom to marry, or whether the sick will live, for example, they consult an oracle. They prepare for these consultations by following a strictly prescribed ritual. First a substance is gathered from the bark of a certain type of tree. Then this substance is prepared in a special way during a seancelike ceremony. The Azande then pose the question in a form that permits a simple yes or no answer, and feeds the substance to a small chicken. The Azande decide beforehand whether the death of the chicken will signal an affirmative or negative response, and so they always receive an unequivocal answer to their questions.

For monumental decisions, the Azande add a second step. They feed the substance to a second chicken, asking the same question but reversing the import of the chicken's death. If in the first consultation sparing the chicken's life meant the oracle had said yes, in the second reading the oracle must now kill the chicken to once more reply in the affirmative and be consistent with its first response.

Our Western scientific knowledge tells us that the tree bark used by the Azande contains a poisonous substance that kills some chickens. The Azande have no knowledge of the tree's poisonous qualities. They do not believe the tree plays a part in the oracular ceremony. The ritual that comes between the gathering of the bark and the administration of the substance to a fowl transforms the tree into an oracle. The bark is but a vessel for the oracle to enter. As the ritual is completed the oracle takes possession of the substance. The fact that it was once a part of a tree is irrelevant. Chickens then live or die, not because of the properties of the tree, but because the oracle "hears like a person and settles cases like a king" (Evans-Pritchard, 1937:321).

The Westerner sees insuperable difficulties in maintaining such beliefs when the oracle contradicts itself. Knowing the oracle's bark is "really" poison, we wonder what happens when, for example, the first and second administration of the oracle produces first a positive and then a negative answer. Or, suppose someone else consults the oracle about the same question, and contradictory answers occur? What if the oracle is contradicted by later events? The house site approved by the oracle, for example, may promptly be flooded; or the wife the oracle selected may die or be a shrew. How is it possible for the Azande to continue to believe in oracles in the face of so many evident contradictions to his faith?

What I have called contradictions are not contradictions for the Azande. They are only contradictions because these events are being viewed from the reality of Western science. Westerners look at oracular practices to determine if in fact there is an oracle. The Azande *know* that an oracle exists. That is their beginning premise. All that subsequently happens they experience from that beginning assumption.

The Azande belief in oracles is much like the mathematician's belief in certain axioms. Gasking (1955:432) has described such unquestioned and unquestionable axioms as *incorrigible propositions:*

> An incorrigible proposition is one which you would never admit to be false whatever happens: it therefore does not tell you what happens. . . . The truth of an incorrigible proposition . . . is compatible with any and every conceivable state of affairs. (For example: whatever is your experience on counting, it is still true that $7 + 5 = 12$.)

The incorrigible faith in the oracle is "compatible with any and every conceivable state of affairs." It is not so much a faith about a fact in the world as a faith in the facticity of the world itself. It is the same as the faith many of us have that $7 + 5$ always equals 12. (cf Polanyi, 1958:190–193; 257–261).

Just as Gasking suggests we explain away empirical experiences that deny this mathematical truth, the Azande too have available to them what Evans-Pritchard (1937:330) calls "secondary elaborations of belief." They explain the failure of the oracle by retaining the unquestioned absolute reality of oracles. When events occurred that revealed the inadequacy of the mystical faith in oracles, Evans-Pritchard tried to make the Azande understand these failures as he did. They only laughed, or met his arguments:

> sometimes by point-blank assertions, sometimes by one of the evasive secondary elaborations of belief . . . sometimes by polite pity, but always by an entanglement of linguistic obstacles, for one cannot well express in its language objections not formulated by a culture (Ibid.:319).

Evans-Pritchard (Ibid.:319-320) goes on to write:

> Let the reader consider any argument that would utterly demolish all Zande claims for the power of the oracle. If it were translated into Zande modes of thought it would serve to support their entire structure of belief. For their mystical notions are eminently coherent, being interrelated by a network of logical ties, and are so ordered that they never too crudely contradict sensory experience, but, instead, experience seems to justify them. *The Zande is immersed in a sea of mystical notions, and if he speaks about his poison oracle he must speak in a mystical idiom.* (italics mine.)

Seeming contradictions are explained away by saying such things as a taboo must have been breached, or that sorcerers, witches, ghosts, or gods must have intervened. These "mystical" notions reaffirm the reality of a world in which oracles are a basic feature. Failures do not challenge the oracle. They are elaborated in such a way that they provide evidence for the constant success of oracles. Beginning with the incorrigible belief in oracles, all events *reflexively* become evidence for that belief.[1]

The mathematician, as Gasking suggests, uses a similar process:

> But it does lay it down, so to speak, that if on counting 7 + 5 you do get 11, you are to describe what has happened in some such way as this: Either "I have made a mistake in my counting" or "Someone has played a practical joke and abstracted one of the objects when I was not looking" or "Two of the objects have coalesced" or "One of the objects has disappeared," etc. (Gasking, 1955; quoted in Pollner, 1973:15–16).

Consider the analogous case of a Western scientist using chloroform to asphyxiate butterflies. The incorrigible idiom called chemistry tells the scientist, among other things, that substances have certain constant properties. Chloroform of a certain volume and mix is capable of killing butterflies. One evening the scientist administers the chloroform as usual, and is dismayed to see the animal continue to flutter about.

Here is a contradiction of the scientist's reality, just as oracle use sometimes produces contradictions. Like the Azande, scientists have many secondary elaborations of belief they can bring to bear on such occurrences, short of rejecting the Western causal belief. Instead of rejecting chemistry they can explain the poison's failure by such things as "faulty manufacturing," "mislabeling," "sabotage," or "practical joke." Whatever the conclusion, it would continue to reaffirm the causal premise of science. This reaffirmation reflexively supports the reality that produced the poison's unexpected failure in the first place.

The use of contradictions to reaffirm incorrigible propositions can be observed in other branches of science. In the Ptolemaic system of astronomy, the sun was seen as a planet of the earth. When astronomers looked at the sun, they saw it as an orb circling the earth. When the Copernican system arose as an alternative to this view, it offered little new empirical data. Instead, it described the old "facts" in a different way. A shift of vision was required for people to see the sun as a star, not a planet of the earth.

Seeing the sun as a star and seeing it as a planet circling the earth are merely alternatives. There is no a priori warrant for believing that either empirical determination is necessarily superior to the other.

How is a choice between equally compelling empirical determinations made? The convert to the Copernican system could have said: "I used to see a planet, but now I see a star" (cf. Kuhn, 1970:115). But to talk that way is to allow the belief that an object can be both a star and a planet at the same time. Such a belief is not allowed in Western science. So, instead, the Copernican concludes that the sun was a star all along. By so concluding, the astronomer exhibits an incorrigible proposition of Western thought, the *object constancy assumption*.[2] This is the belief that objects remain the same over time, across viewings from different positions and people. When presented with seemingly contradictory empirical determinations, the convert to Copernicanism does not consider that the sun changed through time. Instead he says: "I once took the sun to be a planet, but I was mistaken." The "discovery" of the sun as a star does not challenge the object constancy belief any more than an oracular "failure" challenges the ultimate reality of Azande belief.

The reaffirmation of incorrigible propositions is not limited to mystical and scientific ways of knowing. This reflexive work operates in commonsense reasoning as well. Each time you search for an object you knew was "right there" the same reflexive process is operating. Say, for example, you find a missing pen in a place you know you searched before. Although the evidence indicates that the pen was first absent and then present, that conclusion is not reached. To do so would challenge the incorrigibility of the object constancy belief. Instead, secondary elaborations—"I must have overlooked it," "I must not have looked there"—are invoked to retain the integrity of the object constancy proposition.

Without an object constancy assumption, there would be no problems about alternative determinations. But, with this assumption as an incorrigible proposition, the person faced with alternative seeings must choose one and only one as real. In choosing one, the other is automatically revealed as false. The falsehood of the rejected alternative may be explained in various ways. It may be due to a defective sensory apparatus, or a cognitive bias, or idiosyncratic psychological dynamics. We explain the inconstancy of the experienced object by saying that inconstancy is a product of the experiencing, not a feature of the object itself.[3]

Once an alternative seeing is explained away, the accepted explanation provides evidence for the object constancy assumption that made the explanation necessary in the first place. By demanding that we dismiss one of two equally valid empirical determinations, the object constancy assumption leads to a body of work that validates that assumption. The work then justifies itself afterward, in the world it has created. This self-preservative reflexive process is common to oracular, scientific, and commonsense reasoning.

So far I have approached the reflexive feature of realities as if it were a form of reasoning. But reflexivity is not only a facet of reasoning. It is a recurrent fact of everyday social life. For example, *talk itself is reflexive* (cf. Garfinkel, 1967a; Cicourel, 1973a). An utterance not only delivers some particular information, it also creates a world in which information itself can appear.

Zimmerman (1973:25) provides a means for understanding the reflexivity of talk at the level of a single word. He presents three identical shapes:

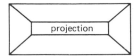 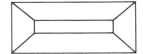 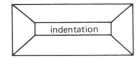

The first and third differ from the second: they each contain single words. These words interact with the box in which they appear so as to change the nature of that box. In so doing, they reflexively illumine themselves. For example, the word "projection," appearing in some other setting, would not mean what it does here. For me it means that I am to see the back panel and the word "projection" as illustrative of a projection. The word "projection" does not merely appear in the scene reporting on that scene. It creates the scene in which it appears as a reasonable object.

Similarly, the word "indentation" not only takes its meaning from the context in which it appears, it reflexively creates that very context. It creates a reality in which it may stand as a part of that reality.

These examples only hint at the reflexivity of talk. [Escher's "Drawing Hands" (see frontispiece) provides another visual intimation of reflexivity.] Actual conversations are more complex than single words. The social context in which talk occurs, while analogous to one of these static boxes, is enormously ambiguous and potentially infinitely referential. Nonetheless, conversation operates like the printed "projection" and "indentation." An analysis of greetings can be used to show how talk partially constitutes the context and then comes to be seen as independent of it.[4]

To say "hello" both creates and sustains a world in which persons acknowledge that (1) they sometimes can see one another; (2) a world in which it is possible for persons to signal to each other, and (3) expect to be signaled back to, by (4) some others but not all of them. This is a partial and only illustrative list of some of the things a greeting accomplishes. Without the superstitious use of greetings, no world in which greetings are possible "objects" would arise. A greeting creates "room" for itself. But once such verbal behaviors are regularly done, a world is built up that can take their use for granted (cf. Sacks, Schegloff, and Jefferson, 1974).

When we say "hello" and the other replies with the expected counter greeting, the reflexive work of our initial utterance is masked. If the other scowls and walks on, then we are reminded that we were attempting to create a scene of greetings and that we failed. Rather than treat this as evidence that greetings are not "real," however, the rejected greeter ordinarily turns it into an occasion for affirming the reality of greetings. He formulates "secondary elaborations" of belief about greetings. He says, "He didn't hear me," "She is not feeling well," "It doesn't matter anyway."

Reflexivity provides grounds for absolute faith in the validity of knowledge. The Azande takes the truth of the oracle for granted, the scientist assumes the facticity of science, the layman accepts the tenets of common sense. The incorrigible propositions of a reality serve as criteria to judge other ways of knowing. Using his absolute faith in the oracle, the Azande dismisses Evans-Pritchard's Western science contradictions. Evans-Pritchard, steeped in the efficacy of science, dismissed the oracle as superstitious. An absolute faith in the incorrigibility of one's own knowledge enables believers to repel contrary evidence. This suggests that all people are equally superstitious.

REALITY AS A COHERENT BODY OF KNOWLEDGE

The phenomenon of reflexivity is a feature of every reality. It interacts with the coherence, interactional, fragility, and permeability features I describe in the rest of this chapter. These five features are incorrigible propositions of the reality of ethnomethodology. They appear as facts of the external world due to the ethnomethodologist's unquestioned assumption that they constitute the world. In other words, these features themselves exhibit reflexivity.

This reflexive loop constitutes the interior structure of ethnomethodology. This will become clearer as I describe the second feature of realities, their exhibition of a coherent body of knowledge. To illustrate this feature I will extrapolate from the work of Zimmerman and Wieder (n.d.), who investigated the life of a number of self-named "freaks," frequent drug users within America's counterculture. Both freaks and their academic ethnographers (e.g., Reich, 1970; Roszack, 1969) describe freaks as radical opponents of the straight culture from which they sprang. As Zimmerman and Wieder (n.d.:103) write:

> From the standpoint of the "straight" members of society, freaks are deliberately irrational. . . . they disavow an interest in efficiency, making long-

range plans, and concerns about costs of property (etc.) which are valued by the straight members of American society and are understood by them as indicators of rationality.

On first appearance, here is a reality that seems anarchical. Nonetheless, Zimmerman and Wieder (Ibid: 102–103) found that:

> when it comes to those activities most highly valued by freaks, such as taking drugs, making love, and other "cheap thrills," there is an elaborately developed body of lore. Freaks and others use that knowledge of taking drugs, making love, etc., reasonably, deliberately, planfully, projecting various consequences, predicting outcomes, conceiving of the possibilities of action in more or less clear and distinct ways, and choosing between two or more means of reaching the same end.

The most vivid illustration that freaks use a coherent body of knowledge comes from Zimmerman's and Wieder's discoveries about the place of drugs in the everyday freak life. At first glance such drug use appears irrational. Yet, among freaks, taking drugs "is something as ordinary and unremarkable as their parents regard taking or offering a cup of coffee" (Ibid:57). Freak behavior is not a function of the freaks' ignorance of chemical and medical "facts" about drugs. The freaks studied knew chemical and medical facts well. They organized these facts into a different, yet coherent corpus of knowledge.

One of the team's research assistants, Peter Suchek, was able to systematize the freaks' knowledge of drugs into a taxonomic schemata (Table 2).

What the freak calls "dope," the chemist calls "psychotropic drugs." Within the family of dope, freaks distinguish "mind-expanding" and "body" dope. Freaks further subdivide each of these species. In addition, freaks share a common body of knowledge informing them of the practicalities surrounding the use of each type of dope. All knowledge of dope use is grounded in the incorrigible proposition that dope is to be used. One must, of course, know how to use it.

Zimmerman and Wieder (Ibid.: 118) found the following knowledge about "psychedelic mind-expanding dope" to be common among freaks:

> The folk pharmacology of psychedelic drugs may be characterized as a method whereby drug users rationally assess choices among kinds of drugs, choices among instances of the same kind of drug, the choice to ingest or not, the time of the act of ingestion relative to the state of one's physiolo-

**Table 2   The folk pharmacology for dope
(after Zimmerman and Wieder, n.d.: 107)**

Types of Dope	Subcategories
Mind expanding dope	(Untitled)
	"grass" (marijuana)
	"hash" (hashish)
	"LSD" or "acid" (lysergic acid)
	Psychedelics
	Mescaline
	synthetic
	organic
	natural, peyote
	Psilocybin
	synthetic
	organic
	natural, mushrooms
	"DMT"
	miscellaneous (e.g., Angel's Dust)
Body dope	"speed" (amphetamines)
	"downers" (barbiturates)
	"tranks" (tranquilizers)
	"coke" (cocaine)
	"shit" (heroin)

gy and relative to the state of one's psyche, the timing relative to social and practical demands, the appropriateness of the setting for having a psychedelic experience, the size of the dose, and the effectiveness and risk of mixing drugs.

Freaks share similar knowledge for the rest of the taxonomy. Being a freak means living within the auspices of such knowledge and using it according to a plan, as the chemist uses his. Both the freaks' and the scientists' realities are concerned with "the facts." Though the facts differ, each reality reflexively proves its facts as absolute.

Consider how the freak assembles the knowledge he uses. He is not loath to borrow from the discoveries of science. But before accepting what the scientist says, he first tests scientific "facts" against the auspices of his own incorrigible propositions. He does not use the scientists' findings to determine the danger of the drug, but rather to indicate the particular dosage, setting, et cetera, under which a drug is to be taken.

Scientific drug researchers frequently attend to the experiences of freaks in a comparable way. They incorporate the facts that freaks report about dope into their coherent idiom. The two then are like independent teams of investigators working on the same phenomenon with different purposes. They are like artists and botanists who share a common interest in the vegetable kingdom, but who employ different incorrigibles.

The freak's knowledge, like all knowledge, is sustained through reflexive interactional work. For example, the knowledge contained in the drug taxonomy (Table 2) sometimes "fails," that is, it produces not a "high" but a "bummer." The incorrigible propositions of freak pharmacology are not then questioned. Instead, these propositions are invoked to explain the bummer's occurrence. "For example," Zimmerman and Wieder (Ibid.: 118) write:

> a 'bad trip' may be explained in such terms as the following: it was a bad time and place to drop; my head wasn't ready for it; or it was bad acid or mescaline, meaning that it was cut with something impure or that it was some other drug altogether.

The reflexive use of the freak taxonomy recalls my previous discussion of the Azande. When the oracle seemed to contradict itself, the contradiction became but one more occasion for proving the oracular way of knowing. The reality of oracles is appealed to in explaining the failure of the oracle, just as the reality of freak pharmacology is used to explain a bad trip. It would be as futile for a chemist to explain the bad trip scientifically to a freak as it was for Evans-Pritchard to try to convince the Azande that failures of the oracle demonstrated their unreality.

The coherence of knowledge is a reflexive consequence of the researcher's attention. Zimmerman and Wieder, in the best social science tradition, employed many methods to construct the freak's taxonomy. Freaks were interviewed by sociology graduate students and by their peers. These interviewers provided accounts of their own drug experiences as well. Additional freaks not acquainted with the purposes of the research were paid to keep personal diaries of their day-to-day experiences. Zimmerman and Wieder used a portion of this massive data to construct the freak taxonomy, then tested its validity against further portions of the data.

Such systematizations are always the researcher's construction (Wallace, 1972; see Chapter 8 below.) To claim that any reality, including the researcher's own, exhibits a coherent body of knowledge is but to claim that coherence can be found *upon analysis.* The coherence located in a reality is found there by the ethnomethodologist's interactional work. The coherence feature, like all features of realities, operates as an incorrigible proposition, reflexively sustained.

Consider the analogous work of linguists (e.g., Chomsky, 1965). Within language-using communities, linguists discover the "rules of grammar." Although the linguist empirically establishes these grammatical rules, speaker-hearers of that language cannot list them. Rules can be located in their talk, upon analysis, but language users cannot describe them.

Similarly, freaks could not supply the taxonomy Zimmerman and Wieder claim they "really" know. It was found upon analysis. It is an imposition of the researcher's logic upon the freak's logic.

Castaneda's (1968, 1971) attempts to explain the reality of Yaqui sorcery further illustrates the reflexity of analysis. In his initial report, *The Teachings of Don Juan,* Castaneda (1968) begins with a detailed ethnography of his experiences of his encounter with a Yaqui sorcerer, Don Juan. In this reality it is common for time to stop, for men to turn into animals and animals into men, for animals and men to converse with one another, and for great distances to be covered while the body remains still.

In the final section of his report, Castaneda systematizes his experiences with the sorcerer. He presents a coherent body of knowledge undergirding Don Juan's teachings. Thus Castaneda, like Zimmerman and Wieder, organizes a "nonordinary" reality into a coherent system of knowledge.

In a second book Castaneda describes Don Juan's reaction to his systematization of a peyote session, a "mitote." Castaneda told Don Juan he had discovered that mitotes are a "result of a subtle and complex system of cueing." He writes (1971:37–38):

> It took me close to two hours to read and explain to Don Juan the scheme I had constructed. I ended by begging him to tell me in his own words what were the exact procedures for reaching agreement.

When I had finished he frowned. I thought he must have found my explanation challenging; he appeared to be involved in deep deliberation. After a reasonable silence I asked him what he thought about my idea.

My question made him suddenly turn his frown into a smile and then into roaring laughter. I tried to laugh too and asked nervously what was so funny.

"You're deranged!" he exclaimed. "Why should anyone be bothered with cueing at such an important time as a mitote? Do you think one ever fools around with Mescalito?"

I thought for a moment that he was being evasive; he was not really answering my question.

"Why should anyone cue?" Don Juan asked stubbornly. "You have been in mitotes. You should know that no one told you how to feel, or what to do; no one except Mescalito himself."

I insisted that such an explanation was not possible and begged him again to tell me how the agreement was reached.

"I know why you have come," Don Juan said in a mysterious tone. "I can't help you in your endeavor because there is no system of cueing."

"But how can all those persons agree about Mescalito's presence?"

"They agree because they *see*," Don Juan said dramatically, and then added casually, "Why don't you attend another mitote and see for yourself?"

Don Juan finds Castaneda's account ridiculous. This rejection is not evidence that Castaneda's attempt at systematization is incorrect. It indicates that the investigator reflexively organizes the realities he investigates. All realities may *upon analysis* exhibit a coherent system of knowledge, but knowledge of this coherence is not necessarily part of the awareness of its members.

Features emerging "upon analysis" is a particular instance of reflexivity. These features exist only within the reflexive work of those researchers who make them exist. This does not deny their reality. There is no need to pursue the chimera of a presuppositionless inquiry. Because all realities are ultimately superstitious, the reflexive location of reflexivity is not a problem within ethnomethodological studies. Rather, it provides them with their most intriguing phenomenon.

My discussion of these first two features of realities also shows that any one feature is separate from the other only upon analysis. In my description of reflexivity, I was forced to assume the existence of a coherent body of knowledge. Similarly, in the present discussion I could not speak about the existence of coherent systems of knowledge without introducing the caveat of "upon analysis," an implicit reference to reflexivity. This situation will continue as I discuss the remaining three features. Though I attempt to keep them separate from one another, I will only be partially successful, since the five are inextricably intertwined. Nevertheless, I will continue to talk of them as five separate features, not as one. I acknowledge that this talk is more heuristic than literal—it provides a ladder with five steps that may be climbed and then thrown away (cf. Wittgenstein, 1921).

REALITY AS INTERACTIONAL ACTIVITY

Realities are also dependent upon ceaseless social interactional work. Wood's study of a mental hospital illustrates the reality of this reality work. He discovered that psychiatric attendants shared a body of knowledge. Wood's (1968:36) analysis of the attendants' interaction with the patients uncovered labels like: "baby," "child," "epileptic," "mean old man," "alcoholic," "lost soul," "good patient," "depressive," "sociopath," and "nigger." Though borrowed from psychiatry, these terms constitute a corpus of knowledge which reflects the attendants' own practical nursing concerns. These terms can be arranged in a systematic taxonomy (see Table 3). Each is shown to differ from the others according to four parameters of nursing problems.

Table 3   The meaning of the labels (Wood, 1968:45).

Psychiatric Attendant Label	Nursing Trouble				
	work	clean-liness	super-visory	miscel-laneous	frequency x 60
mean old man	yes	yes	yes	yes	2
baby	yes	yes	yes	—	20
child	yes	yes	—	yes	4
nigger	yes	—	yes	yes	1
epileptic	—	yes	—	yes	4
sociopath	yes	—	—	yes	3
depressive	—	—	—	yes	2
alcoholic	—	—	yes	—	8
lost soul	yes	—	—	—	12
good patient	—	—	—	—	6

Wood's study explored how the attendants used this taxonomy to construct meanings for the mental patients' behavior. One explanation of label use is called a "matching procedure." The matching model of labeling patient behavior is essentially a psychological theory. It treats behavior as a private, internal state, not influenced by social dimensions. The matching model assumes the patients' behavior has obvious features. Trained personnel monitor and automatically apply the appropriate label to patients' behavior.

Wood presents five case histories that show that labels are not applied by a simple matching process. They are molded in the day-to-day interaction of the attendants with one another and with the patients. The labeling of patients is a social activity, not a psychological one.

Wood (Ibid.: 51–91) describes the labeling history of patient Jimmy Lee Jackson. Over the course of his three-month hospitalization, Jackson held the same official psychiatric label, that of "psychoneurotic reaction, depressive type." However, the ward attendants saw Jackson within the web of their own practical circumstances. For them, at one time he was a "nigger," at another a "depressive," and at yet another a "sociopath." These seeings reflected a deep change in the meaning Jackson had for the attendants. When he was seen as a "nigger," for example, it meant that the attendants considered he was "lazy, and . . . without morals or scruples and . . . that the patient is cunning and will attempt to ingratiate himself with the attendants in order to get attention and 'use' them for his own ends" (Ibid.: 52). When Jackson became a depressive type, all these negative attributes were withdrawn. The change in attribution, Wood shows, cannot be explained by a matching procedure. The attendants' social interactional work produced the change, independent of Jackson's behavior. This suggests that realities are fundamentally interactional activities.

One evening Jackson was suffering from a toothache. Unable to secure medical attention, he ran his arm through a window pane in one of the ward's locked doors. He suffered a severe laceration of his forearm which required stitches. When the attendants who were on duty during this episode returned to work the following afternoon, they discovered that the preceding morning shift had decided that Jackson had attempted suicide. Jackson was no longer presented to them as a nigger. The morning shift found that persons who had not even witnessed the event had given it a meaning they themselves had never considered. Nevertheless, the evening shift accepted the validity of this label change.

The label change indexed a far larger change. Jackson's past history on the ward was reinterpreted. He now was accorded different treatment by attendants on all shifts. He was listened to sympathetically, given whatever he requested, and no longer exhorted to do more ward work. All the attendants came to believe that he had always been a depressive and that they had always seen him as such.

A few weeks later Jackson became yet another person, a "sociopath." The attendants no longer accepted that he was capable of a suicide attempt. The new label was once again applied retrospectively. Not only was Jackson believed to be incapable of committing suicide now, he was thought to have always been incapable of it. The attendants agreed that the window-breaking incident had been a "fake" or "con,"—just the sort of thing a sociopath would do. Attendants who had praised Jackson as a hard worker when he was labeled a depressive now pointed to this same work as proof he was a "conniver." Requests for attention and medicine that had been promptly fulfilled for the depressive Jackson were now ignored for the sociopath Jackson, or used as occasions to attack him verbally.

Yet, as Wood describes Jackson, he remained constant despite these changes in attendant behavior. He did the same amount of work and sought the same amount of attention and medicine whether he was labeled a nigger or a depressive or a sociopath. What Jackson was at any time was determined by the reality work of the attendants.

In the final pages of his study, Wood (Ibid.: 137–138) further illustrates the power of interactional work to create an external world:

> The evening that he [Jackson] cut his arm, I, like the PAs [psychiatric attendants], was overcome by the blood and did not reflect on its "larger" meaning concerning his proper label. The next day, when I heard all of the morning shift PAs refer to his action as a suicide attempt, I too labeled Jackson a "depressive" and the cut arm as a suicide attempt. When the label changed in future weeks I was working as a PA on the ward up to 12 hours a day. It was only two months later when I had left the ward, as I reviewed my notes and my memory, that I recognized the "peculiar" label changes that had occurred. While I was on the ward, it had not seemed strange to think that cutting an arm in a window was a serious attempt to kill oneself. Only as an "outsider" did I come to think that Jackson had "really" stayed the same through his three label changes.

As Wood says, Jackson could never have a meaning apart from *some* social context. Meanings unfold only within an unending sequence of practical actions.[5]

The *matching* theory of label use assumes a correspondence theory of signs (cf. Garfinkel, 1952:91ff.; Wieder, 1970; Chapter 9 below). This theory of signs has three analytically separate elements: ideas that exist in the head, signs that appear in symbolic representations, and objects and events that appear in the world. Meaning is the relation among these elements. Signs can stand on behalf of the ideas in the head or refer to objects in the world. This theory of signs implies that signs stand in a point-by-point relation to thoughts in one's mind or objects in the world. Meanings are stable across time and space. They are not dependent upon the concrete participants or upon the specific scenes in which they appear.

Wood's study indicates that labels are not applied in accordance with correspondence principles. Instead, labels are *indexical expressions*. Meanings are situationally determined. They are dependent upon the concrete context in which they appear. The participants' interactional activity structured the indexical meaning of the labels used on the ward. The relationship of the participants to the object, the setting in which events occur, and the circumstances surrounding a definition, determine the meaning of labels and of objects.

The interactional feature indicates that realities do not possess symbols, like so many tools in a box. A reality and its signs are "mutually determinative" (Wieder, 1973:216). Alone, neither expresses sense. Intertwining through the course of indexical interaction, they form a life.

THE FRAGILITY OF REALITIES

Every reality depends upon (1) ceaseless reflexive use of (2) a body of knowledge in (3) interaction. Every reality is also fragile. Suppression of the activities that the first three features describe disrupts the reality. Every reality is equally capable of dissolution. The presence of this fragility feature of realities has been demonstrated by studies called "incongruity procedures" or "breaching experiments."

In one of the simplest of these, Garfinkel used 67 students as "experimenters." These students engaged a total of 253 "subjects" in a game of tick-tack-toe. When the figure necessary for the game was drawn, the experimenters requested the subject to make the first move. After the subject made his mark, the experimenter took his turn. Rather than simply marking another cell, the experimenter erased the subject's mark and moved it to another cell. Continuing as if this were expected behavior, the experimenter then placed his own mark in one of the now empty cells. The experimenters reported that their action produced extreme bewilderment and confusion in the subjects. The reality of the game, which before the experimenter's move seemed stable and external, suddenly fell apart. For a moment the subjects exhibited an "amnesia for social structure" (Garfinkel, 1963:189).

This fragility feature is even more evident in everyday life, where the rules are not explicit. People interact without listing the rules of conduct. Continued reference is made to this knowledge nonetheless. This referencing is not ordinarily available as long as the reality work continues normally. When the reality is disrupted, the interactional activity structuring the reality becomes visible. This is what occurred in the tick-tack-toe game. À usually unnoticed feature of the game is a "rule" prohibiting erasing an opponent's mark. When this unspoken "rule" is broken, it makes its first public appearance. If we were aware of the fragility of our realities, they would not seem real.

Thus Garfinkel (Ibid:198) found that when the "incongruity-inducing procedures" developed in games:

> were applied in "real life" situations, it was unnerving to find the seemingly endless variety of events that lent themselves to the production of really nasty surprises. These events ranged from . . . standing very, very close to a person while otherwise maintaining an innocuous conversation, to others . . . like saying "hello" at the termination of a conversation. . . . Both procedures elicited anxiety, indignation, strong feelings on the part of the experimenter and subject alike of humiliation and regret, demands by the subjects for explanations, and so on.

Another of the procedures Garfinkel developed was to send student experimenters into stores and restaurants where they were told to "mistake" customers for salespersons and waiters. The following is a sample of what the experimenters reported about the results of these procedures.

One experimenter went to have lunch at a restaurant near a university. Her host directed her toward a likely subject. She began by saying to him:

(E). I should like a table on the west side, a quiet spot, if you please. And what is on the menu?

(S). [Turned toward *E* but looked past and in the direction of the foyer.] Eh, ah, madam, I'm sure. [Looked past *E* again, looked at a pocket watch, replaced it, and looked toward the dining room.]

(E). Surely luncheon hours are not over. What do you recommend I order today?

(S). I don't know. You see, I'm waiting . . .

(E). [Interrupted with] Please don't keep me standing here while you wait. Kindly show me to a table.

(S). But Madam—[started to edge away from door, and back into the lounge in a slightly curving direction around *E*].

(E). My good man— [at this *S*'s face flushed, his eyes rounded and opened wide.]

(S). But—you—I—oh dear! [He seemed to wilt.]

(E). [Took *S*'s arm in hand and propelled him toward the dining room door slightly ahead of herself.]

(S). [Walked slowly but stopped just within the room, turned around and for the first time looked directly and very appraisingly at *E,* took out the watch, looked at it, held it to his ear, replaced it, and muttered, "Oh dear."]

(E). It will take only a minute for you to show me to a table and take my order. Then you can return to wait for your customers. After all, I am a guest and a customer, too.

(S). [Stiffened slightly, walked jerkily toward the nearest empty table, held a chair for *E* to be seated, bowed slightly, muttered "My pleasure," hurried toward the door, stopped, turned, looked back at *E* with a blank facial expression.]

At this point, *E*'s host walked up to *S*, greeted him, shook hands, and propelled him toward *E*'s table. *S* stopped a few steps from the table, looked directly at, then through *E*, and started to walk back toward the door. Host told him *E* was a young lady whom he had invited to join them at lunch. (He then introduced her to *S*, who was one of the big names in the physics world, a pillar of the institution.) *S* seated himself reluctantly and perched rigidly on his chair, obviously uncomfortable. *E* smiled, made light and polite inquiries about his work, mentioned various functions he had attended and at which he had been honored, and then complacently remarked that it was a shame *E* had not met him personally. If she had, he said, she would not have mistaken him for the maître d'. The host chattered about his long-time friendship with *E,* while *S* fidgeted and looked again at his pocket watch, wiped his forehead with a table napkin, and looked at *E* but avoided meeting her eyes. When the host mentioned that *E* was studying sociology at UCLA, *S* suddenly burst into loud laughter, realized that everyone in the room was looking in the direction of our table, abruptly became quiet, and said to *E,* "You mistook me for the maître d', didn't you?"

(E). Deliberately, sir.

(S). Why deliberately?

(E) You have just been used as the unsuspecting subject in an experiment.

(S). Diabolic. But clever, I must say [to our host] I haven't been so shaken since ——— denounced my theory of ——— in 19—. And the wild thoughts that ran through my mind! Call the receptionist from the lobby, go to the men's room, turn this woman to the first person who comes along. Damn these early diners, there's nobody coming in at this time. Time is standing still, or my watch has stopped. I will talk to ——— about this, make sure it doesn't happen to "somebody." Damn a persistent woman. I'm not her "good man." I'm Dr. ——— and not to be pushed around. This can't be happening. If I do take her to that damned table she wants, I can get away from her, and I'll just take it easy until I can. I remember ——— (hereditary psychopath, wife of one of the "family" of the institution), maybe if I do what *this* one wants she will not make any more trouble than this. I wonder if she is "off." She certainly looks normal. Wonder how you can really tell? (Garfinkel, 1963:224–226).

The breaching experiments were subsequently refined, such that:

the person [subject] could not turn the situation into a play, a joke, an experiment, a deception, and the like . . .; that he have insufficient time to work through a redefinition of his real circumstances; and that he be deprived of consensual support for an alternative definition of social reality (Garfinkel, 1964; in 1967a:58).

This meant that subjects were not allowed to reflexively turn the disruption into a revalidation of their realities. The incorrigible propositions of their social knowledge were not adequate for the present circumstances. They were removed from the supporting interactional activity that they possessed before the breach occurred.

These refinements had the positive consequence of increasing the bewilderment of the subjects, who became more and more like desocialized schizophrenics, persons completely devoid of any social reality. These refinements produced a negative consequence. They were immoral. Once subjects had experienced the fragility, they could not continue taking the stability of realities for granted. No amount of "cooling out" could restore the subject's faith.

But what is too cruel to impose on others can be tried upon oneself. These self-imposed procedures are discussed in Chapter 12.

THE PERMEABILITY OF REALITIES

Because the reflexive use of social knowledge is fragile and interaction dependent, one reality may be altered, and another may be assumed. Cases where a person passes from one reality to another, dramatically different, reality vividly display this permeability feature.

Tobias Schneebaum, a painter who lives periodically in New York, provides an example of a radical shift in realities in his book, *Keep the River on Your Right* (1969). Schneebaum entered the jungles of Peru in 1955 in pursuit of his art. During the trip the book describes, he gradually lost interest in painterly studies. He found himself drawn deeper and deeper into the jungle. Unlike a professional anthropologist, he carried no plans to write about his travels. In fact, the slim volume from which I draw the following discussion was not written until 13 years after his return.

He happened upon the Akaramas, a stone age tribe that had never seen a white man. They accepted him quickly, gave him a new name, "Habe," meaning "ignorant one," and began teaching him to be as they were.

Schneebaum learned to sleep in "bundles" with the other men, piled on top of one another for warmth and comfort. He learned to hunt and fish with stone age tools. He learned the Akaramas' language and their ritual of telling stories of their hunts and hikes, the telling taking longer than the doing. He learned to go without clothing, and to touch casually the genitals of his companions in play.

When one of the men in Schneebaum's compartment is dying of dysentery, crying out at his excretions of blood and pain, the "others laugh and he laughs too" (Ibid.:109). As this man lies among them whimpering and crying in their sleeping pile at night, Schneebaum writes (Ibid.:129): "Not Michii or Baaldore or Ihuene or Reindude seemed to have him on their minds. It was as if he were not there among us or as if he had already gone to some other forest." When he dies, he is immediately forgotten. Such is the normal perception of death within the Akarama reality. As Schneebaum (Ibid.:109) describes another incident: "There were two pregnant women whom I noticed one day with flatter bellies and no babies on their backs, but there was no sign of grief, no service..."

Gradually, Schneebaum absorbed even these ways and a new sense of time. At one point he left the Akaramas to visit the mission from which he had embarked. He was startled to find that seven months had passed, not the three or four he had supposed. As he was more and more permeated by the stone age reality, he began to feel that his "own world, whatever, wherever it was, no longer was anywhere in existence" (Ibid.:69). As the sense of his old reality disappears, he says, "My fears were not so much for the future . . . but for my knowledge. I was removing my own reflection" (Ibid.:64–65).

One day, a day like many others, he rises to begin a hunting expedition with his sleeping companions. This day, however, they go much farther than ever before. They paint themselves in a new way and repeat new chants. Finally they reach a strange village. In they swoop, Schneebaum too, shouting their sacred words and killing all the men they can catch, disemboweling and beheading them on the spot. They burn all the huts, kidnap the women and children. They then hike to their own village, without pause, through an entire night. At home, a new dance is begun. The meat of the men they have murdered and brought back with them is cooked. As a new movement of the dance begins, this meat is gleefully eaten. Exhausted at last, they stumble together on the ground. Then the last of the meat is put to ceremonious use:

> we sat or lay around the fires, eating, moaning the tones of the chant, swaying forward and back, moving from the hip, forward and back. Calm and silence settled over us, all men. Four got up, one picked a heart from the embers, and they walked into the forest. Small groups of others arose,

selected a piece of meat, and disappeared in other directions. We three
were alone until Ihuene, Baaldore, and Reindude were in front of us, Reindude cupping in his hand the heart from the being we had carried from
so far away, the heart of he who had lived in the hut we had entered
to kill. We stretched out flat upon the gound, lined up, our shoulders
touching. Michii looked up at the moon and showed it to the heart. He
bit into it as if it were an apple, taking a large bite, almost half the heart,
and chewed down several times, spit into a hand, separated the meat into
six sections and placed some into the mouths of each of us. We chewed
and swallowed. He did the same with the other half of the heart. He turned
Darinimbiak onto his stomach, lifted his hips so that he crouched on all
fours. Darinimbiak growled, Mayaarii-ha! Michii growled, Mayaarii-ha!,
bent down to lay himself upon Darinimbiak's back and entered him
(Ibid.:106–107).

Mass murder, destruction of an entire village, theft of all valuable
goods, cannibalism, the ritual eating of the heart before publicly displayed homosexual acts—these are some of the acts Schneebaum partici-
pated in. He could not have done them his first day in the jungle.
But after his gradual adoption of the Akarama reality, they had become
natural. It would have been as immoral for him to refuse to join his
brothers in the raid and its victory celebration as it would be immoral
for him to commit these same acts within a Western community. His
reality had changed. The moral facts were different.

Schneebaum's experience suggests that even radically different realities can be penetrated.[6] We would not have this account, however,
if the stone age reality had completely obliterated Schneebaum's Western
reality. He would still be with the tribe. The more he permeated the
Akaramas' reality, the more suspect his old reality became. The more
he fell under the spell of the absolutism of his new reality, the more
fragile his old reality became. Like the cannibals, Schneebaum says: "My
days are days no longer. Time had no thoughts to trouble me, and
everything is like nothing and nothing is like everything. For if a day
passes, it registers nowhere, and it might be a week, it might be a month.
There is no difference" (Ibid.:174).

As the vision of his old reality receded, Schneebaum experienced its
fragility. He knew he must leave soon, or there would be no reality
to return to. He describes his departure:

A time alone, only a few weeks ago, with the jungle alive and vibrant
around me, and Michii and Baaldore gone with all the other men to hunt,

I saw within myself too many seeds that would grow a fungus around my brain, encasing it with mold that could penetrate and smooth the convolutions and there I would remain, not he who had travelled and arrived, not the me who had crossed the mountains in a search, but another me living only in ease and pleasure, no longer able to scrawl out words on paper or think beyond a moment. And days later, I took myself up from our hut, and I walked on again alone without a word to any of my friends and family, but left when all again were gone and I walked through my jungle . . . (Ibid.:182).

The Akarama would not miss him. They would not even notice his absence. For them, there were no separate beings. Schneebaum felt their reality obliterating "the me who had crossed the mountains in a search." Schneebaum was attached to this "me," and so he left.

In the previous section, I listed three conditions necessary for successful breaches: There can be no place to escape. There can be no time to escape. There can be no one to provide counter evidence. The same conditions are required to move between realities. That is, as Castaneda's (1968, 1971, 1972) work suggests, in order to permeate realities, one must first have the old reality breached. Castaneda has named this necessity the establishment "of a certainty of a minimal possibility," that another reality actually exists (personal communication). Successful breaches must establish that another reality is available for entry. Thus, as Don Juan attempted to make Castaneda a man of knowledge, he first spent years trying to crack Castaneda's absolute faith in the reality of Western rationalism.

Castaneda's work suggests many relations between the fragility and permeability features. It is not my purpose to explore the relations of the five features in this book. But I want to emphasize that such relations can be supposed to exist.

I relied on the "exotic" case of a person passing from a Western to a stone age reality to display the permeability feature of realities. However, any two subsequent interactional encounters could have been used for this purpose. All such passages are of equal theoretic import. Passages between a movie and freeway driving, between a person's reality before and after psychotherapy, between a "straight" acquiring membership in the reality of drug freaks, or before and after becoming a competent religious healer, are all the same. The differences are "merely" methodological, not theoretical. Studying each passage, I would concentrate on how the reflexive, knowledge, interactional, and fragility features effect the shift.

All realities are permeable. Ethnomethodology is a reality. This book is an attempt to breach the reader's present reality by introducing him to the "certainty of a minimal possibility" that another reality exists.

ON THE CONCEPT OF REALITY

Many ethnomethodologists rely on Schutz's concept of reality (e.g., 1962, 1964, 1966). I review a portion of this work in Chapter 5. My use of "reality" contrasts with Schutz's view. For Schutz (e.g., 1962:208ff.), the reality of everyday life is the *one* paramount reality. Schutz says that this paramount reality consists of a number of presuppositions or assumptions, which include the assumption of a tacit, taken for granted world; an assumed practical interest in that world; and an assumption that the world is intersubjective (e.g., 1962:23). Schutz argues that other realities exist, but that they derive from the paramount reality. For example, he discusses the realities of "scientific theorizing" and of "fantasy." These realities appear when some of the basic assumptions of the paramount reality are temporarily suspended. The paramount reality of everyday life has an elastic quality for Schutz. After excursions into other realities, we snap back into the everyday.

My view of realities is different. I do not wish to call one or another reality paramount. It is my contention that every reality is equally real. No single reality contains more of the truth than any other. From the perspective of Western everyday life, Western everyday life will appear paramount, just as Schutz maintains. But from the perspective of scientific theorizing or dreaming, or meditating, each of these realities will appear just as paramount. Because every reality exhibits the absolutist tendency I mentioned earlier, there is no way to look from the window of one reality at others without seeing yourself. Schutz seems to be a victim of this absolutist prejudice. As a Western man living his life in the Western daily experience, he assumed that this life was the touchstone of all realities.

My concept of reality, then, has more in common with Wittgenstein (1953) than with Schutz. Wittgenstein (e.g., 1953:61, 179) recognizes that human life exhibits an empirical multitude of activities. He calls these activities language games. Language games are forever being invented and modified and discarded. The fluidity of language activities do not permit rigorous description. Analysts can discover that at any time a number of language games are associated with one another. This association, too, is not amenable to rigorous description. Instead, language games exhibit "family resemblances." One can recognize certain games going together. But one could no more articulate *the* criteria for this resemblance than one could predict the physical characteristics of some unseen member of a familiar extended family. Wittgenstein (Ibid.: 119, 123) calls a collection of language games bound together by a family resemblance, a *form of life*.[7] Forms of life resemble what I call "realities." Realities are far more aswarm than Schutz's terms "finite" and "province" suggest. Forms of life are always forms of life forming.[8] Realities are always realities becoming.

NOTES

1. See Pollner's (1970, 1973) discussions of the reflexive reasoning of the Azande, and Polanyi's (1958:287–294) examination of the same materials. In the Apostolic Church of John Marangue, illness is not bodily malfunction, it is sin. Sin is curable not by medicine, but by confessional healing. When evangelists' attempts to heal church members were not accompanied by recovery, Jules-Rosette (1973:167) reports that church members did not lose their faith in the confessional process. They looked to other "causes" of the "failure." They said things like: Other persons must have been implicated in the sin, and untrue confession must have been given. Once again, contradictions that could potentially challenge a basic faith do not, as the basic faith itself is not questioned.

2. See Gurwitsch (1966) for a more technical discussion of the object constancy assumption. Later in this chapter and in Chapter 5, I show that the object constancy assumption is not a belief that exists in the head. A body of interactional work is required to achieve a constant world.

3. The pen–not pen and planet-star examples are adapted from Pollner (1973). Much of this discussion of reflexivity derives from Pollner's thinking on these matters.

4. Riel (1972) illustrates how talk reflexively constitutes the context it then seems to independently reference. Trying to make a certain point, she reports turning away from an inadequate sentence she had written to explore notes and texts again. Forty-five minutes later she wrote the now-perfect sentence, only to discover it was exactly the same sentence she had rejected before.

5. Cicourel (1968) examines the interactional work that accomplishes external objects in greater detail. He shows that juvenile delinquents and crime rates are constituted by the social activities of law enforcement personnel.

6. For an account of a reality shift in the other direction, from the stone age to industrial Western society, see Kroeber's *Ishi in Two Worlds* (1961). Again the transition was never total, but this was a result of a political decision on the part of the author's husband. As Ishi's official keeper, he wished to keep him primitive for his own and anthropology's benefit.

7. Blum (1970b) has previously explored the importance of Wittgenstein's notion of "form of life" for social science.

8. This phrase, like much of this chapter, has been adapted from the unpublished lectures of Pollner. For Pollner's published writings see Zimmerman and Pollner, 1970; and Pollner, 1970, 1973, 1974.

PART TWO

STUDIES
IN
ETHNOMETHODOLOGY

CHAPTER THREE

The
Imposition
of
Reality

Western science is a reality that has as its essential concern the investigation of other realities. Because to some extent ethnomethodology has developed as a rejection of the social science approach to the study of realities,[1] much ethnomethodological research has been devoted to describing the social scientific reality. These investigations have determined that social science is committed to attempting a *causal* analysis of the various realities it studies. Such analyses are then typically used to disparage the integrity of the realities studied. These phenomenal realities are either explicitly or implicitly compared with the reality of social science. Invidious comparisons judge them to be less rational, more superstitious, less exact than social science.

The scientific reality is used as *the* standard against which all other realities are compared. For example, the social science reality is used to reduce the reality of Yaqui sorcery (Castaneda, 1968, 1971, 1972) to a bizarre function of aberrant drug use, to dismiss the Azande's oracles as primitive superstition, and to relegate the Arakamas' eating and sleeping habits to the evolutionary barbaric past.

Ethnomethodology treats social science as one more reality among the many. It suggests that social science distorts other realities because it views them only through the lenses of its own system. In reflecting upon the results of social science research, the ethnomethodologist has come to the conclusion that *the imposition of one reality on another necessarily distorts the reality studied.*[2]

A simple and paradigmatic example of this distortion has been examined in a series of studies on educational situations (Cicourel et al., 1974; Jennings, 1972; Leiter, 1971; MacKay, 1973, 1974; Mehan, 1973; J. Handel, 1972; Roth, 1972). I want to examine several of these situations in detail and then elaborate their general implications before turning to a discussion of the larger issues they raise for social science. Later chapters describe alternative work ethnomethodologists have undertaken.

OFFICIAL DISTORTION OF THE CHILD'S REALITY

Educational tests are used to make critical judgments about children in American schools. The Southern California elementary schools studied by Cicourel et al. (1974) used reading, intelligence, and language development tests to assess the children's development. After these tests were given to first grade children in the two schools studied, MacKay (1974), Mehan (1973), and Roth (1972) examined the children's own perceptions and understandings of testing materials.

In the California reading tests, words, sentences, or paragraphs, contained in an arrow, appear along the left side of the page. The arrow points to a series of three pictures arrayed along the right side of the page. The child is told to mark the picture that "goes best" with the words in the arrow.

One question has the word "fly" in the arrow pointing to pictures of an elephant, a bird, and a dog. The correct answer to this question is the bird. The answer sheets of many of the first grade children showed they had chosen the elephant alone or along with the bird as a response to that question. When Mehan asked them why they chose that answer, they replied, "That's Dumbo." Dumbo, of course, is Walt Disney's flying elephant, well known to children who watch television and read children's books as an animal that flies.

In a related classroom exercise, the first grade children were shown the picture of a medieval fortress—complete with moat, drawbridge, and parapets—along with three initial consonants: D, C, and G. The children were instructed to circle the correct initial consonant. C for "castle" was the correct answer, but many children chose D. After the exercise, when

Mehan asked the children what the name of the building was, they replied, "Disneyland."

The phenomenon these examples illustrate is found in the Basic Concept Inventory (BCI). This test is used to measure the children's "language development." The child is shown a series of pictures and is asked to point to the picture that best represents the question asked. One question asks the child to "find the ones that talk" in a picture of a man, a boy, a dog, and a table. Children frequently included the dog along with the man and boy in answers to this question. For those children who have learned to say that their pets "speak" or "talk," it is not an unlikely choice.

These three examples recall a feature exhibited in our discussion of "knowledge systems" in the previous chapter. Drug freaks and pharmacologists, I pointed out, while sharing knowledge, use it in differing ways according to the realities in which they live. In the last test example, for instance, the child has used the word "talk" with reference to "dogs." The test is designed to test the child's ability to abstract. "Talking" is used to distinguish between humans and animals. Because the child has pointed to the picture of the dog, the test results indicate that the child has not yet developed the ability to use the concept correctly. However, when the child points to the dog, it is not, as the tester must conclude, that the child does not know how to abstract and categorize. This answer indicates instead that the child is operating within a different reality, one in which pets can talk. The child is able to abstract, but is using different features to do the abstracting.

Similarly, when the child applies the word "fly" to an elephant, or "D" for Disneyland to a fortress, this is evidence to the tester that the child cannot abstract similar features of objects. According to this criterion, the child who does not answer such questions properly has been found to be an inadequate adult, a nonresident of the tester and teacher reality. But to therefore conclude that the child's reading and conceptual abilities are "impoverished" is to deny the actual complexity and richness of the child's day-to-day life.

To see the child as a "more or less competent adult" is to distort the reality of the child. The distortion thereby obscures the very phenomenon—the child's competence—that the test hopes to measure. These tests measure only adult competence, the reality in which the world of play, fantasy, television, and work are rigorously separated. The tests do not capture the intricate and subtle ways children use language or concepts within their own realities. A few more examples will make the character of this distortion clearer.

Another item on the California reading test displays a picture of a house cat followed by a songbird on a perch in the first box, a tree and a flower in the second, and a ball and a doll in the third. The

question is to identify "pets." One child Mehan interviewed after the test had not marked any of the three pictures. When Mehan asked the child what the word in the arrow was, he replied "pets." When he was asked what was in each of the pictures, he replied that the first picture showed a *tiger* and a bird, the second a flower and a tree, the third a doll and a ball. When Mehan asked him which picture he had marked, the child pointed to a picture of a baby chick on a row above. Mehan then asked him why he had chosen that picture and the child replied: "Because the question says pets and that's a tiger. A tiger can't be a pet; it belongs in the zoo." This child knew what the word "pets" meant, yet he was scored wrong. His incorrect answer did not result from a lack of conceptual sophistication, though testing theory would say this when wrong answers appear. He got his question wrong because he saw the object in one of the pictures differently than the adult tester who constructed the test. The child and the tester inhabit different realities. Where the tester saw a cat, this child saw a tiger. Because the child saw differently from the tester, he was not able to link the question to the picture as the adult reality would expect. Nonetheless, he undertook a complex and accurate reasoning process. He found an answer, eschewing the frame assumed to be in effect by the tester, and considering pictures from the entire page in order to find two animals he could call pets.

Numerous other examples exist that show how the California reading test masks the complexities of these first graders' realities. One question shows pictures of a girl walking with a briefcase, a plate of cookies, and a dog barking. The question asks the child to locate the picture

| bake | | | |

that best represents "bake." From the tester's point of view, the picture of the cookies is the correct answer, because cookies are baked. Many of the children Mehan examined after the test chose either the picture of the girl or marked both the girl and the cookies. When questioned, the children indicated that the picture of the girl was chosen because they did not identify the second picture as "cookies." Some children called them "buttons," and others called them "potatoes," neither of which are unequivocally associated with the baking process. Some of the children said they chose the girl because "she bakes." Other children chose the girl and the cookies and constructed a story around them. They saw the girl "walking to the store to buy cookies" or "going to the bakery." These children answered these test questions "incorrectly" because, within their reality, the "same" objects possessed meanings different from those they held within the tester's reality.

One arrow on the reading test contains the words: "Mother said, 'The cat has been out in the rain again!' " The first picture shows a dripping wet raincoat hanging on a coat hanger. A puddle of water is collecting beneath the coat. The second shows a cat playing with a ball in the yard with the sun shining. The third shows the interior of a room with a door, a floor with footprints on it, and a wall with dotted wallpaper. The correct answer is the third picture, presumably because in order to have muddy footprints on the floor, the cat had to be outside in

| Mother said, "The cat has been out in the rain again!" | | | |

the rain. One of the children MacKay interviewed had answered this question correctly, but did not identify the third picture as the *inside* of the house. He said it was the *outside* of the house. What the tester saw as "dotted wallpaper" he saw as "sprinkles." The child had marked the third box, and therefore got the question right. Here is an instance where the child's different definition of test objects did not prohibit him from obtaining a "correct" answer. This example indicates once again that the child does not necessarily see objects in the way assumed by the test.

One question on the Basic Concept Inventory asks pupils to decide which child in a group is the tallest. Because the children's heads are obscured in the picture, the test taker is supposed to reply, "I don't know," or "I can't tell." However, many pupils examined selected one specific child in the picture as the tallest. When Mehan asked the children why they had chosen that boy, they replied that he was the tallest because "his feet are bigger." Investigating the thread of reasoning used by the children, then, shows that they understood the *intent* of the question—to discriminate and compare—but that they were not using the same criteria as the tester. The children were making comparisons based on shoe size. Because they were not using the criteria intended but never explicated by the tester, answers that indicated that one child was taller than another were marked wrong. In this case, a wrong answer does not index a lack of reasoning ability, but rather the use of an alternative scheme of interpretation.

Another item in the California reading test shows the branch of a tree in the first box, a birdhouse in the second, and a bird nest in the third. The words are, "The bird built his own house." One child

The bird built his own house.

MacKay interviewed checked the third box (the correct answer), but when the child was asked why he answered as he did, he said: "Because owls are too big—they can't fit into the house." MacKay (1974:240) concludes:

> In this item, the student marked the correct answer, but the reasoning would be incorrect, I assume, from the point of view of the test constructor. The student displays the correct skill—identifying an illustrative instance—

but does not know one word. The complexity of what the child knows is not recoverable from the test results.

TABULATING THE CHILD'S REALITY

The educational test is constructed with the assumption that children share the adult reality. More specifically, it is assumed that the child's factual knowledge can be organized only in the way that the adult organizes factual knowledge. But these examples show that the child does not necessarily share the tester's adult reality. This disparity between adult and child realities suggests that making policy decisions on the basis of tests which have imposed the adult point of view on the child's world may be dangerous. Children know "facts" about educational materials, but often organize them in their own manner.

School officials usually have little awareness of how tests distort and mask the complexities of the child's reality. The answers to test questions are regularly compiled into a table of test scores. School officials then use these tabulated results to make decisions about the child's progress and career in school (see Chapter 4). The table of correct scores is presumed to stand on behalf of the child's underlying ability or competence—the higher the score, the greater the ability. The examples described in this chapter demonstrate the danger in assuming that correct and incorrect answers index the child's abilities. Examining only a document that tabulates correct and incorrect scores makes it impossible to determine the child's abilities.

Social science research uses tabulated results derived from interrogation procedures that are similar to educational tests.[3] Just as educational test results obscure the child's reasoning procedures, social science research results obscure the interactional activities that produce the results. Just as an educational test imposes adult logic on the child, social science methods assume people employ "scientific rationality" in their daily lives. Adult testers treat children as more or less competent versions of adults; social scientists treat other realities as more or less competent versions of their own. But the data they handle is no nearer to reflecting the day-to-day activities of their subjects than the test is to displaying the complexities of the child's reality. I now attempt to substantiate this claim.

THE ETHNOMETHODOLOGICAL CRITIQUE OF SOCIAL SCIENCE

Sociologists depend on the deductive model of explanation. Such explanations demand causal terms. A theoretical premise proposes a causal relationship between events. An empirically testable hypothesis is derived from a theoretical statement. Operational definitions of the theoretical concepts are written. Intervention methods that allow the observation of instances of the operationalized concepts are devised. Observations are made, and the results are compared to those predicted by the originating theoretical hypothesis. The theoretical statement is modified, confirmed, or denied.

This idealized model notwithstanding, sociologists are aware that the concepts and relations that their theories describe cannot be directly observed. As a result, they have adopted a strategy quite foreign to the work of their natural science cousins. While the latter typically measure their phenomena directly, sociologists speak of measuring their concepts through *indicators*. The following account is prototypic:

> Morale cannot be measured directly, but its presence and strength can be *indicated* by directly observable events that usually accompany high and low levels of morale . . . (Trow, 1963:13).

Trow is saying that sociological concepts, in this case "morale," are not directly observable. Morale becomes the theorized *cause* of certain behaviors, even though it does not naturally or unequivocally appear in the lives of those for whom its causative powers are supposed to be operating. Sociologists are forced to depend upon indicators because their commitment is to causal explanation, not to the experiential substance of scenes.

As Trow goes on to say:

> An empirical indicator is an *observable* sign that some *un*observable characteristic of an individual or group exists. To rely on empirical indicators in sociology is like relying on the observation of smoke as an indicator or natural sign of the probable existence of fire (Ibid.).

Trow's analogy is apt. Smoke, we know, is not the phenomenon of interest, fire is. Similarly, what sociologists measure with their indicators is not a direct measurement of the phenomena that interest them. Sociologists theorize about "morale," "marital stability," "reading achievement," and the like, but they cannot claim that their instruments directly measure these phenomena. The measurements are only indicators, the smoke arising from the theorized, but never to be seen, fire.

For example, what relation does a social science view have to the day-to-day life of the respondent? The sociologist dare not pursue this question; perhaps "marital stability," for example, cannot be unequivocally seen over the breakfast table. So the sociologist concentrates on more constrained scenes—paper and pencil test, or a questionnaire, or an interview—and runs these through a measurement grid that produces numbers. These may not measure the phenomenon as a physicist measures the speed of light, but the sociologist is willing to assume they indirectly indicate it. On this sociologists build their discipline.[4]

Sociologists carry this reality with them as they enter their research worlds. They are thus like adult testers entering the child's world. Both impose a foreign, abstracted scheme on their subjects.

Such general claims need now to be substantiated. Nothing at first glance seems more basic than birth and death. It seems no imposition of the social scientist's reality on others to exhibit an abiding concern for these facts. But the sociologist has not merely sought to explore the meaning of birth and death in various realities; the sociologist has posited cause and effect linkages. Theories are built, for example, about the factors that influence the rate of births and family size. Propositions, such as "in a period of declining population, the greater the family's income, the fewer the children there are likely to be in the family," ensue. And, conversely: "The lower the socio-economic status (SES) of the family, the higher the fertility rate" (cf. Blake, 1961). Having made such theoretical statements, the sociologist seeks to check them against the lives of people to see how economic factors influence family size.

One way to determine how people make decisions and carry them out in their daily lives would be to observe their actions. Another is to ask people about what they do. Direct observation, whether in the field or in a laboratory, is not typical in sociology. The sociologist, for the most part, asks people questions. Phillips (1971:3) points out that more than 90% of studies in the *American Sociological Review* between 1962 and 1969, and 92% of studies in the *American Journal of Sociology* and *American Sociological Review* in 1965–1966 used the survey research technique. I will spend my time accordingly detailing the distortion inherent in this approach. Nonetheless, the ethnomethodological criticisms of this measurement practice apply as well to participant observation and laboratory techniques (Cicourel, 1964; Crowle, 1971; Jennings, 1972).

Tabulating Social Phenomena

In the survey method, the sociologist constructs a set of questions. The answers provide indicators of relationships. To determine the economic position of the family, for example, the sociologist might ask a series of questions concerning the occupation of the head of the household, how much money is earned, and how long that person has been employed. To determine the family's attitude toward family size, the sociologist might ask about the family's attitude toward children, optimal family size, and the actual number of children in the family.

The answers are not claimed to constitute "economic position" and "attitude toward family size" respectively. Rather, they are claimed to indicate these theoretical "things," as smoke does fire. The sociologist selects a representative sample of respondents and solicits their cooperation in answering the questions. When an adequate number of questionnaires have been completed, the sociologist tabulates the answers. The answers are replaced by "objective" numerals, which are placed in tables. Mathematical operations are conducted on the tabulated numerals to see whether the originating theory fits the data, whether the sociologist's reality has been matched by the reality found "in the field."

A typical example of the way data is displayed in sociological studies appears in Table 4.[5] This table represents data collected by Cicourel in his study of fertility and family planning in Argentina. The study was designed as a replication of Blake (1961) and Stycos (1955). Its method of presentation is similar to that found in most sociological studies.

Table 4 shows that 90% of the men and 83% of the women interviewed designated cities of over 100,000 as their birthplace. In general, this sample would be characterized as *urban*. The religious preference of the majority of respondents is Catholic, according to the table. Few divorces, separations, or second marriages are reported by the respondents. Sociologists traditionally hold that family stability is important for low fertility and family planning. Thus they might argue from this table that since Argentine marriages are stable, family planning efforts would be likely to succeed (cf. Blake, 1961). The family stability hypothesis is given further support by the urban character of the sample.

Table 4 General Characteristics of Cicourel's Argentina Sample

Characteristics	Men	Women
Place of birth		
Rural Argentina	3	15
Urban Argentina	67	102
Semiurban Argentina	7	13
Rural area in foreign country	—	—
Urban area in foreign country	23	22
Semiurban area in foreign country	—	—
Religion		
Catholic	78	124
Protestant	4	9
Other Christian religions	2	5
Jewish	6	8
Other	—	—
None	9	4
No information	1	—
Marital status		
Common-law	1	2
Married	95	138
Separated	2	5
Divorced	1	3
Widowed	1	9
Number of unions		
One	93	147
Two	7	5
Three or more	—	—
Totals for each characteristic	100	152

Cicourel argues that tables like this do not reveal the reality of every-day interaction which leads to decisions about having children, sexual intercourse, or terminating marriages. Such tables distort family life, just as school tests obscure the reality of children. For example, the stability of Argentine families inferable from this table is deceiving, because there is no legal means to obtain a divorce in Argentina. Cicourel reports that some members of the middle class or upper middle class do obtain "mail order" divorces from Mexico, and some go to Uruguay, but such activities are mainly ceremonial. The lower classes rarely go through any formal procedure. Instead, when marriages are troubled, both parties may take up other relationships while retaining the "fact" of their own marriage. These entangling alliances produce highly complicated lives, especially for the *villa miseria* poor who live in Buenos Aires and other large cities.

Table 4 provides no evidence of the negotiated living arrangements that occur especially among the poor. Common-law marriages are common. These living arrangements produce complicated kinships, for children may be exposed to maternal kin only. Fathers may come and go over the course of a few years. In these common-law arrangements the wife's problem is to hold on to the husband long enough so that he contributes to the support of the household while the children are growing up. "Holding on" might mean providing the husband with sex on demand, a bed, food, and clothes cleaned and repaired, while requiring from him minimal responsibility for raising children. Because divorce is illegal, and because the poor are unwilling to defy church divorce dogma while engaging in extramarital relations, the *reported* stability of marriage does not reflect the actual instability of the family patterns of the people studied.

In sum, Cicourel claims that sociological tables of data no more reflect the manifold realities of everyday life than a battery of test scores provides an accurate picture of the abilities and sensibilities of a child. This critique of social science research is not merely a complaint that the sociologist is "abstracting" from his phenomenon. The ethnomethodological discovery is not that the results of sociological studies are not themselves the phenomena they attempt to describe. All science necessarily abstracts from its phenomena. The trouble with sociology is that its abstraction systematically distorts what common sense tells us was the beginning phenomenon of interest: the actual day-to-day social life of human beings. In the sociologist's tables of data, and even more in the theories made up about those tables, one cannot find a sense of the person's daily activities that produced the various phenomena those tables talk about.

Constructing Data in the Interview

To obtain the computer printouts and subsequent tables on which socio-logical explanations are built, the sociologist must first transform respondents' answers into quantifiable data. Such coding processes conceal the respondent's experience of the social scene that is being asked about. In addition, coding processes always necessarily mask the embodied symbolic character of the social interaction between the interviewer and the respondents that produced the answers in the first place.

Surveys dip into everyday life and take a reading as if people were oil in an engine and the interview a calibrated dipstick. The sociologist presumes that what adheres to the stick is itself not important, except for what it indicates about "something else." The interviewer is not interested in the interview. The information there is not seen as a part of that particular interaction, but is rather made to stand on behalf of other activities that the researcher never observes. For example, as in Cicourel's replication, the concern may be with births and deaths, but the researcher does not observe people courting or flirting or touching, preparatory to creating a baby. Neither does he observe the day in, day out sanitary habits of his subjects, acts affecting their mortality rates. Rather than look at such activities, the sociologist asks subjects to tell about them, and accepts these descriptions as indicators of the activities themselves.[6]

This is not a complaint about the veracity or reliability of subjects; it is not a matter of whether they are "telling the truth." To "tell the truth" about one's behaviors, no matter how candidly and completely, is never a direct exhibition of the behaviors themselves. It is a gloss for them, a breaking down of the ongoing flow of life into a set of verbal categories. By concentrating on talk rather than on the activities themselves, social scientists ease their way toward the kind of causal descriptions to which they are committed. They further aid their commitment by directing subjects' conversations: the interviewer will ask the questions, supply the topics, mention key words. All this is carefully preplanned by the researcher to assure that whatever happens in the interview will be translatable into the preestablished coding categories. Such research is never directly concerned with the general question of the relations between everyday descriptive talk—the talk in an interview—and events in the world. Neither are these researchers interested in describing how the interview itself unfolds.

Table 5 summarizes the length of time Cicourel's Argentine respondents were engaged prior to their present marriage. This table shows that 75% of the couples had courtships that lasted one year or more. The sociologist would typically hypothesize that fewer children would be produced by this sample.

Table 5   Duration of Engagement Prior to Present Marriage from Cicourel (1973b:92)

Duration of Engagement	Frequency
Less than six months	12
Six months to one year	29
One to two years	45
More than two years	80
No information	4
Total	170

Cicourel (1973b:92ff.) analyzes part of an interview of an older couple who satisfy the modal categories reported in Table 5. The wife's interview schedule shows the following:

Age:	69
Occupation prior to marriage:	chef
Age when met present husband:	43
Children:	none

These data seem neat and obvious. But such coded results do not reveal how the interviewer accomplished the intricate work of turning the wife's answers into his coding categories. For example, when the woman was asked at what age she began to go out with men, she replied: "Eighteen." She said she had a boyfriend at that age who visited "once or twice a week." Then, when asked about her parents' actions toward the boyfriend, she replied: "I would receive him in my house, he would come in the early evening two times a week. My parents were very [sensitive] 'delicate.' " Cicourel said that the implication of this remark is that her parents were strict. Thus, the sociologist might draw the conclusion that in this case premarital intercourse was unlikely. When the woman was subsequently asked: "How frequently would you see each other? Where?" the woman answered: "Every 15 or 20 days because the parents were 'delicate,' they did not want us to see each other every day."

Cicourel interprets this remark as contradicting the earlier statement about the boyfriend visiting twice a week. The next question asked was: "Was this the first man you had sexual relations with?" The woman answered: "No." The second part of the question was a probe: "Could you tell me something more about this?" The question produced the response: "My present husband wants to have relations every four days, but he can't and becomes very nervous. He attempts it [sexual relations] when he is well, but not when he is angry. He then bangs [himself, his head] against the wall."

Cicourel (Ibid.:93–94) analyzes the woman's answer to this question:

> By using the open-ended questions we attempted to generate details and broad conceptions about everyday family life in the hope of eliciting as much ethnographic background as possible to offset the static question-answer format. Since the woman's remark did not appear to be a response to the probe, we might speculate along one or any number of the following lines: that she did not have anything to report about the first man with whom she dated socially, that she did not want to bring up the affair again, that her present marriage was felt to be more "interesting" for the interviewer, that her remarks were intended to open up a more serious problem than the original question and probe touched on, or that she viewed the questions as invitations or excuses for getting at her present circumstances.

Because the woman's answer to the question is ambiguous, it is difficult for the interviewer to code her response and tie it to the research hypothesis about the relationship between economic factors and fertility. "The interviewer and the respondent must engage in interpretive work in deciding if a response is appropriate" (Ibid.:94). Yet this interpretive work is neither part of sociologists' theory nor of their method.

The interview situation is a chunk of time from one reality that is separate from the lived reality of the lovemaking, courtship, financial troubles, and so forth, which the interview is assumed to index. The interview's purpose is to capture lived experiences outside the interview. Yet, the interview itself is a new experience only vaguely related to the experiences it is supposed to represent. Even when the interviewer and respondent share the same reality—in the sense of "class" background, language, age—distortion is inevitable.

Cicourel's interview schedule contained a number of questions on premarital sexual relations. These were designed to lead the respondent into revealing information that fixed-choice questions would either preclude or structure in an unknown way. The exchange between this same female respondent (R) and the interviewer (I) follows (Ibid.:96–99):

I.   Did you (the two of you) ever talk about getting married? [At some time did (the two of you) talk about getting married?]

R.   Yes.

I.   What did you say?

R.   That if he had good intention(s) I would accept him. I was distrustful (of him) because there are men with bad intentions. "If you come with good intentions I accept, if not, no." [As if she were telling the interviewer how she spoke to her husband to be.] I treated him with *Usted* [formally, by using the polite form of address]. I treated him this way [formally] for two or three months. After two or three months when we became "promised" to each other, we began to *'tutear* [we became intimate on a first name basis, using the familiar form of address].

I.   How did you come to marry him?

R.   [They became married at the outset. The interviewer did not write down the answer verbatim, but paraphrased the respondent's remarks.]

I.   What made you want to be married to him?

R.   Because I worked, and it was very difficult to stay employed; it is better to work in one's home. I would have liked to marry a man but the opportunity never presented itself.

I.   Surely you did not help them [men] find you, were you afraid of them?

R.   Yes, I was afraid of them.

I.   Why were you afraid of them?

R.   Because of what people would say. In addition, my mother would always tell me to be careful because men always want to fool [trick] one.

I.   Did the marriage have something to do with your being pregnant?

R.   I did not have [sexual] relations before getting married.

I.   Who was more interested [anxious] in getting married?

R.   He was more interested because his daughter was leaving home, because she was getting married, and only he and his sons would remain at home.

The questioning begins with a question about premarital plans:

I.   Did you ever talk about getting married?
R.   Yes.

The woman's "yes" answer tells us nothing about the discussions, their frequency, or their emotions. A fixed choice answer of "seldom," "occasionally," and "often" tells us little more because behavioral scenes are not captured by such headings. The probe question ("What did you say?") supplies more information. It suggests that a "proper relationship" existed between the woman and her husband-to-be. The use of the Spanish polite form of address and a long engagement provide documentation for this "proper" relationship. However, as Cicourel (Ibid.:97), says:

> we have no other details about their day-to-day physical and verbal communication. The age of the couple may have been one reason for the seemingly exaggerated formality of the relationship, or perhaps the woman was simply afraid of men as was suggested earlier; perhaps too all courtships were more formal at the time the couple met, or there may have been some combination of the three, even a dozen more possibilities. The particular statements we call questions and answers are sufficiently ambiguous yet they also seem sufficiently plausible to allow us to construct a rather large number of convincing explanations.

The next question asks: "What made you want to be married to him?"

R.   Because I worked, and it was very difficult to stay employed; it is better to work in one's own home. I would have liked to marry a man but the opportunity never presented itself.

This question was designed to encourage respondents to provide spontaneous details about their marriage. It was intended to get beneath an idealized normative answer. This woman's explanation of the "practical" need to get married seems convincing. However, the interviewer questioned the respondent further:

I.   Surely you did not help them find you, were you afraid of them?
R.   Yes, I was afraid of them.

A plausible reason for this woman's marriage at this time now emerges: she had a long-standing fear of men, especially their concerns with sex.

She was working, but felt her job lacked security. Her husband-to-be seemed to have allayed her fear by maintaining a proper relationship for a number of months. The fact that the woman was not pregnant and that the husband's daughter was leaving home provide more evidence for this interpretation of the woman's account.

However, propriety constrains the interviewer from exploring another equally plausible account of this marriage: the woman was getting old and had not yet landed a man; this one came along, and was grabbed for convenience (Ibid.:98). The interview format requires the interviewer to accept the unstated conditions provided by the respondent and precludes exploring answers very deeply.

There is an acceptable way one can and should talk to a stranger who enters one's home in science's name. Such polite talk is not false talk. It merely reminds us that the interviewer expects this woman to give the interviewer an explanation of her marriage that she would not give her best female friend. She might well have two more plausible stories she tells—one to her husband, another to her mother. Though substantially different, none would be a lie. The interviewer, too, gets a valid account of this woman's past. But clearly, the real phenomenon of interest emerging here is that of accounting, of talk and the interview interaction itself. One cannot extrapolate from the woman's talk to a causal theory of fertility rates, without ignoring how plausible stories constitute the social order.

To think that these "problems" can be resolved by adding this one woman's response to thousands of others and transforming them all from "sloppy" conversation into numerals seems not so much hopeless as absurd. I have as many stories about my life as there are occasions in which to tell them. So does everyone. The "true" causes undergirding such stories will not be known until we have solved the problem of the relation between everyday talk and the "things" and "events" and "feelings" that talk is supposed to be about. But surely we will first have to solve the far simpler problem of the relation between scientific symbols and the realities they symbolize. I shall argue that this "simpler" problem may not permit any general solution.

Spontaneous Interviewing

Aware of the way interrogation structures meaning, Shumsky (1972) attempted to obtain spontaneously generated descriptions of the "same" object. The persons chosen were all members of an encounter group that Shumsky led. He arranged for one session of the group to be video-taped, and produced a "hot-seat" experience within it. He devised a novel "interviewing" technique. He had participants removed from the group after the hot seat had been played out, but while the group was continuing. The participant was met by Shumsky's confederate in an adjoining room. A videotape of the hot seat experience was available to the interviewer and participant for viewing.

Shumsky wanted the interviews to unfold without the imposition of categories on the respondents' descriptions. The interviewer was to merely point the respondent toward the video monitor. A few open-ended questions were to elicit the participants' descriptions. These self-generating accounts were to constitute Shumsky's data on naturally oc-curring descriptions.

This simple design was difficult to carry out. The interactional work required to obtain naturally occurring descriptions opposed the work required to sustain the interview itself. This tension is illustrated in the following exchange between the Interviewer and Jay. Jay had just been exposed to the hot-seat experience.

(1)	*Jay.*	I'm being psychoanalytically indoctrined.
(2)	*Interviewer.*	Yeah sit down.
(3)	*Jay.*	Do you have a match?
(4)	*Interviewer.*	Eh yeah. I do as a matter of fact. I got one uh let's see ah uh here we go.
(5)	*Jay.*	What are you seeing here?
(6)	*Interviewer.*	Ah oh this is a re-play. How about that. We're really ——— man.
(7)	*Jay.*	You were watching.
(8)	*Interviewer.*	No. I can't watch it we got one tape out okay.
(9)	*Jay.*	Yeah.
(10)	*Interviewer.*	Okay. Not very clear is it?
(11)	*Jay.*	This isn't from the beginning.
(12)	*Interviewer.*	Uh almost uh not from the very beginning but when they started I was trying to get ah a certain place here ah let me just uh find it.
(13)	*Jay.*	Have you already seen this?
(14)	*Interviewer.*	No no I haven't seen it cause he just gave it to me yeah he just gave it to me yeah now its ah it's

		shorter than what we thought all right it's shorter (turns off video recorder). Let me I mean let me ask you something first uh I was interested in how you uh was talking to Erv was it Erv about his engagement to Sherry.
(15)	*Jay.*	Yeah.
(16)	*Interviewer.*	Is this a long standing deal? I didn't uh couldn't understand it. Is it like I got later that uh you guys had talked him out of it at one point? Is that what you said?
(17)	*Jay.*	This was a year ago in group.
(18)	*Interviewer.*	Oh.
(21)	*Jay.*	We were very turned off to this you see.
(22)	*Interviewer.*	Oh I see.
(23)	*Jay.*	You can hear it all on the tape. I don't have to reiterate you know.
(24)	*Interviewer.*	No I heard it okay but I didn't see it on the tape but uh I couldn't understand what uh what got that started.
(25)	*Jay.*	Oh I see. Oh yeah that's what did. See only Tom, Gina, and I, and Erv and and uh uh Marshall know (Shumsky, 1972:197–198).

The exchange shows that the interviewer could not just point to the scenes on the video monitor. He also had to relax the respondent (2 and 4). These competing demands worked against each other and the success of the interview. Jay (5) then asks the interviewer the sorts of questions Jay himself is supposed to answer.

The interviewer then tries to focus the respondent's attention without being too specific (12). The interviewer refers to the event to be described as "a certain place" not "that part of the tape that shows you on the hot seat." The interviewer wants the respondent to "fill in" these vague references in the way he ordinarily would describe such a situation. But, in attempting to leave room for the respondent to supply the description, the interviewer ends up doing most of the describing. The interviewer's evasiveness fails to produce well-formulated descriptions. The respondent responds vaguely to vague questions (see especially 21 to 25).

This phenomenon is illustrated by a second interview Shumsky presents. Vickie, the respondent, is an experienced encounter group member. She arrived too late to witness Jay's hot-seat experience. The interviewer shows her that portion of the videotape. This is part of the exchange that followed:

(204) *Vickie.* And Erv knew where he was at.

(205) *Interviewer.* Oh.

(206) *Vickie.* You know it's strange.

(207) *Interviewer.* What do you think Marsh is doing?

(208) *Vickie.* Marshall?

(209) *Interviewer.* Yeah.

(210) *Vickie.* Well he uh um I don't know he's um you know asking Jay un you know why does there have to be a time element (Interviewer: oh) why does there have to be all these things like why you know I don't see you getting involved you're always retreating and going back.

(211) *Interviewer.* Going always retreating going back?

(212) *Vickie.* Right only before like getting really involved with someone and thinking (Interviewer: eh) there has to be a time element.

(213) *Interviewer.* What do you think Marshall's up to by making that kind of a remark those kinds of remarks to Jay?

(214) *Vickie.* I don't know. Marshall's really incredible sometimes.

(215) *Interviewer.* Do you think he's just talking or do you think he's doing it for some reason or you know if you were sitting eh there.

(216) *Vickie.* I don't know what (Ibid.:211–212).

This exchange displays the tension created by attempting to obtain self-organizing descriptions while simultaneously maintaining the interview as a sensible conversation. The interviewer wanted to shift the topic from the incident in the session that preceded the hot-seat experience (the group's discussion of one participant's impending marriage) to the procedures the group leader used during the hot-seat experience. At the same time, the interviewer did not want to impose a particular way of seeing the experience. The essentially vague statement "What do you think Marsh is doing?" (207) is the result. Vickie (210) does not provide a specific response to the question. The interviewer repeats her final comment ("always retreating and going back") as an attempt to encourage the respondent to continue.

The interviewer's comment "What do you think Marshall's up to" (213) attempts to focus attention in an unfocused way. Like the first question (207), it does not elicit a substantial description (214). Apparently thwarted by the lack of openness met by the previous questions (207 and 213), the interviewer imposes a choice of alternatives on the respondent: "Do you think he's just talking or do you think he's doing it *for some reason* or do you know if *you were sitting there*". Even this attempt to organize the respondent's perceptions was not sufficient to overcome the vagueness of the previous questions.

The interviewer provides so little structure that he does not get the description he desires. Nevertheless, the respondent remarks on his attempts to structure her perceptions:

(225)	*Interviewer.*	But then I know that pulling you out like that you know kind of puts you on the spot here with me and I don't want to make you feel uncomfortable but at the same time I'm really interested in how you see things.
(226)	*Vickie.*	Well it's good because like you stop and you clarify points that I haven't even thought of.
(227)	*Interviewer.*	Ah well how did I do that?
(228)	*Vickie.*	And you make me think (Interviewer: yeah) well why is someone doing this and why is someone doing that because usually I just I I understand the whole thing I'm thinking about what I would say to the person and bringing someone out um you try and get something from another person.
(229)	*Interviewer.*	Oh but you do? I'm telling you these things that uh maybe you wouldn't ordinarily think about.
(230)	*Vickie.*	Yeah.
(231)	*Interviewer.*	Yeah but in that case then I'm it's not me maybe it's just not you it's me that's talking see I in other words I'm concerned that . . .

(232)   *Vickie.*   Yeah.

(233)   *Interviewer.*   That if I'm giv if I'm feeding you this stuff then hell that doesn't do me any good cause after all I can go and see it and say to you well Vickie what do you make of it so you think then that I've really uh suggested things to you that you wouldn't have thought of otherwise.

(234)   *Vickie.*   Right.

(235)   *Interviewer.*   Oh that's interesting uh see in other words I'm trying to figure out.

(236)   *Vickie.*   See when you question something.

(237)   *Interviewer.*   Yeah.

(238)   *Vickie.*   It it makes me have to clarify it in my mind and then clarify it to you (Ibid:212–213; italics omitted).

Vickie indicates that she feels the interviewer is structuring her experience by saying:

(226)   *Vickie.*   Well it's good because like you stop and you clarify points that I haven't even thought of.

(228)   *Vickie.*   And you make me think . . . well why is someone doing this and why is someone doing that because usually I just . . . understand the whole thing. . . .

The respondent says she normally experiences the group's activities as a coherent whole. But she explains that she appreciates the interviewer's structuring:

(236-238)   *Vickie.*   See when you question something. . . . it makes me have to clarify it in my mind and then clarify it to you.

Shumsky's work provides a social science analog for an argument prominent in the later philosophy of Wittgenstein. This argument is summarized in Wittgenstein's (1953:14e) observation that "an ostensive definition can be variously interpreted in every case." Shumsky's study illustrates the relevance of Wittgenstein's argument for the social sciences. Shumsky's transcripts make evident that interviewers cannot merely ask their respondents to match "signs" with them. Mere ostensive pointing to a phenomenon such as the hot-seat experience can always be misunderstood. The researcher must supply the respondent with the "right" context. By creating such contexts, researchers structure respondents' talk. This is an unavoidable consequence of talking.

Structured interviews produce descriptions. But such impositions do not produce naturally occurring descriptions. Unstructured interviews generate naturally occurring talk. But this talk is rarely about the specific research topic. One way to avoid this circularity is to treat talk itself as a phenomenon (Garfinkel, 1967a; Sacks, 1963; Zimmerman and Pollner, 1970; cf. Chapter 6).

The Interpretation of Secondary Data

Sociologists have attempted to avoid these methodological problems by analyzing materials like census reports and crime statistics that have already been collected for other purposes. After a review of the literature in one research area that uses such secondary data, Garfinkel (1960, in 1967:211) concludes that the findings from these studies are built upon "long chains of plausible inference which require the researcher *to presuppose a knowledge of the very social structures that are presumably being described in the first instance.*"

These studies examined psychiatric clinic records to see if characteristics such as sex, age, social class, and referral method distinguished outpatients who were accepted from those who were rejected. Garfinkel points to three inadequacies in these studies that are endemic to all sociological uses of "secondary data." First, these studies use different sets of characterizing categories or parameters. None uses the entire set that can be compiled from the 23 studies collected together. Therefore, the concept "client," so central to the research, is never adequately described.

This vagueness in social science parameters should be compared to the use of parameters in natural science. In physics, for example, "sound in general" is defined by three parameters: amplitude, frequency, and duration. In any specific instance one need not determine the quantitative values of all three parameters. But in using the concept one must know that the three parameters define it, and that each of them must be measured when the concept is exhaustively described (Garfinkel, 1967a:210).

Sociological concepts are not so defined. The parameters that one study uses to define a "client," for example, are not those of some other study. It is not simply that each study chooses to measure different parameters: they do not even agree on the parameters in the first place.

A second difficulty arises after researchers have performed their mathematical operations on the data. They have "results" before them, a series of numbers exhibiting statistical significance. The problem is to translate these into findings that inform the researchers about the procedures of clinic personnel which can only be done by adopting one of a number of models of the way the clinic works. To conform to the rigorous demands of science, this choice must be made independent of the mathematical data. But depending on the model of clinic activities that the sociologist adopts, different results will be obtained. More alarmingly, *different models will result in different findings*, even when the mathematical results remain the same.

For example, the data Garfinkel collected in his replication of this work showed that the age distribution of those accepted and those rejected did not vary significantly. The typical research model of clinics would transform these results into the finding that clinic personnel do not use age as a criterion. "On the other hand," Garfinkel (Ibid.:243) points out, "the identical non-significant chi-square could be treated as a contrasting finding, i.e., that the clinic personnel made their selections with respect to the age distribution of the original cohort." That is, one could suppose that the clinic personnel acted to assure that at each stage of the clinic's activities, the patients in treatment were representative of the entire population of persons who ever contacted the clinic. There are "good reasons" to suppose this indeed was the case: clinic personnel were aware that politically powerful persons were monitoring their actions to make sure they were unprejudicially serving the "community at large." The question that oriented these studies—how do clinic personnel select clients—is not resolved by the mathematical results. The results can be used to support alternative models; the choice between these models must be made on extramathematical grounds.

The best model to interpret the results would presumably be the one that best fits actual clinic personnel activities. But after reviewing three candidate models, each of which give a different meaning to the mathematical research results, Garfinkel raises a third difficulty with these types of studies. In actual clinic procedures, he suggests, prospective clients cannot be unequivocally grouped into two classes, one of which is undergoing treatment, the other not. The treatment of persons by clinics is more fluid than this. No one is a client once and for all; no person is ever finally rejected.

But researchers, on the other hand, must treat clinic events as "essentially discrete events," otherwise their mathematical procedures make no sense. When they do this, clinic personnel complain that such formulae do not describe "adequately *their* interest in cases and *their* ways of handling clinic affairs" (Ibid.:254). In other words, researchers hear the complaint that their quantitative parameters are not the things that personnel use to conduct their daily work. The researchers, they feel, distort their reality.

In general terms, the critique of social science presented so far may be summarized as follows.

First comes the initial and irrevocable step of the data gathering encounter. The ethnomethodologist says that the interview imposes a structure on the respondent that may not be consistent with the respondent's daily life. The structure of the interview is based on a formal logic that does not necessarily recover the way in which people make decisions in their daily lives. The *talk* about sexual activities is assumed to provide a scientifically adequate description of the *doing* of sexual activities. Of course, researchers build checks for reliability and validity. But these checks assume that everyday language can accurately describe social actions, if only persons are properly motivated, or encouraged, or probed. I have tried to illustrate the arbitrariness of this assumption. Much of the original work of ethnomethodology explicitly eschews the assumption of the separation of words and things. This work is the subject of later chapters.

A second step away from everyday interaction occurs during the sociological coding process. At this juncture, the results of the interview, experiment, or field study are run through a grid to remove the ambiguity of everyday life and substitute the either-or logic of science. This transforms a real human situation into a collection of logical categories. In this collection, one is no longer able to recover the logic of everyday life.

Next comes the manipulation of the "objectified data" produced by the coding process. These categories are treated as indicators of "factors" and "causes" which were never directly observed within the data collection situation. Equally strange, these data are now manipulated as if the coding process has merely been a "technical" problem. Previously, data collection models had to be assumed by the coders in order to get the coding done. Now, similar models must be employed by the researchers as they interrogate their data. However, neither of these models are made an explicit feature of the research. The model used by the coders to turn the raw data into the objective data may well differ from that used by sociologists to interpret this data.

In the fourth and final stage, the sociologists codify the various "findings" that have emerged from their interrogation of the objective data. They offer these to the public and to their colleagues as descriptions of social life. But such descriptions rest upon this four-fold progression of increasing abstraction away from the everyday lives of human beings. In order for a theory relating economic factor to family size to be persuasive, for example, we would have to be able to observe economic factors in the here and now affecting the subtle negotiations that lead to sexual intercourse. The claim that lower social class causes the propagation of children tells us nothing of the everyday loves of people.

That is, in attempting to do a social *science*, sociology has become alienated from the social. Bittner (1973:115), writing about modern interpreters of Marx, summarizes this implication of my critique:

> Positivists cannot understand that the realities of society and culture are a function of passion and of judgment, and that without passion and judgment they cannot be apprehended in their true nature. It is of the greatest importance that dealing with human matters from a distance and by means of instruments is no mere innocent mistake, it is artful deception . . ., the ultimate effect of which cannot be anything but the further spiritual deracination of man and the increase of the sum total of alienation in society.

While most ethnomethodologists accept this critique, it marks as well one of the many points from which individual paths begin to diverge. Having "found social science out" in this way, the question arises whether we are now ready to develop a superior social science. Some of the researches my later chapters describe strive to avoid the problems this critique raises. Others take the critique so seriously that they are not within the social science tradition. They are hybrids of science and art.

Understanding these differences and the depths of the critique calls for an examination of the ultimate scaffolding of the natural and social sciences: formal logic.

LOGIC AND REALITY

Logic and Social Research

Sociology seeks models of explanation like those in the natural sciences. Such scientific explanations establish causal relationships among literally defined concepts. Unfortunately, when the logical requirements of causal relations and literal description are applied to social phenomena, they distort those phenomena.

A causal model requires that each event have an antecedent. Every change must have a cause. The causative agent can be stated as the subject of the proposition, for example, "The man broke the window." The subject is indispensable in the propositional sentence. It is the causative agent of the action reported by the predicate. If it is not stated, it is implied. "The window broke" implies a causative agent: a man, the wind, etc. Formulations of thought based on such logic do not allow an uncaused event. Even though the exact factual cause may not be apparent, the assumption remains that something or someone caused the event to occur, and that the causative agent is located in the linearly recoverable past.

Causal models require literally defined concepts. Literal measurement (Cicourel, 1964; Wilson, 1970) specifies a category or class and identifies properties that objects must possess in order to be included in that class. Literal measurement requires that phenomena being treated conform to the "law of the excluded middle" and the "law of identity."

The law of the excluded middle operates as a kind of logical division. The first operation of logical division separates objects dichotomously: those that are something from those that are not, those that possess a certain attribute from those that do not. The conventional way of representing this dichotomous division is: $p/not\ p$. The division $p/not\ p$ is not equivalent to p/q, for those in q may not be in p. This conclusion points to the need for mutual exclusiveness in logical definitions.

A logical definition specifies the properties of an object in propositional form. For example: "This object is yellow and hard." Yellowness and hardness are the attributes of the object. They are in the object. The properties are assumed to be stable, discrete, and permanent. An object defined as yellow and hard will be defined in the same way at a later time and will be the same object to all competent observers.

Once an object has been defined as having certain properties it retains those properties, because an object cannot be two things at once according to the law of the excluded middle.[7]

A causal model requires that the phenomenon being studied conform to the law of identity. A classic formulation of the law of identity is Leibniz's law: "This holds basically that identical 'things' share all the same properties. No property will distinguish one identical thing from another" (Schwartz, 1971:49; after Lewis, 1918). That is, A is always A.

Within natural sciences the assumption of causes and literal description has proved efficacious. The results within social science have been more equivocal. Ethnomethodological studies suggest there is a principled reason for this equivocality: social events are not networks of caused events, nor are they amenable to literal description.

Consider, for example, the search for causes. The natural science model claims that every event must have a determinate antecedent. In sociological studies of family size, "economic conditions" are frequently offered as the antecedent cause of a certain number of children. Cicourel's work illustrates that this "cause" is not experienced as a factor by men and women as they woo one another. They do not make love and have children or abortions because of economic conditions.

To seek any cause for their behavior requires the assumption that they experience the world and each other through the use of literally defined concepts. If a sociological explanation is to describe social relations, it must describe portions of lived social realities. But persons do not use concepts or speak to one another (or interviewers) in conformance with the laws of the excluded middle and identity. This does not mean that people are irrational. It does mean that they are rational in a way that is incompatible with the requirements of literal description.

Everyday objects do not display constant and stable properties. The meanings of real world events flow. Cicourel's work illustrates, for example, that the activity "having children" did not have the same meaning for the researcher and for the marital partners, as the law of the excluded middle required. The meaning shifted over the course of every interview. Similarly, the meaning shifts over the duration of any person's day, as over their life. "Having children" means one thing to a virgin, another to the same woman during her pregnancy, yet another when she is giving birth—still another when she is talking to an interviewer, and so forth. The law of the excluded middle requires constancy. Sociological explanations adapt meanings from everyday life and impose that constancy. This destroys the experiential essence of everyday life, its constant ebb and flow.

The law of identity is not applicable to everyday life since, according to this logical principle, every word must mean the same to every person. But Cicourel's work illustrates that different respondents heard the "same" questions differently. A question or cluster of questions was not an identical stimulus object to all respondents. Meanings in everyday life are bound to context and personal history. These integral parts of every meaning undermine the requirements of the law of identity—that same "things" be indistinguishable from one another.

As everyday meanings do not meet the canons of logic, they are transformed by literal description. These transformed meanings are amenable to causal models. Everyday life is not.

Logic as a Commonsense System

As I have just indicated, sociologists assume that formal logic is a natural scaffolding upon which to hang explanatory descriptions of human phenomena. They simultaneously assume that formal logic is a system intrinsically superior to any other reasoning. Each assumption reflexively provides for the other.

Ethnomethodologists, on the other hand, have come to think of formal logic as just one more system among many. It is no more (or less) universally applicable than the Tarot, or astrology, or Yaqui sorcery. There is no a priori reason why logic should be used as a general apparatus for collecting descriptions of all other realities that appear. One could just as well investigate events in order to translate them into an explanation using astrology, Yaqui sorcery, or the Akarama or Azande cosmologies.

Schwartz (1971) argues that if logic, or any system, is to deserve the faith of universal application, two separate criteria must be met. The first requirement is that the system not be grounded in the vagaries and ambiguities of common sense. After all, if the candidate system is but one more commonsensical system, it will be impossible to claim that its laws and explanations transcend common sense and exhibit truths more fundamental than everyday talk. Schwartz argues that logic depends on common sense.

The second requirement for a system claiming to be universal is that it must demonstrate that objects are constant, independent of its methods of apprehension. Schwartz argues that formal logic has not found a general solution to this problem of object constancy.

Schwartz develops these two arguments by focusing on the history of the problem that the law of identity has posed for logic. The law of identity was described above as: *A* is *A;* that is, identical objects have all properties in common. This definition permits impressive technical formulations. But as a *definition* of identity, it has posed problems for logicians. It has led to some logically valid conclusions that are inconsistent with common sense.

The law of identity, for example, permits the following valid syllogism:

1. The number of planets = 9
2. Kepler did not know that the number of planets was greater than 6
3. (Therefore) Kepler did not know 9 was greater than 6 (after Kalish, 1959:229; in Schwartz, 1971:67).

In attempting to solve such contradictions, logicians appeal to their commonsense knowledge of the world. This sense dictates that the conclusion (no. 3) is a fallacy, and so the logician begins the technical work of seeking a mechanism to undo the paradox. Logicians look for ways to redefine the law of identity so that it will produce conclusions that are consistent with common sense.

In attempting to solve contradictions between logic and common sense posed by the law of identity, logicians begin with an unquestioned commonsensical faith. They assume that objects are independent of the methods by which they are observed. Logicians do not treat this belief as a theoretical problem. They do not first undertake an empirical investigation to see if more than one kind of identity relation appears in the world.

Logicians assume as well that identity permits a general formulation. As Frege (in Schwartz 1971:62) wrote, "it is inconceivable that various kinds of it should occur." And yet they seek no evidence for this either. It is an incorrigible proposition in their knowledge system, as unchallengeable as the Azandes' belief in the power of their oracle.

Schwartz discusses three famous correctives for the law of identity, those of Russell, Frege, and Husserl. It is clear that each of these thinkers based their solutions on what they assumed about the world, independent of logic or science. They each seek to reconcile these commonsense assumptions with the rigorous criteria of logic. Once they have established their principled solutions, they then use these solutions to denigrate the messy way people in their everyday lives talk and reason. But these "formal semantic interpretations of a concept only obtain their preferred status over commonsense understandings after the legislation [of a corrective for common sense] is accomplished and the results tried and accepted." "Before that," Schwartz goes on to say, "the situation is quite the reverse" (1971:76). It is common sense that is given the "preferred status."

Schwartz shows that logical investigations "proceed by considering some conception from ordinary language use, mathematics, science, traditional logic and philosophy, or commonsense reasoning, and try to shape and fashion it so that it satisfies constraints, sometimes from all these areas simultaneously!" (Ibid.:67). Clearly, to see logic in this way is not to denigrate its practice. It only indicates the futility of appealing to logic in an effort to find a system that will be independent of common sense. Where else could logic come from than from the everyday world? Why should we expect any single syntactic system to arise, upon which all other realities could be placidly hung?

Once logical systems are lowered from the illusory imperial heights and are understood as human phenomena like any other, they do not lose their usefulness. They become interesting in a way they never were before. One of the principles of ethnomethodology is that objects are not constant, but instead are the creation of a ceaseless body of reality work. When logic enters the picture, it explicitly seeks to deny this principle and build a discipline wherein the constancy of objects is assumed and raised to the place of highest honor. Any reality so absolutely committed to this fundamental principle thus becomes a phenomenon of special fascination to ethnomethodologists. They would suppose that the attempt to so deify object constancy would forever fail, and that these recurrent failures would be exactly the most visible occasions wherein the principle of object constancy would be reflexively invoked in order to justify the failure it has produced.

This is the phenomenon Schwartz describes. The problem of identity has never found a general solution in logical theory, yet no one within the discipline has ever used this fact to suggest that there is no such thing. From the beginning, as an incorrigible proposition, logicians assumed that language, or at least logical language, is an *entity,* not an activity (cf. Schwartz, 1971:104). Logicians have failed to formulate non-paradoxical criteria that specify the logical relations which constitute an identical bunch of things. Yet this failure is not taken as grounds for rejecting the faith in entities as such. Rather, it is taken as further proof that the work of logic is not yet complete.

As Schwartz (1971) suggests, logic is thus like a theology. Or, as I said in Chapter 2, the faith in logic is held superstitiously. The failure of theologians to describe the attributes of God never leads to rejection of the God idea. Instead, these failures are pointed to as exhibiting once more the marvelous reality of that Being. The failure of an oracle never leads to the rejection of the oracle. The failure of an experiment never leads to a rejection of the scientific method. Just so, logicians are forever running their heads up against the fact that their objects seem only to reside in the ways that they talk about those objects. They never then reject the externality and independence of these objects. They instead appeal to their failures as proofs of the importance of their problems.

Ethnomethodologists see in logic a further demonstration of two of their own incorrigible propositions: (1) "it is impossible to distinguish and thus contrast, the interpretation of a thing from the thing itself . . . because the interpretation of the thing *is* the thing" (Ibid.:14). And (2) each knowledge system has absolute faith in its basic propositions. Logic is no more and no less superstitious than other knowledge systems in this regard.

When logic is thus seen as but one more instance of the process of reflexivity, it can be expected that in the face of "troubles" there will be a variety of "secondary elaborations of belief" (see Chapter 2) that can be invoked to save the reality's integrity. In the particular case of the problem of identity, these elaborations have typically centered around the invocation of "mental" constructs, unseen and unseeable. Rather than question the identity proposition, realms of "denotation" or "sense" or "noemas" have been proposed. Such realms are neither the thing nor the name for the thing. Such a realm remains forever constant. Identity relations are placed in such realms.

The elegance of these formulations lies in their irrefutability. No one can touch a hypothesized realm, and so the identity problem is solved.

No proof can deny that in Plato's heaven of Forms, for example, objects are constant. When contradictions occur in our world, it is to truths beyond that disputants appeal. One of these truths for the Azande is oracles, one for logicians is identity. Both truths permit no refutation and enable their realities to persist. From my point of view, these practices are identical, and thus I choose not to choose between them.

THE INEVITABILITY OF REALITY IMPOSITION

The social scientist and the educational tester impose formal logic on those they study and test. The imposition of a logic that is foreign to a reality creates distortions. The examples presented in Chapter 2 from Castaneda, Schneebaum, and others could also be used to show that every person's experience of the world is always from the point of view of the reality that person has learned. By imposing their reality, all individuals resemble the social scientist and the educational tester—they, too, are distorting the reality they are viewing.

These observations lead to the conclusion that such distortion is inevitable. One reality cannot investigate another without running it through its own knowledge and reasoning system. This distortion is as inevitable for the ethnomethodologist studying social science or educational testing as it is for the educator examining children, or for the Akarama hearing a phonograph record for the first time (Schneebaum, 1969).[8]

The studies by ethnomethodologists that seem to attack social science thus must be understood as points of view rather than as attacks. Any one person looking at another implies, in the final analysis, the imposition of one reality on another.

Distortion is inevitable and cannot be remedied; *ignorance* of this distortion is not inevitable and can be remedied. That understanding is a contribution of the ethnomethodological studies described in this chapter. Once the veil of ignorance is removed, and the necessity of distortion is understood, perhaps social scientists will no longer use their strength as academics to recast other cultures and subcultures in their own image.

But if this is the personal and political meaning of these studies, there is also a theoretic meaning. They point to a new range of phenomena previously untouched by social science: the phenomenon of distortion itself. Distortion is a phenomenon unlike phenomena in the sociology of knowledge. Questioning the methods of questioning the phenomenon are not excluded. The phenomenon and the method are mutually constitutive.

TOWARD THE STUDY OF EVERYDAY LIFE

Three related but separate discoveries seem to have emerged from ethnomethodology's explorations into the reality of social science. First, there is the methodological discovery that sociology's measurement is based on indicators and a process of abstraction that differs fundamentally from the measurement practices of the natural and life sciences.

Second, there is the claim that formal logic is an inappropriate model of the everyday actor within the flow of social life. In Chapter 4 I present as further evidence to support this claim an argument based on an "occasioned" concept of rules.

The third discovery stems from treating formal logic as but one more reality. Such an approach reveals that logic is based on common sense and has a self-preservative reflexive character. It is an independent reality upon which "lesser" forms can be hung only with distortion.

This critique of sociology is not so much ethnomethodology itself as it is a way of understanding the grounds upon which ethnomethodology has been built. These discoveries indicated the possibility that researchers could "cease treating the scientific rationalities as a methodological rule for interpreting social actions" (Garfinkel, 1960, in 1967a:279), and instead begin to seek "to discover the natural logic of common sense meanings" (Cicourel, 1964:103). However, the way to build such an alternative program is not obvious. Not one but several promising alternative paths have been charted. In the next chapter I review one of these paths, by discussing several studies that have created a new ethnographic sense for the nature of social rules. In Chapter 5 I detail the model of the actor that replaces for ethnomethodologists the overrationalized sociological model.

Chapter 6 describes an empirical program that treats the naturally occurring language practices of everyday speakers without a priori commitment to the scaffolding of formal logic. In Chapters 7 and 8 I examine six disparate programs that have concentrated on the phenomenon of reflexivity.

In Chapter 9 I offer an ethnomethodological alternative approach to the Hobbesian problem of social order. In Chapter 12 I discuss a research methodology that complements this theory. Chapter 10 provides a codification of ethnomethodology's philosophical groundings, while in Chapter 11 I attempt an appraisal of the moral import of ethnomethodology.

NOTES

1. The dialectical growth of ethnomethodology out of the body of social science is considered in Chapter 11. In Chapter 10, I offer an understanding of the dialectical relations among the basic concepts of ethnomethodology. Pollner (1970) has earlier explored the importance of dialectical thinking for ethnomethodology.

2. Within ethnomethodology, the most influential statement of this is Garfinkel's (1960, in 1967a:262–285), "The Rational Properties of Scientific and Common Sense Activities." Elaborating on Schutz (1962), Garfinkel describes 14 common meanings for the concept "rationality." He argues that four of these meanings are peculiar to the attitude of scientific theorizing. "By contrast, actions governed by the attitude of daily life are marked by the specific absence of these [four] rationalities" (Garfinkel, 1967a:270). Social scientists typically confuse these two attitudes and judge the actions of persons in everyday life by the criteria of the scientific rationalities. Thus, in the name of science they distort the phenomenon their theories are supposed to be about. Compare Cicourel, 1964; Blum, 1970a; and McHugh, 1970.

3. See Jennings and Jennings (1974), who draw the parallel between the social science experiment and the educational test.

4. This argument—that the natural sciences measure directly and the social sciences only indirectly—is a methodological specification of Schutz's (1962) discussion concerning the necessary use of "second-order" concepts in social science.

An early reader of this chapter raised the objection that the idea that the natural sciences measure directly is "old fashioned" philosophy of science. This is true. It is now *au courant* for philosophers of science to elaborate on Norman Campbell's ([1920] 1957; [1921] 1952) old ideas to maintain that measurement, like all else in science, emanates from a common-sense model, Campbell's (1957:113–158) "analogy." An introduction and bibliography to this "new" philosophy of science can be found in Prosch (1973). Most prominent among its proponents are Feyerabend (e.g., 1965a, 1965b) and Polanyi (e.g., 1958, 1966, 1969). I discuss this "movement" in Chapter 11.

But my discussion here is not concerned with such issues. When I maintain that the natural and life sciences measure directly I am not offering a philosophy of science but rather an empirical statement. I am not concerned with the various "reconstructed logics of science," to use Kaplan's (1964:10ff.) term. These philosophies have never been of much interest to the practicing natural scientist, anyway. Social scientists frequently mistake these reconstructed logics for empirical descriptions.

Lazarsfeld's (e.g., 1958, 1966) apologia for a social science based on indicators illustrates this. Lazarsfeld relies on the "old" philosophy of science. He accepts Carnap and Hempel's theories about science as empirical descriptions of actual practice. Thus Lazarsfeld is able to ignore the fact that practicing scientists normally assume they are measuring directly. This belief is so pervasive that it reaches beyond the laboratory into the minds of such grand theorists as Planck and Einstein. These two gentlemen rejected the Copenhagen interpretation of the quantum precisely because they maintained it did not lead to direct measurements. The idea of measurement which only "indicated" the presence of the quantum was so foreign to Einstein's conception of science that he argued that Bohr and Heisenberg were not doing science by proposing it. Philosophers of science such as Nagel (1961) both support Einstein's position against Heisenberg and argue that a dependence on indicators is not peculiar to social science. A more consistent view is to acknowledge that natural and social scientists differ importantly on this issue.

5.   This is Table 3 from Cicourel (1973b). Other studies that locate distortion as data is removed from its originating context are Cicourel (1973b, 1973d), Kitsuse and Cicourel (1963), Douglas (1967), Garfinkel (1967a, 1967b), Leiter (1969), and Mehan (1973, in preparation).

6.   This masking operation is not limited to social science research. Kitsuse and Cicourel (1963) located a similar phenomenon in the procedures used by such organizations as the police and FBI to assemble tables of statistics, or more specifically, rates of deviant behavior. Kitsuse and Cicourel (1963:138) say:

> criminal statistics fail to reflect the decisions made and the discretion used by law enforcement personnel and administrators, and the general accommodations that can and do occur. An offender's record, then, may never reflect the ambiguous decisions, administrative discretions, or accommodations of law enforcement personnel; a statistical account may thus seriously distort an offender's past activities.

7.   This discussion of logic in natural and social science (which benefits from the help of Sam Edward Combs) is an elaboration of the discussion of object constancy in Chapter 2.

8.   Schneebaum (1969:123-24) describes the manner in which stone age people "distort" the meaning of a phonograph. Their reality makes it into a box with tiny people inside. This description does not capture what Westerners know it to be any more than a Westerner's description of stone age reality captures the lived meaning of those phenomena.

CHAPTER FOUR

Reality
as a
Rules System

Many ethnomethodologists have studied everyday rule use. This work must be understood against the background of the sociological study of rule use with which it dialectically converses. This antithetical theory is the "normative conception" of action. Wilson (1970) has argued that it is the bedrock of all present-day sociologies, whether their theoretical orientation is functionalist, symbolic interactionist, or exchange, and whether their preferred methodology is surveys, experiments, or field observation (see Blum, 1970a).[1]

The normative theory of action employs three core concepts: actors, rules, and situations. It is assumed that *actors* know and follow *rules* in *social situations*. Rules are assumed to exist independently of actors and of situations. They are "external and objective" constraints, a species of the sociological conception of "social facts" articulated by Durkheim. Because rules are assumed to be independent of the scenes in which they appear, explanation within the normative theory of action amounts to a listing of the relevant, empirically determined rules. These rules take the form of motives, norms, folkways, expectations, et cetera, and are represented as the *causes* of sociologically relevant actions (see Blum, 1970a:335).

This theory also treats situations as independent of either the rules or the actors. Therefore, this mode of explanation makes persons within everyday life into "judgmental dopes" (Garfinkel, 1967a:66–75). In the normative theory of action, actors are thought to enter situations, define them, recognize which rules are applicable, and act automatically. The normative theory says that actors make no judgment in order to "know" what kind of situation they have entered. The normative theory does not make actors a constitutive part of that situation. The actor's presence there does nothing to inform the meaning of the situation.

The normative theory further assumes that once a situation is properly identified, no judgmental work is required to determine which rules are appropriate to it this time. To follow rules in the normative theory of action, the actor need only employ a simple "matching procedure." Once the situation's meaning is apparent, itself an automatic occurrence, the germane norms just flash in front of the actor like traffic signals, telling the person "walk" or "don't walk" (Cicourel, 1973a:11–41; Wieder, 1970.)

This normative theory of action intertwines with the overrationalized model of the actor discussed in the previous chapter. To assume that meaning in everyday life can be understood according to the model of meaning assumed in formal logic is to treat the elements of action as stable and finite "things."

Ethnomethodology has rejected formal logic as a model of action. The concept of rule has been central to all previous social theories. Therefore, a body of work was begun to construct an alternative description of rule use. This work has commonly employed the ethnographic method. It has lead to the general claim that rule use is neither automatic nor consistent. Whenever a rule is applied, it must be applied within a specific social situation. Relevant rules do not merely emerge once a social situation is determined. Actors, rules, and situations ceaselessly inform one another. The situation is not independent of the actors who are within it. And because of actors' ever-shifting corpus of social knowledge and practical interests (see Chapter 5), a situation is never judged once and for all. Every judgment is situationally absolute, based on the realization that some later determinations may change the certainty of the here and now.

The very invocation of a rule alters the situation. Rules, like actors and situations, do not appear except in a web of practical circumstances. Intertwined, the actor, rules, and the present definition of the situation *constitute* the situation. No single one of these can be abstracted out and treated as either cause or effect. Actors cannot be seen as outside of the situations judging them, for they are an integral and reflexive constituent of those situations. In short, the ethnomethodological ethnographies of rule use demonstrate that descriptions of realities as rules systems are unavoidably and necessarily incomplete.

Ethnomethodological studies of rule interpretation have been conducted in many settings, including legal, medical, educational, bureaucratic, and social scientific settings.[2] In each of these settings, the three analytic elements—actors, rules, and situations—are prominent. For example, in the legal setting, the actor producing the behavior is the suspect. The observer determining the appropriateness of the actor's behavior is the policeman or judge. The rules are the legal code. In the medical situation, the actor producing the behavior is the patient, the observer is the doctor or psychiatrist, the rules are disease terms. In bureaucratic situations, the actor producing the behavior is the client or customer, the observer is the administrator, the rules are the administrative procedures.

To study rule use, ethnomethodologists have chosen to research situations where the rules have been well codified. Discoveries of *essential incompleteness* in these rules are presumed to imply a similar incompleteness in *all* normative proscriptions, regardless of formality or legality. If formal rules require appeal to situational constraints, then less formal prescriptions, such as conversational rules, must also be essentially incomplete.

RULE USE IN LEGAL SETTINGS

On the Beat

As a policeman approaches a grocery store that he passes every night on his beat, he suddenly stops. He says to his partner: "Something's wrong; we gotta check that store out." When the policeman investigates he may find the grocer working late on his income tax, certainly no crime. Or, a robbery may taken place. The policeman does not know what is "wrong" as he begins his investigation. He does not know what "told" him that "something's wrong." He is not simply following a rule. He is *doing* his job, constructing his life.

The policeman accomplishes this work by developing and using a background of knowledge that he has come to take for granted (Bittner,

1967a:705, 707, 709; Cicourel, 1968; Sacks, 1972b). The policeman develops expectations about what should appear in the territory he works. The cop on the beat "knows" the routine actions of the people he normally encounters. He "knows" when the grocer opens his store and when he closes it. He "knows" that all the shades should be drawn and only one light should be burning. He "knows" when the living-room drapes in certain houses are usually open and when they are closed. These expectations constitute part of an unspoken background of the policeman's knowledge of his territory. The policeman cannot necessarily say in so many words what features he uses to make decisions, to investigate a situation, to stop a person walking on the street, or to pull a car over to the side of the road. The policeman does not chronicle the daily happenings of the people he sees. If an off-duty policeman were interviewed in his own living room, he would not necessarily be able to explain why he decided to investigate particular situations.

Although the policeman cannot provide a detailed report of the daily routines of his beat when he is removed from it, the policeman can *see* an unusual event or action as it happens. The policeman recognizes when occurrences stand out from the texture of the routine. He uses that perceptual anomaly as a signal to investigate. This indicates that he knows far more than is contained in any list of rules, no matter how large. The corpus of what he knows requires reference to all the situations he may enter. "How long," we might ask him, "have you known that that particular storekeeper leaves on the second and only the second tier of lights each night?" "Not until tonight," he might reply, "when I saw the first tier lit and *felt* something was wrong."[3]

If an anomaly had never appeared, he would not have become aware of his knowledge. The particular situation of this night made it appear. If the policeman were training a rookie on his beat, he would not tell him a list of things to look for, or a list of rules. He would take him on his rounds and *show* him how he does it. This showing might well include the formulation of some rules, but he could never tell him everything, nor would he need to. The rookie would learn to see and to feel as his teacher showed him. He would learn how to *do* the beat, how to use what partial set of rules he was told, and most importantly how, in the day-to-day work at the scene, to generate new rules as previously unmet situations arose.

A list will neither capture how the rules are used and understood, nor show what they mean at any particular time. Thus, to understand social interaction, the actor's interpretation of social rules in social situations must be investigated.

Here is a further example of rule interpretation in a legal setting, adapted from Cicourel (1968:170ff.). A particular town has a curfew law which says that any child under the age of 16 must be home by 10:00 P.M. on week nights. Although the policeman may not be able to quote the legal terminology found in the law books, he knows that youngsters are supposed to be home at night in his town.

As a policeman is cruising around at 10:15 P.M., he sees a couple of kids darting around the corner of a building. The kids' movement is an instance of a unique feature emerging from the background of routine features. The background of experience for that policeman is that "everything is supposed to be quiet in this neighborhood; no one is supposed to be around." So he investigates. He does not necessarily know if a law has been violated at this point, or what particular law applies. He only recognizes that something unusual is happening.

Although according to the written law, any youngster who is under age and out after curfew should be treated in a similar manner, the policeman does not rely on the law alone when deciding to bring a youth to the station house. Instead, the policeman always encounters the objective features of the law against a background of situational features, which include what is said between the policeman and the suspect, the behavior of the suspect, the place of the encounter, et cetera. Because the objective features of the law are seen against a background of situational features, "objectively similar" displays will be treated differently, and hence have different meanings. Thus the formal rule is not complete in itself, in that it does not include background features.

Garfinkel (1967a:210–223) calls this aspect of rules their "et cetera aspect." Every rule is used and usable only within a web of practical circumstances which "fill in" the incompleteness, particularizing the empty but promissory et cetera aspect. A policeman does not use the curfew law as a rule that says "Anywhere and always arrest anyone you see out after curfew." The curfew law instead includes within it an et cetera provision, which indicates that the law as a rule is to be used under particular circumstances. Depending on these practical contingencies, the same act may sometimes be seen as a rule infraction, and on other days it may not be seen in this way. The sense in which the incompleteness of rules is filled in according to the particular problem at hand is amplified in my next example.

In the Court

The legal rules that the policeman uses on his beat are incomplete. Ethnomethodological research has also shown that these rules are incomplete guides for understanding how cases are settled in courts of law. When settling cases, courtroom participants, like the policeman in the field, interpret the law against emerging situational features, such as the suspect's demeanor, courtroom relations, et cetera.

A case file of a suspect accused of breaking and entering might disclose the following facts:

Violation: breaking and entering
Name of defendant: Phillip Kingston
Age: 18
Sex: M
Race: Negro
Place of offense: Madison Avenue Presbyterian Church, 1660 Madison Avenue
Date and time of offense: 9:00 P.M., January 19
Arresting officer: Walter Crumckee (cf. Emerson, 1969:116).

The case file does not reveal the practical, often dangerous circumstances the policeman faced. It does not display the tentativeness of his decisions. It does not reveal the swarm of particulars the policeman used to reach what now appears to be an objectively clear, unambiguous conclusion. As Bittner (1967a:710) says, "patrolmen do not really enforce the law when they invoke it, but merely use it as a resource to solve certain pressing practical problems in keeping the peace." They use the rules of law as a guide for and means of "controlling trouble" (Bittner, 1967a, 1967b).

When the policeman must describe the circumstances of his beat to the court, he finds himself in a different practical situation. In the court he is required to say different things, to think different ways, to invoke the law differently than he did during the original arrest (Bittner, 1967a, 1967b; Cicourel, 1968). The following testimony, given by the policeman in this breaking and entering case, shows the way meaning shifts in practical circumstances:

Policeman. On the evening of January 19 I responded to a call from the night watchman of the Madison Avenue Presbyterian Church. He reported hearing someone on the roof of the church. I found the accused

> on the roof of the church while a church social was
> in progress. He had wirecutters and other tools with
> him. He said he had been drinking and did not
> know how he got up there. . . . He wouldn't say
> anything (Emerson, 1969:116).

The laws that were used on the beat to control trouble are used in
the court to talk in a legal way. They are used to justify prior actions
to observers—judges, lawyers, juries—who did not witness the "trouble,"
who perhaps have never seen such troubles firsthand, or ever witnessed
an arrest. Hence the "same law" means one thing to the policeman when
he is faced with the practical concerns of controlling trouble, and something else when he uses that law as a guide for his talk on the witness
stand. The meaning of the law shifts with practical circumstances.

The following sentencing discussion between the public defender and
the prosecuting attorney shows how the same event can also have different meanings at the same time. The public defender is attempting to
obtain a light sentence for the juvenile:

*Public
    defender.*   This is a good boy, your honor, he hasn't been in
                        trouble for three years.

*Prosecuting
    attorney.*   (Interrupting.) That's not quite true, your honor,
                        there have been several recent parole violations.

*Public
    defender.*   (Continuing.) I think that this is another case of
                        idle hands where this boy has nothing to do. I—

Judge.   (Interrupting.) Idle hands? How can you say it's a
                        case of idle hands when he went out buying these
                        tools? These are professional tools. It's not just a
                        kid breaking into a place with a crowbar. These
                        are professional tools (Ibid.:116–117).

Although each of these courtroom participants has the same information about the juvenile's activities, they do not treat that activity in the
same way. The defense attorney, working to have the case seen as an
unusual event in an otherwise normal childhood characterizes the
juvenile's life as "trouble free." The defense attorney, seeing the

juvenile's acts as a "uniquely misguided event," focuses on the juvenile's biography. The judge, seeing the juvenile's life as "trouble," brings the juvenile's use of tools from the background of the defense attorney's account into the foreground. He ignores the biographical aspects of the defense attorney's account.

These diverse interpretations of the "same" event in the juvenile's life indicate that the factual matters of the case comprise only a part of the apparatus which the courtroom participants employ to decide the case. The factual features of the case are part of a perceptual swarm which also include the juvenile's courtroom demeanor, his past history of involvement with the police, his school record, the dynamics of court-room relationships, and each participant's conceptions of "normal crimes" (Sudnow, 1965). The courtroom participants see the juvenile's activities against these practical circumstances. As different aspects of the swarm are highlighted, the juvenile's actions appear differently.

This example raises the question of what it means to speak of an event as unitary. The normative approach to social action claims that events are the same at different times, and are the same for different people at the same time. Ethnomethodological rule studies suggest that the "same event" is seen differently under the auspices of different prac-tical concerns, and/or in the light of different bodies of knowledge. In addition, the same person can see events differently at different times.

Garfinkel (personal communication) once illustrated how meaning changes through time by asking his students to listen to the ringing of a telephone. The first, second, or any ring is the same, we say. Physics encourages this belief. Yet, if we listen we hear that each ring means something different, because time passes. Previous hearings change what the next hearing can be.

Every person at every moment is approaching his world with shifting practical concerns and with some swarm of social knowledge. These in-terests and facts are always brought to bear on the events we see before us, whether we be law enforcement personnel, judges, or scholars writing expositions of other scholars' studies.

EDUCATIONAL DECISION MAKING

In the United States, students follow different paths in school. Although all students must enter school in the primary grades, they leave at different points. The different patterns raise an important question. How is it that some students continue in school, while others, for example, drop out in their junior year of high school?

One set of explanations of differential school performance patterns deals with students' characteristics. School success and failure is said to be the result of hereditary factors (Herrnstein, 1971; Jensen, 1969). Another set of explanations suggests that school performance is a function of the structure of the school environment (Holt, 1964; Silberman, 1970). The conventional school is characterized as authoritarian, teacher centered, and compartmentalized, an atmosphere which stifles certain students and accounts for their poor school performance.

The ethnomethodological interest in rule use suggests a third approach: Students' careers emerge from the interactional work of school administrators and teachers. This perspective suggests that student's performance cannot be understood independently of the assessment procedures that produce accounts of their abilities.

Placement Decisions

Cicourel and Kitsuse (1963) illustrate the power of this approach in their study of high school guidance counselors. The counselor helps the student decide which classes to take the following year. Typically, the classes available are arranged in a hierarchical order. One classroom (or perhaps "skill group" within a class) is reserved for the "better" students, another for the "average" students, a third for the "poor" students, and so on. The counselor's assessment of the student's record determines the student's classes. Thus, the educational counselor channels students into courses of instruction which determine their future career possibilities.

Now the question becomes: What is the basis upon which the counselor or other school official makes such administrative decisions? Do Jensen's "genetically provided[11] or Holt's "structural" factors account for these decisions? Leiter's (1974) extension of the Kitsuse and Cicourel (1963) work indicates that neither of these clusters of factors, alone or together, can explain how actual educational decisions are made.

Leiter tape-recorded the discussions between a principal and his kindergarten teachers as they decided to place "graduating" kindergarten students into one of three first grades. The principal placed the name of the three first grade teachers on a large piece of cardboard, and gave the following instructions:

Principal.	Here are the pictures of [Teacher 1's students]. Now what I want you to do is to take each one of these and on the back with a felt pen or something write two or three descriptors. (Picks up a picture.) What's outstanding about this child, Pa (———): sunny, cheerful, aggressive, retiring?
Teacher 2.	Would you please write a long list that we could choose from, those are great (laughs).
Teacher 1.	No, she's outgoing, an' strong, academically strong.
Principal.	Okay, then that goes on the back here. Now recognizing that [jet overhead masks out talk.] [First Grade Teacher A] is a different kind of person, who would be good for this child? Now does this child need somebody strongly oriented academically? Does she need that kind of strong hand? Here's a warm mother (tapping First Grade Teacher B's card): I came into the auditorium and she had Li on her lap. Li had gotten money at lunch time but she didn't bring it quite by accident because the student teacher thought she'd brought money for her lunch and she had to take it back, which just crushed her. And First Grade Teacher B, instead of saying "It's all right now you just get in line and go," there she was sitting there with this child—you know it was beautiful.

Now we're going to have some kids in here who are going to need a Momma type. All right, here's our Momma (tapping First Grade Teacher B's card). Here's a gal we want to protect (pointing to First Grade Teacher C, to be the new teacher). We don't want to give her really tough ones. I will not have her picking up all the kids that are difficult. |
| *Teacher 1.* | Hummm. |
| *Principal.* | People who have the experience, people who have the know-how pick up the tough ones because they know more and can protect against that kind of child. So these are the two that we give the really difficult kids to and now you know how First Grade |

	Teacher A teaches: it's very open and noisy and undisciplined. (Now holding Su's picture.)
Teacher 1.	Couldn't stand it—
Principal.	Well, this is right. What kids will benefit by being—
Teacher 1.	Su should go right there (puts picture on First Grade Teacher B's card).
Principal.	All right, you'd have Su over here, see. Now when you get these—you slip them in like this . . . (Leiter, 1974:34-35).

This short passage indicates the extremely complicated processes by which children get sorted in schools. The teachers and principal are engaged in telling stories about the children and other teachers, while relying on the "rules" of good pedagogy. They are doing this within a particular scene, at a particular time, with particular interests. We are not told here who are friends, who enemies. We do not know if any of the participants are in a hurry to finish, or whether the teachers are letting the principal do most of the talking because they respect him, or because they know he does not really care for their opinions, or because they do not wish to cooperate with him, et cetera.

Anyone who has met with persons to make "official" decisions will recognize in these examples the influence of the great web of practical circumstances. These teachers and principal have not come together to talk about the students as outsiders to the school or as strangers to each other. It is a situation of "passion and judgment," as Bittner (1973:115) phrases it. In addition to talking about the children, the participants are displaying for each other how they feel about their jobs, this particular meeting, and about each other. Their sorting of the children is a function of their practical circumstances. The ongoing course of the meeting forever alters these circumstances. Leiter (1974:72) concludes from these materials that the child's compositely judged abilities are not "so much a product of the situated practices of interaction." (cf. Shumsky and Mehan, 1974).

Classroom Decisions

In a language development lesson designed to teach children how to use prepositional phrases, the teacher divided her first grade class into four small groups. She instructed one group at a time while the remainder of the students worked at their desks. Each group was given similar materials to work with and each group was asked similar questions.

In each lesson, the teacher demonstrated the spatial relationship of two or more objects. She placed one object over the other, under the other, below the other, or above the other. She then asked the children to do the same. Then the teacher asked the children to report on their work.

Analysis of a videotape of the lesson (Mehan, 1974) showed that the teacher treated the children's similar responses in different ways. Both before and after the lesson, the teacher told Mehan that she expected the children to report about their work in a complete sentence. The model sentence was, "The square is over the line." Phrases such as "under the grass," "it's on there," and "there" were, according to the teacher's stated goals, not acceptable. Nevertheless, during the course of the lesson, some of these "deviant" answer types were accepted.

In addition, the child's answer was supposed to be given in one turn. On six occasions, the children produced all of the correct parts of the answer, but they appeared across two or more turns:

(1) *Teacher.*   Diana, where is the red flower?
    Diana.   The red flower . . .
    Teacher.   The red flower . . .
    Diana.   . . . is under the tree
    Teacher.   Now look at the . . .

(2) *Teacher.*   Listen, Romona, can you remember what I said?
    Romona.   Put it above . . .
    Teacher.   Above what?
    Romona.   The green line . . .
    Teacher.   All right, Romona, tell us what you did.
    Romona.   Put a square a, a, a, put a square above the green line.

(3) *Teacher.*   Okay, Janice, can you tell me what you did?
    Janice.   I put a blue triangle above.
    Teacher.   Above what?
    Janice.   The green line.
    Teacher.   OK, I put a, a pink diamond above the green line.

(4) *Teacher.*   All right, Janice, tell me what you did.
    Janice.   I put a blue, unn . . .
    Romona.   Square
    Janice.   Square
    Teacher.   Square
    Romona.   I'm not going to tell you guys.
    Janice.   Above the green line
    Teacher.   Paul, what did you do . . .?

(5) *Teacher.*   In some cases I can see the rug is under the . . .
    Romona.   Cabinet.
    Teacher.   Right!
    Romona.   Under the cabinet.
    Teacher.   OK, say it all by yourself now.
    Romona.   The rug is under the cabinet and the TV.
    Teacher.   All right, Janice . . .

(6) *Teacher.*   Paul, can you tell me something that is under something else?
    Paul.   The boxes.
    Teacher.   What are they under?
    Paul.   Under the flat blocks.
    Romona.   They are under the wood . . .
    Teacher.   OK, the big blocks are under the flat blocks . . .

                                                                    (Mehan, 1974:109)

When the child's answer was spread across a number of turns as these answers were, the teacher's plan was to have the child combine the parts into a complete sentence. However, on only two of the six occasions (2 and 5) where answers appeared across turns did the teacher demand that the child complete the answer. In the remaining four exchanges, the child's incomplete answers were allowed to pass. Similar results were also observed when the children responded with only phrases, pointings, or pronouns. These were accepted even though the teacher's rule disallowed them.

The teacher's differential treatment of the same answer types cannot be explained by differences among the lessons or by differential expectations for the children's performances. The history of the children's performance in this lesson, on this particular day, on previous days, all contribute to the teacher's moment-to-moment decisions about answers. These and other factors do not enter neatly into a calculus of values weighed according to a prearranged plan. The teacher's attention is demanded in too many places to make calculated decisions during the flow of conversation within a lesson. The determination of a correct answer is negotiated each moment of teacher-child interaction. Before a lesson starts, the teacher may have an overall plan in mind. The teacher may be able to say what criteria will be used to judge correct answers. But as the lesson gets underway, decisions to accept or reject a child's answer become influenced by the child who is answering the question, when in the lesson the question occurs, and the child's immediate past performance. These and still other features compose a set that is irrevocably indefinite and unspecifiable. Garfinkel (in Hill and Crittenden, 1968:248) has called such a collection a "swarm set."[4]

MEDICAL DECISION MAKING

The textbook version of hospital procedures is similar to the textbook version of legal procedures. Justice is presumed blind. So too, medicine is supposed to treat all patients impartially. A set of biological symptoms is supposed to instruct the doctors' proper medical action.

Sudnow (1969) conducted a comparative analysis of a private hospital in a suburban area, and a lower class public hospital in an inner city. He observed emergency room procedures in both hospitals, and found that patients' biological symptoms alone were not sufficient to account for the staff's medical action.

For example, a Bowery drunk reeking of alcohol and vomit and a pubescent girl smelling of sunshine and Musk oil, both suffering from a heart problem that requires mouth-to-mouth resuscitation, could be brought into an emergency room. Medically, both require the same treatment, but medical decisions are always informed by more than biological symptoms. Biological symptoms never appear in the world as abstractly as they do in textbooks. They are always embedded in a social context that includes factors such as the age, social status, and "desirability" of the patient, the number of other patients in need of help at that moment, the number of staff on hand and their training, et cetera.

Aspects of a patient's case are informed by social and organizational features. These factors do not compose a neat calculus of treatment possibilities, however. They no more conform to formal logic than the features that contribute to a policeman's arrest decisions, or a teacher's classroom decisions. The factors which contribute to medical decisions are organized anew in each situation and are influenced by practical and fortuitous circumstances. Although it is possible to conduct a causal analysis that correlates, say, the race and age of a patient with the race and attitudes of a doctor, such an analysis would not reveal how medical decisions are made in the ongoing flow of hospital life. It would represent the imposition of the reality of Aristotelian logic on a reality that does not depend on that logic.

BUREAUCRATIC RULE INTERPRETATION

An applicant approaching the reception counter of a welfare agency is in many ways like a child approaching a school. Certain career options are made available and others are denied, depending on the outcome of decisions that the public welfare agent makes.

The welfare agent must first decide if assistance is warranted in each case. If it is, then the agent must decide the appropriate category of assistance. The "rules" of the welfare agency are established by the Social Security Act, and specify the general conditions for granting aid to needy persons (Zimmerman, 1970b:322). In addition to these administrative procedures, the welfare agent must satisfy the supervisor's definitions of acceptable work (Ibid.:324). Decisions to distribute money, groceries, or medicine are similar to school decisions to assign pupils to certain classes.

The caseworker consults official records such as employment forms, rent receipts, bank statements, and other biographical information obtained from the client to determine the suitability of the request. However, the official facts are never sufficient to decide the suitability of cases. The welfare agent must rely on background knowledge of community actions and schedules to make official facts and requests real. For example, Zimmerman (Ibid.:331–332) writes:

> On New Year's Eve, an APTD applicant appeared in the office seeking carfare. His assigned worker was in the field, and another worker in the

unit was designated to handle the matter temporarily. His request for carfare was supposedly in order to keep a doctor's appointment (a quite ordinary and appropriate request for applicants in this category awaiting final determination of eligibility). The worker consulted with the supervisor on the request and was directed to defer issuance of the carfare pending a review of the case record. The supervisor noted that he could not meet his scheduled appointment on time in any event. She also told the worker to contact the doctor to verify the existence of the appointment.

The amount of money at issue would total at the most two dollars, and probably would be less. At the time, the caseworker involved could not comprehend the effort extended by the supervisor to monitor the expenditure of such a small amount. She was not "skeptical" of the request. (It should be added that the author was also puzzled by the insistence on checking out such an apparently routine request.)

As it turned out, the case record depicted the man as a "chronic alcoholic." Furthermore, it was also learned that the doctor with whom the man claimed to have had an appointment was on vacation. This information recast the situation as that of a drunk attempting to secure liquor on New Year's Eve.

The applicant's request was seen against different backgrounds by the supervisor, the researcher, and the caseworker. The caseworker and the researcher saw the applicant's case as legitimate. The "more experienced" supervisor, juxtaposing the account against a background of skepticism, obtained a different meaning for the request.

These differences in substantive meaning echo what we have learned about the nature of rule following in legal, medical, and educational settings. Both the observer and the caseworker (on the one hand) and the supervisor (on the other) were filling in information around the applicant's request. The meaning of an event (or object, word, or action) cannot be decided in isolation. The meaning of an event cannot be separated from the mode of its apprehension. The mode of apprehension is reflexively related to the particular reality of the apprehender. To make sense of the rules, these realities always include an ongoing use of the context within which the rules are found.

Zimmerman's study, then, like the others reviewed above, illumine Garfinkel's (1967a:41) claim that all rules have about them "surrounding fringes" (or "outer horizons"), which must be filled in by particular actors according to their practical concerns at the time. Without this work, a rule has no meaning, no life at all.

Such "et cetera" features of rules, which Garfinkel (1967a:22) at other times names "ad hoc features", are essential constituents of all rules and cannot be eliminated. As Garfinkel writes:

> To treat instructions as though *ad hoc* features in their use were a nuisance or to treat their presence as grounds for complaint about the incomplete-ness of instruction, is very much like complaining that if the walls of a building were only gotten out of the way, one could see better what was keeping the roof up (Ibid.).

The normative theory of rules described at the outset of this chapter explains social action by rules and situations. In the ethnomethodological theory of rules, actors, rules, and situations are conceived to be mutually constituting.

Hence, the first discovery of the ethnomethodological exploration of the normative theory of rules is that any discussion of social action must include situationally provided et cetera features as well as norms, actors, and situations. A second discovery of the ethnomethodological approach to rule use is that these components are dialectically determinative. The actor himself constitutes a part of the situation; the situation contains this particular actor *now,* with his here-and-now concerns. The rule is invoked as an additional constituent of actor-situation-context *now.* Rules appear in no other place. They never "speak for themselves." Only in being tied to particular scenes by particular actors do they find a voice.

ORDINARY LANGUAGE INDEXICALITY

Rule use in institutionalized settings has been talked about in this chapter. But I claim as well that *all* symbolic forms (rules, linguistic utterances, gestures, actions) carry a fringe of incompleteness that must be filled in, and filled in differently every time they occur (Garfinkel and Sacks, 1970:348–350). This is not to maintain that what is filled in can be explicitly articulated by either participants or researcher. In fact, the incompleteness *cannot* be exhaustively articulated. All offered completions themselves carry a horizon of incompleteness.

Garfinkel (1967a:38–42) offers an illustration of this essential incompleteness in ordinary conversation. He asked students to record a short conversation. One student brought Garfinkel (Ibid.:38–39) the following:

Husband.	Dana succeeded in putting a penny in a parking meter today without being picked up.
Wife.	Did you take him to the record store?
Husband.	No, to the shoe repair shop.
Wife.	What for?
Husband.	I got some new shoelaces for my shoes.
Wife.	Your loafers need new heels badly.

Although we are not familiar with the circumstances, participants, or topics of this conversation, we obtain a sense of what happened. For me, it is a routine exchange between a husband and wife about events that took place during the day. I know that the parties in the conversation are husband and wife because those labels are provided along with the text. I doubt that I would be able to infer this relationship just from the words spoken in the conversation. Another person, called Dana, also figures in the events. It is not clear to me who he is. The significance of the phrase "picked up" in the first utterance is also confusing.

Garfinkel (Ibid.:38–39) provides an interpretation of this text which was written by the husband in the exchange. It goes as follows:

| *Husband.* | Dana succeeded in putting a penny in a parking meter today without being picked up. | This afternoon as I was bringing Dana, our four-year-old son, home from the nursery school, he succeeded in reaching high enough to put a penny in a parking meter when we parked in a meter zone, whereas before he had always had to be picked up to reach that high. |
| *Wife.* | Did you take him to the record store? | Since he put a penny in a meter that means that you stopped while he was with you. I know that you stopped at the record store either on the way to get |

him or on the way back. Was it on the way back, so that he was with you, or did you stop there on the way to get him and somewhere else on the w a y back?

Husband.	No, to the shoe repair shop.	No, I stopped at the record store on the way to get him and stopped at the shoe repair shop on the way home when he was with me.
Wife.	What for?	I know of one reason why you might have stopped at the shoe repair shop. Why did you in fact?
Husband.	I gót some new shoelaces for my shoes.	As you will remember I broke a shoelace on one of my brown o x f o r d s the other day so I stopped to get some new laces.
Wife.	Your loafers need new heels badly.	Something else you could have gotten that I w a s thinking of. You c o u l d have taken in your black loafers, which need heels badly. You'd better g e t them taken care of pretty soon.

Obviously, a person who was a party to the conversation obtained a different sense of what happened than I did. Some of the differences in meaning concern factual matters: The husband knows who Dana is, knows the particulars of the trip reported, et cetera. Other differences in meaning stem from the way in which the husband and wife fit the specific events into a larger pattern of activities and relationships within the family. For example, she ties the prior plans for the day, the scheme of organizing daily activities, to the distribution of responsibilities for the family.

The gap between what was "actually said" and what was reported by one of the conversationalists as "what happened" led Garfinkel (Ibid.: 39) to the conclusion that has been located again and again throughout this chapter with regard to normative rule application: "there were many matters that . . . partners understood they were talking about that they did not mention . . . [and] many matters that . . . partners understood were understood on the basis not only of what was actually said but what was left unspoken."

That is, all the information that conversationalists need in order to understand each other is not located in the linguistic utterances exchanged between them. Because of the sketchiness and vagueness of spoken utterances, conversationalists must "look elsewhere than to what was said in order to find the corresponding contents" (Ibid.:27). They must attend to contextually provided features, which include knowledge of "the biography and purposes of the speaker, the circumstances of the utterance, the previous course of the conversation, or the particular relationship of actual or potential interaction which exists between user and auditor" (Ibid.:40).

What the husband has filled in for us above is not all that he knows. Garfinkel set his students the additional task of filling in what the first filling-in meant, and then the further task of filling in the circumstances of that filling-in. The students despaired and gave up, and rightly so.

> They did not wait around to see of what the problem consisted. They said immediately that the very way of doing it multiplied that text as a texture of relevances; that is, they found themselves in a tree where the very fact that they were in the tree was the thing that stirred its branches. That is what I understand that these things—the et cetera, the unless, the let it pass—are all about (Garfinkel, in Hill and Crittenden, 1968:222).

They had come to see that the incompleteness of symbols is irreparable. Every attempt at repair increases the number of symbols that needs to be repaired.[5]

THE UNIVERSALITY OF INDEXICAL EXPRESSIONS

Symbolic forms have been found to be incomplete. Utterances that require contextual information to be understood are called "indexical expressions" (Bar-Hillel, 1954; Peirce, 1933; Russell, 1940:134–143).

The question arises whether *any* utterances are independent of contextual information. Bar-Hillel (1954) addresses this question by talking about the truth value of statements. Statements that are true for all times, all places, and for all observers are not indexical, he says, but are "universal" or "objective." Bar-Hillel suggests that statements such as "ice floats on water" meet this criterion of universal truth. But the truth value of a statement such as "it is raining" is dependent upon the situation in which it is uttered. Likewise, a determination of the truth value of the statement "I am hungry" depends upon knowledge of the state of the person making the utterance.

However, there is a way in which all three of these utterances rely on the contextual use of background knowledge to be understood. To understand the statement "ice floats on water," the hearer must know what "ice" is, must know what "water" is, and must know what the process of "floating" is. He must also add to these "knowings" a conditional sloppy domain of *ceteris paribus*. This domain protects him with the caveat, "all other things being equal." For example, yes, ice floats on water, but not a single ice cube with a weight on top of it. Or, yes, it is "universally true" that ice floats on water, but only if there is "enough" water, the et cetera of our *ceteris paribus* adds. That an iceberg will not float on the water in my bathtub flatly contradicts this universal truth. But this fact will not be counted as a contradiction to that truth, at least not by reasonable people. And that reasonableness is the key to the reality of nonindexical expressions. They do exist, but only within a swarm of never-specified caveats, et cetera clauses, and *ceteris paribus* assumptions. Universal statements exists, but only within some particular reality that accepts the incorrigibility of the unstated et cetera clauses. To claim that a statement such as "ice floats on water" is universal is to assume that the universe of discourse provided by Western science is universal. The statement "ice floats on water" is universal within that reality at the present time; but the truths of that reality are not timeless. Western science provides *one* view of the world, it does not provide the only view. The history of science itself is full of examples of universal explanations which have been replaced by other universal explanations.[6] Each of these explanations was true at its time. Each of these explanations was part of a reality; none had meaning out of the context of some reality (cf. Ten Houten and Kaplan, 1973).

A feature of knowledge systems described in Chapter 2 was the belief that the way one looks at the world is the way all peoples should look at the world if they want to see truly. This feature of absolutism is evident in Bar-Hillel's analysis. He assumes that the Western science way of seeing the world is universal. My position—that many realities exist—relativizes this absolutism. From within a reality, it is necessary to assume such universality in order to interact. But when more than one reality is taken into account, when any one statement is examined from the perspective of another, then the universal indexicality of all symbols becomes apparent. Every person in every reality, be he Bar-Hillel doing logic, or Don Juan doing sorcery, operates out of a web of shifting interests and knowledge. Every person is required to fill in the rules and laws and to make them, in the here and now, universal.

CONCLUSION

The various ethnomethodological ethnographies of rule use arose in conversation with the normative theory of action that I described in the opening pages of this chapter. These studies attempt to build an alternative model of rule use. This alternative displays the mass of situated, practical circumstances that constitute everyday "rule-governed" action.

At the time that these ethnomethodological ethnographies were being written, a related program was also being developed. While the ethnographers were concentrating on the *scenic* details of rule use, others were constructing a *general* model of the actor that would be compatible with the discoveries of these ethnographies. This model sought to avoid the problems that arose from the normative sociological model's commitment to formal logic and scientifically rational explanations of action. This alternative ethnomethodological model of the actor is the focus of the next chapter.

NOTES

1.   Symbolic interaction conceptions, by putting the "objects" of social scenes into the act itself, on a par with the actor (Blumer, 1971; Manis and Meltzer, 1967), are frequently asserted to avoid the major troubles of normative sociological theories. This theory, however, does not avoid the difficulties I describe here. The following formulation describes the symbolic interactionist conception of normatively guided action: The actor takes an action. Another responds. The actor perceives the other's responses and modifies his subsequent behavior according to his perception of the other's response.

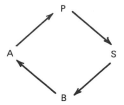

Kinch (1963) diagrams this notion as shown. *B* is the actor's behavior, *A* is the other's responses toward him, *P* is the actor's perception of that response, and *S* is the actor's "self concept," or modified subsequent behavior.

This model of action is subject to all the criticisms to be made against normative theories of action in this chapter and elsewhere (Cicourel, 1964, 1973; Garfinkel, 1967a; Wilson, 1970; Zimmerman and Pollner, 1970 Zimmerman and Wieder, 1970). It treats action as discrete, as automatically applicable, as easily and mutually understood by all parties to the situation. It does not recognize the indexicality and reflexivity of action.

2. Studies conducted in legal settings include Bittner (1967a, 1967b), Cicourel (1968), Emerson (1969), Garfinkel (1967a:105–115), Pollner (1970), Sacks (1972b), Sudnow (1965), and Wieder (1973). Those conducted in medical settings include Garfinkel (1967a:186–207), Sudnow (1969) and Wood (1968). Those conducted in educational settings include Cicourel and Kitsuse (1963), Leiter (1974), and Mehan (1974). Examples of studies in bureaucratic settings include Bittner (1965), Garfinkel (1967a:12–18), and Zimmerman (1966, 1969, 1970a, 1970b). Social scientific settings have been represented by Garfinkel (1967a:20–24) and Leiter (1969). Each of these studies offers investigations of not only rule use, but a variety of other phenomena as well. I have focused on but one common theme in these studies. In so doing, I may often be ignoring the major thrust of the author's own interest.

3. The ethnomethodological position on the use of social knowledge is reminiscent of Wittgenstein:

> Suppose it were asked: *"When* do you know how to play chess? All the time? or just while you are making a move? And the *whole* of chess during each move?—How queer that knowing how to play chess should take such a short time, and a game so much longer? (1953:59e)

> But what does this knowledge consist in? Let me ask: *When* do you know that application? Always? day and night? or only when you are actually thinking of the rule? do you know it, that is, in the same way as you know the alphabet and the multiplication table? (Ibid.:58e)

> We also say "Since yesterday I have understood this word." "Continuously," though?— To be sure, one can speak of an interruption of understanding. But in what cases? Compare: "When did your pains get less?" and "When did you stop understanding that word?" (Ibid.:59e)

> If there has to be anything "behind the utterance of the formula" it is *particular circumstances,* which justify me saying I can go on—when the formula occurs to me. (Ibid.:60e)

4. I refer to Hill and Crittenden (1968) throughout this volume. Their work is a valuable introduction to ethnomethodology, as it contains transcriptions of informal conversations between ethnomethodologists and interested sociologists. However, because the remarks were informal, transcribed from an inadequate recording, and edited by Hill and Crittenden and not by the speakers, all quotations from this source are suspect. I quote from this volume only as a way of providing a source for ideas that ethnomethodologists frequently share among themselves.

5.   This discovery is vividly illustrated in John Barth's novel *Giles Goat-Boy* (1966:443–455). When the goat-boy arrives on campus for student orientation he is directed to a console where he listens to the president's welcoming speech. For any questionable phrase, he can push the "hold" button and then one of the various university department's buttons to get a gloss on that aspect of the speech. Having, for example, pressed the philosophy button to learn about the president's meaning in saying "Ockham's razor" only to hear an unknown Latin term used there, the goat-boy presses another hold—to hold the philosophy gloss—and requests a gloss on the philosophy gloss from the Latin department. Whereupon he finds he must get yet another gloss from the history department, which leads to a need to put them on hold so as to get a gloss from the agricultural department on the gloss from the history department on the gloss from the Latin department on the gloss from the philosophy department on the meaning of the phrase from the president's speech which is on hold. At last, like each of us in everday life, the goat-boy decides to "let it pass" in the hopes that he will understand it all later, or that it is not important, or that no one will notice that he does not understand.

6.   Since remote antiquity most people have seen one or another heavy body swinging back and forth on a string or chain until it finally comes to rest. To the Aristotelians, who believed that a heavy body is moved by its own nature from a higher position to a state of natural rest at a lower one, the swinging body was simply falling with difficulty. Constrained by the chain it could achieve rest at its low point only after a tortuous motion, and a considerable time. Galileo, on the other hand, looking at the swinging body, saw a pendulum, a body that almost succeeded in repeating the same motion over and over again ad infinitum. . . . He saw differently from the way he had seen before (Kuhn, 1970:118–119). During the seventeenth century, when their research was guided by one or another effluvium theory, electricians repeatedly saw chaff particles rebound or fall off, the electrified bodies that attracted them. . . . Placed before the same apparatus, a modern observer would see electrostatic repulsion (Ibid.:117).

Or, again, after the assimilation of Franklin's paradigm, the electrician looking at a Leyden jar saw something different from what he had seen before. The device had become a condenser, for which neither the jar nor the glass were required. Instead, the two conducting coatings—one of which had been no part of the original device—emerged into prominence (Ibid.:117–118).

. . . a course of action which is perfectly rational from the point of the actor may appear non-rational to the partner or observer or vice-versa. Both attempts to induce rain by performing the rain dance or by seeding clouds with silver iodine, are subjectively seen, rational actions from the point of view of the Hopi Indian or the modern meteorologist, respectively, but both would have judged as non-rational by a meteorologist 20 years ago (Schutz, 1962:29).

CHAPTER FIVE

The
Reality
Constructor

In Chapter 2, I described the appearance of "impossible objects": a pen at once absent and present, the sun as a satellite of the earth and the earth as a satellite of the sun. To resolve the contradiction of such appearances, persons act as if an object cannot be two things at once. The work that achieves this "object constancy assumption" is so successful that it is neither noticed by persons doing it nor by social scientists who study everyday life.

Much ethnomethodological theorizing has explored the work entailed in achieving the object constancy belief and other fundamental propositions of daily life. The ethnomethodologist finds that persons are constructing social structures without being aware of this work. This reality work is explicated by the construction of a "model of the actor."

In the normative model, rules, actors, and situations are assumed to be independent entities. In the ethnomethodological model, persons are treated as reality constructors. Rules are dependent upon the ceaseless, ongoing activities of persons within social situations. The ethnomethodological model is a characteristization of the way persons *create* situations and rules, and so at once create themselves and their social realities.[1]

A CONSTRUCTION OF THE REALITY CONSTRUCTOR

I will now attribute some minimal requisites for social interaction to a model of the actor. The attributions are *constitutive*. They both create interaction and the possibility of interaction. These features have been culled from the writings of Schutz (1962, 1964, 1966, 1967, 1970a), from Garfinkel's (1963, 1967a) distillation of these writings, and from Cicourel's (1973a) further elaboration of this work.[2] My purpose is not to provide an accurate historical sequence in the development of the model. It is rather to provide a single, unified formulation so that the use of this device can be better understood.

This model of the reality constructor is composed of (1) social knowledge and (2) interpretive procedures that operate on that social knowledge.

Social Knowledge

The properties of social knowledge can be summarized as follows:

1. Social knowledge provides *a practical interest* in the world. Garfinkel describes this feature as follows:

> Events, their relationships, their causal texture are not for [the person] matters of theoretic interest. He does not sanction the notion that in dealing with them it is correct to address them with the interpretive rule that he knows nothing, or that he can assume that he knows nothing "just to see where it leads." In everyday situations what he knows is an integral feature of his social competence (1967a:273).

That is, as people conduct the affairs of their daily life, they are *not* constrained by the canons of the "scientific rationalities" (Garfinkel, 1967a:262–283). They are *not* concerned with semantic or conceptual clarity for its own sake, or insuring that their actions conform to the demands of formal logic.

2. Social knowledge is *socially distributed*. Garfinkel describes this feature as follows:

> There corresponds, thereby, to the common intersubjective world of communication, unpublicized knowledge which in the eyes of the actor is distributed among persons as grounds of their actions, i.e., of their motives or, in the radical sense of the term, their "interests," as constituent features of the social relationships of interaction. He assumes that there are matters that one person knows that he assumes others do not know. The ignorance of one party consists in what another knows that is motivationally relevant to the first. Thereby matters that are known in common are informed in

their sense by the personal reservations, the matters that are selectively withheld. Thus the events of everyday situations are informed by this integral background of "meanings held in reserve," of matters known about self and others that are none of somebody else's business; in a word, the private life (Ibid.:276).

This feature of social knowledge provides that some people know some things, but not everybody knows all things. Interactants recognize this. Nonetheless, biographically specific meanings are treated as irrelevant for the purposes of communicating the here-and-now event to others.

3. Social knowledge is *tacit*. Garfinkel points out that any "event means for both the witness and the other more than the witness can say" (Ibid.:56). This feature of social knowledge provides that what both persons know in common cannot be said in so many words. This common, tacit knowing is used by people to build interaction.

4. Social knowledge *takes the world for granted*. Garfinkel writes:

a relationship of undoubted correspondence is the sanctioned relationship between the-presented-appearance-of-the-object and the-intended-object-that-presents-itself-in-the-perspective-of-the-particular-appearance (Ibid. :55).

And he writes elsewhere:

Schutz finds that in everyday situations the "practical theorist" achieves an ordering of events while seeking to retain and sanction the presupposition that the objects of the world are as they appear. The person coping with everyday affairs seeks an interpretation of these affairs while holding a line of "official neutrality" towards the interpretive rule that one may doubt the objects of the world as they appear. The actor's assumption consists in the expectation that a relationship of undoubted correspondence exists between the particular appearances of an object and the intended-object-that-appears-in-this-particular-fashion (Ibid.:272).

That is, people expect the world beyond to be accurately pictured by their way of looking at it. This feature of social knowledge makes it possible for objects to be accepted for what they appear to be on the surface.

This discussion establishes that the reality constructor has social knowledge, but this conception is static. People do not use all their knowledge in every situation. They do not apply all that they (tacitly) know at once. Therefore, our model must have a mechanism that activates the situationally relevant aspects of this constantly changing stock of knowledge.

Borrowing from Schutz, this feature has been talked about in various ways: as "constitutive rules" (Garfinkel, 1963), as "interpretive rules" (Garfinkel, 1967a), as "interpretive procedures" or "basic rules" (Cicourel, 1973a).[3] I will use the term "procedure," because it best conveys the sense that these are descriptions of interactional activities that are *done* by people in interaction.

Interpretive Procedures

Three interpretive procedures have been described by the ethnomethodologist:

1. *Searching for a normal form.* Cicourel (1973a:86) describes this interpretive procedure as follows:

> when discrepancies or ambiguities appear, speakers will attempt to normalize the presumed discrepancies . . . . this commonsense principle provides each member with instructions for unwittingly (and sometimes deliberately) evaluating and striving for a reciprocally assumed normal form judgment of his utterances and perceptions.[4]

2. *Doing a reciprocity of perspectives.* Cicourel (Ibid.:85–86) describes the reciprocity of perspectives as doing the work of sustaining the assumption that:

> (i) each would have the same experiences if they were to change places, and (ii) that until further notice they can disregard any differences that might arise from their respective personal ways of assigning meaning to objects and events.[5]

3. *Employing the et cetera principle.* Cicourel (Ibid.:87) describes this interpretive procedure as follows:

> The participants to a conversation must "fill in" meanings throughout the exchange and after the exchange when attempting to recall or reconstruct what happened because of the inadequacies of oral and non-oral communication, and the routine practice of leaving many intentions unstated (Garfinkel, 1964). Vague or ambiguous or truncated expressions are located by

members, given meaning contextually and across contexts, by their retrospective-prospective sense of occurrence. Present utterances or descriptive accounts that contain ambiguous or promissory overtones can be examined prospectively by the speaker-hearer for their possible meaning in some future sense under the assumption of filling in meanings now and imagining the kinds of intentions that can be expected later. Or, past remarks can now be seen as clarifying present utterances.[6]

Hence, the et cetera principle has three interrelated parts. In some versions of the model, these features are treated as separate entities.

a. Unclear information is allowed to pass while clarifying information is sought.

b. Contextual information is sought over time to fill in the ambiguity of indexical expressions.

c. The filling in is accomplished by retrospective-prospective means. When vague, ambiguous, or unclear utterances occur, the vagueness is not immediately challenged or questioned. The hearer allows the unclear utterance to pass. He assumes that subsequent events will clarify the present ambiguity. If and when subsequent information becomes available, that present information is used to clarify the previously unclear events.[7]

DISPLAYING THE REALITY CONSTRUCTOR

The model of the reality constructor can be used as an analytic tool. I will illustrate this by providing a hypothetical account of an everyday event. A man driving to work sees a fuzzy object. After several minutes during which the object's appearance baffles him, he determines that it is a freeway sign. To account for this occurrence, I will attribute to the model of a freeway driver some of the elements necessary for driving the freeway in an acceptable manner.

Before this man can begin driving his car, in fact, even before he can leave his bed in the morning, put on his clothes, or drink his coffee, he must assume that objects are what they appear to be on the surface. If the motorist had scientifically rational doubts about the nature of objects appearing before him, he would not be able to act at all. If the motorist doubts that the floor under his bed is a floor, he will be unable to stand on that floor. If our motorist does not see the long ribbon of black ooze as a "freeway," the brightly colored mass hurtling toward him as a "car" with a competent driver who will drive past, not at him, he may be unable to negotiate the roadway.[8] These suggest the taken-for-granted features of social knowledge I summarized above.

As the motorist drives the freeway, he is confronted by swirls of colors and sounds. Our motorist must transform these stimuli into meaningful wholes. This is the interpretive procedure "searching for a normal form." As an individual goes through a social situation (as the motorist drives his car), the individual searches for and selects features of the world which can be placed in a familiar schemata. Casting for coherent forms is an interpretive procedure performed on all knowledge systems.

When first confronted by swirling colors, the motorist sensed the presence of a "something," but its specific form, content, and dimensions were unknown. The assumed presence of *"some* object there" enabled the motorist to continue to look for features that would help him identify "the something" as a *specific* thing. In the language of the interpretive procedures discussed above, the motorist allowed unclear events to pass while seeking clarification. He waited to see what the object would mean then.

Although an object may not have a *specific* meaning at the time that it is initially apprehended, it has some meaning. For example, it is "an unclear object." Its specific meaning may become clear with subsequent events. After these events occur, the motorist is able to see in retrospect what the object was "all along." This retrospective filling in is an aspect of the interpretive procedure: employing the et cetera principle.

Of course, this now specific, clear meaning is also subject to subsequent reinterpretation. The object may not be a freeway sign, but a scaffold, or a truck; any subsequent determination will modify previous ones. "What it is now" will be "what it was all along."

The meaning of an object, event, or utterance is also "prospective." When a person does not immediately know the normal form meaning of an object, he assumes that its meaning will become clear later. The practice of "waiting until later to see what was intended now" is the "prospective" interpretive procedure.

The motorist knows this swirling object was a sign all along. He also knows that this object will be the same object the next time he confronts it. It will be the same object on all subsequent occasions. It will be the same object to any and all others who look at it. He maintains this knowledge by employing the "reciprocity of perspectives" interpretive procedure.

Now suppose our motorist needs to go from one part of the city to another. He might ask a gas station attendant for directions:

How do I get to Jack-in-the-Box from here?

The gas station attendant might give the following directions: See this street here? That takes you to the freeway. Stay on the freeway until you see the sign for Mazeville Road. Get off there. Jack-in-the-Box will be on your right, a few blocks down.

In order for the gas station attendant to tell our motorist this, the attendant must treat the freeway sign as a constant object. That is, the gas station attendant must also employ the reciprocity of perspectives interpretive procedure, which provides that the meaning of the objects, utterances, or events that he has encountered are the same that others have encountered. And, in order for the motorist to follow those directions, he must treat the signs, streets, and buildings he encounters and calls by certain names, as the same objects the gas station attendant or anybody else names in the same way.

Now, the motorist who follows these instructions may have had peculiar experiences with that particular street exit. For example, he may once have had a flat tire or an accident there. The gas station attendant may be having "a bad day," or he may have just won money at the racetrack. But the motorist is not interested in these biographical features. He is interested in getting to Jack-in-the-Box. If the gas station attendant were to begin to provide the motorist with the details about his declining business, the rising prices of his products, or what he will do with his winnings, the motorist would see that as strange. Likewise, the gas station attendant is not interested in *why* the motorist wants to go to Jack-in-the-Box. It is irrelevant for his purpose of giving instructions whether the motorist is going to Jack-in-the-Box to make a purchase, to meet someone, or to rob it. Both the motorist and the gas station attendant must treat any such biographically specific meanings as irrelevant for the purposes at hand. They must employ the socially distributed aspect of social knowledge.

The motorist who asks the gas station attendant for directions has a "practical interest in the world" (see the first property of social knowledge, above). He wants to go from one place to another. That practical problem occupies his time. He is not interested in theoretical matters about the journey, the freeway, or the sign, such as the laws of physics that explain how the sign is able to stand in high winds, or the principle that explains how the asphalt is able to support the weight of cars on it, or the kinetic theory that explains why the sign "lights up" when headlights shine on the sign at night. Theoretical reflection and practical problem-solving are separate activities. It is difficult to engage in both simultaneously. On another occasion, at another time, say, when the motorist and a friend are sipping coffee after dinner, they might engage in a discussion of the physical principles of light reflection. But at the moment when the motorist is trying to navigate unfamiliar streets and heavy traffic, he is hardly interested in such theoretical matters.

The motorist is able to concentrate on his practical concerns of finding streets and signs and does not need to worry about asphalt strength and principles of light reflection because he "knows" that other people have these theoretical matters as *their* practical concerns. This is another facet of the social distribution of social knowledge. No member of society need know all society's knowledge in order to interact. But in order to function in everyday life, each must rely on the fact that some people have some knowledge of the world, and that others have other knowledge.

Likewise, no person need have a *formal* acquaintance with any of that knowledge. Just as a speaker of a language need not know the rules of grammar to speak that language (Chomsky, 1965), a person need not be able to list the rules of society to act in it. This illumines the meaning of the "tacit" feature of social knowledge.

Now let us examine the conversation between the motorist and the gas station attendant, especially the instruction the gas station attendant gave to the motorist so that he could go from one part of town to another.

Motorist.	How do I get to Jack-in-the-Box from here?
Gas station attendant.	See this street here? That takes you to the freeway. Stay on the freeway until you see the sign for Mazeville Road. Get off there. Jack-in-the-Box will be on your right, a few blocks down.

To ask the gas station attendant for directions, the motorist would need to know at least the following about socially distributed social knowledge: that there are people who can legitimately be asked for directions; that there are places where directions can be legitimately asked; and that there are times when such questions can legitimately be asked. If a priest hearing confession were asked for directions to Jack-in-the-Box, the person asking the question might be considered bizarre, a stranger, or incompetent. Knowing that there are people who can and cannot be asked for instructions, and knowing that there are those who *can* legitimately be asked for directions, and knowing that such a person has certain obligations to respond is presumably knowledge that "everyone (who is a competent member of society) knows."

The ethnomethodologist is not interested in compiling a list of the "background" knowledge required for successful interaction. The list I have begun above for the motorist merely scratches the surface of what he would have to know to ask that question. As I explain in a later section of this chapter, it seems unlikely that a complete list could ever be constructed.

To ask for directions, the motorist must consult his normal forms, which guide his selection of a person who would be likely to help him. The initial selection is prospective, for the person selected for instructions may be a stranger, a pathological liar, or a robber. Subsequent events will retrospectively inform the motorist if his initial prospective selection was accurate.

What does the gas station attendant's instruction tell the motorist? It seems to tell him everything that he needs to know. It tells him to turn at a certain street of a certain freeway. But notice that far more is implied by the utterance than is stated in words. The utterance assumes that the hearer can supply contextual information (see interpretive procedure 3b)—for example, that he knows the meaning of "freeway" and can recognize one when he sees one, and that he knows what a car is and can use one. It assumes that the person knows about making turns, and can make one, et cetera.

The instruction refers to a few landmarks, a freeway, and a particular sign. It does not provide a detailed map on which every building and street is identified with its dimensions, age, and number of dollars spent in its construction. The hearer must go beyond the information given in the instruction itself and fill in with particulars from his own past experience, and with normal forms that he gains along the way. Thus, the instructions, and the phenomena examined in Chapter 4, are incomplete. The operation of interpretive procedures on social knowledge show how such symbolic forms are managed by the actor.

EXPLORING THE MODEL THROUGH ETHNOGRAPHIES

No studies describing the use of social knowledge and interpretive procedures in actual settings have been conducted.[9] However, the model of the reality constructor need not be restricted to free inventions. It is a schemata that enables actual social scenes to be examined at a greater depth than is usual in sociological field studies. It suggests a way of investigating particular scenes in order to *see general* features. Sociology presently searches particular scenes for *particular* features.

Consider, for example, the works of Becker, Whyte, and Goffman, acknowledged masters of the field study technique. Becker's (1953) analysis of marijuana users is typical. He describes how jazz musicians use "the smoke" to get "high" and improve their performance. Becker's (1968) later analysis of LSD use also describes how particular activities get done. He is not interested in using those particular activities as a vehicle for exploring the general features of all activities. Whyte (1955) provides descriptions of how gang members behave on street corners. Goffman's (1959, 1961, 1969) work reaches toward a deeper level, but it does not to seek features that appear in all situations.[10]

The model of the reality constructor, like Goffman's model, is "only" a schemata. However, it differs from Goffman, Becker and Whyte in directing the researcher's attention to transsituational features of particular situations. It provides a method for attempting ethnographies of the general problem of social order.

The choice between these alternative approaches must be made on extratheoretical grounds. The model of the reality constructor is *not* a higher ontological truth. (I return to this ontological issue at the end of this chapter.) For those interested in the particular features of particular scenes, traditional field work schemata are efficacious. For those interested in the general problem of social order, a model like the reality constructor is indicated.

EXPLORING THE MODEL THROUGH BREACHING

Field work studies are only one method of refining the reality constructor model. A second method is the use of "incongruity" or "breaching" procedures (see Chapters 2 and 12). The logic of the procedures derives from the claim that social structures are created by social structuring activities, work that is not apparent under normal circumstances. A corollary of this suggests that suppressing any of the models' features should "produce anomic effects and increase disorganization" (Garfinkel, 1963:215). I will adapt Garfinkel's breaching procedures to illustrate the necessity of the features of social knowledge, and interpretive procedures.

Breaching Social Knowledge

One of the features of everyday knowledge is that it provides a practical interest in the world (see p. 99 above). Garfinkel (1964, in 1967a:41–44) instructed a number of persons to converse while repressing this feature. He told them to adopt a *theoretic* interest in the conversation. This entailed seeking meanings "for their own sake," "just to see where it might lead." They were to show no regard for the practical circumstances surrounding the conversation.

The people who followed this procedure typically found that social order halted. This is the report of one person (*E*) who attempted to suppress the practical interest feature of social knowledge:

E   My friend and I were talking about a man whose overbearing attitude annoyed us. My friend expressed his feeling:

S.   I'm sick of him.

E.   Would you explain what is wrong with you that you are sick?

S.   Are you kidding me? You know what I mean.

E.   Please explain your ailment.

S.   (He listened to me with a puzzled look.) What came over you? We never talk this way, do we? (Ibid.:44).

The experimenter is not allowing what he knows to be "an integral feature" (Ibid.:273) of the scene. As a result, the ongoing interaction is swiftly disrupted. The subject demands to know "what came over" the experimenter, and points out that "We never talk this way." The repression of this feature of social knowledge breaches the subject's sense of normality, indicating that this feature is vital for the construction of everyday scenes.

A second feature of social knowledge is that it is socially distributed (see p. 99 above). Persons recognize that some persons know some things that others do not. These *personal* disparities in knowledge are supposed to be irrelevant in everyday interaction. Where they are not, it is assumed that the party with relevant personal knowledge will inform the other.

Garfinkel (Ibid.:75) demonstrated the importance of this feature by using the following procedure:

the experimenter engaged others in conversation while he had a wire recorder hidden under his coat. In the course of the conversation the experimenter opened his jacket to reveal the recorder saying, "See what I have?" An initial pause was almost invariably followed by the question, "What are you doing with it?" ... The fact that the conversation was revealed to have been recorded motivated new possibilities which the parties then sought to bring under the jurisdiction of an agreement that they had never specifically mentioned and that indeed did not previously exist.

The subjects knew that the experimenter knew things they did not, just as they knew they had knowledge the experimenter did not. But the subjects assumed as well that these disparities in knowledge were irrelevant to the interaction at hand. The appearance of the tape recorder made this taken-for-granted feature visible. By breaching it, Garfinkel demonstrated its importance to everyday interactions where it exists but is unnoticed. (For allied procedures breaching this feature, see Garfinkel, 1963:201–206; 1967a:71–73.)

The third feature of social knowledge I described above (p. 100) is its tacitness. Social knowledge is assumed to be shared by parties to an interaction. Though this shared knowledge is never exhaustively articulated, persons assume that they know a single world in common.

Garfinkel (1967a:51) designed a procedure to reveal the importance of this feature of social knowledge:

> Students were instructed to engage someone in conversation and to imagine and act on the assumption that what the other person was saying was directed by hidden motives which were his real ones.

In other words, students were asked to suspend the assumption that a body of knowledge was being tacitly held in common. The other person was seen as having a hidden body of knowledge ("motives") which were coloring all that person was doing.

Reviewing 35 instances of the implementation of this breaching procedure, Garfinkel concludes:

> The attitude was difficult to sustain and carry through. Students reported acute awareness of being "in an artificial game," of being unable to "live the part," and of frequently being "at a loss as to what to do next." ... One student spoke for several when she said she was unable to get any results because so much of her effort was directed to maintaining an attitude of distrust that she was unable to follow the conversation. She said she was unable to imagine how her fellow conversationalist might be deceiving her because they were talking about such inconsequential matters (Ibid.).

In sum, students found that they could not suppress the belief that they held a corpus of knowledge in common with the other. Even attempting to breach this feature disrupted the interaction. Common tacit knowledge is thus indicated to be essential to social scenes.

A fourth and final feature of social knowledge is that it takes the world for granted (see p. 100 above). A real world exists independent of the knowledge of the world. This world is in direct correspondence with the knowledge. Knowledge and world picture each other (cf. Wittgenstein, 1921).

Garfinkel (Ibid.: 46) breached this feature by asking subjects to enter their homes with the attitude of a boarder. The home was a familiar world. The attitude of a boarder required the use of unfamiliar knowledge. The procedure was designed to explore the clash of foreign knowledge and a familiar world.

Some of the students were instructed only to observe their homes as a boarder. They were not to act on this attitude:

> Many reported that the attitude was difficult to sustain because with it quarreling, bickering, and hostile motivations became discomfitingly visible. Frequently an account that recited newly visible troubles was accompanied by the student's assertion that his account of family problems was not a "true" picture; the family was *really* a very happy one. Students were convinced that the view from the boarder's attitude was not their real home environment (Ibid.).

The fourth feature of knowledge maintains that there is an undoubted correspondence between knowledge and world. Thus, students found that if they adopted a boarder's knowledge, they experienced a boarder's world. They were anxious to assure themselves that the world that appeared under the aegis of the different knowledge was not the "real" world. That new world offered troubles that were not visible through a family member's knowledge.

Garfinkel's procedure does not suggest that one or the other of these experiences of the home is true. It suggests instead that any knowledge will produce the experience of a world that corresponds with that knowledge. An omnipresent feature of all social knowledge is that it matches a real and external reality.

Breaching Interpretive Procedures

The first of three interpretive procedures I described was "searching for a normal form" (p. 101 above). This refers to the work people do to transform discrepancies and ambiguities into similar patterns. I have adapted another of Garfinkel's (1963:229–235; 1967a:59–67) procedures to illustrate the results of frustrating normal forming.

Garfinkel's subjects were 28 premedical students. They were separately introduced to a purported expert on medical school admissions, who said he was interested in decreasing student anxiety over medical school admissions interviews. He solicited the student's opinion on how this might be done.

After a casual hour's discussion, the interviewer asked the students if they would like to hear a recording of an actual admisssions interview. All of the students had such interviews in their future and leaped at the opportunity as a possible means of increasing their chances of admission.

The applicant the students heard was excessively boorish. He used poor grammar and was stupid. He was pushy and abrasive, contradicting the interviewer when not being evasive. He degraded other schools and professions. On top of it all, he demanded to be told at the end of the interview how he had done. At this point the recording ended.

The students were asked to write a detailed assessment of this tape-recorded applicant's performance. They described him much as I did above. This was, then, a first and initially successful attempt at normal forming. The interviewer-experimenter then breached this procedure. He presented the subject with the fake applicant's "official records," which showed superior grades and recommendations. Before the subjects could begin to attempt to normalize this information, they were inundated with more. They were handed the fake interviewer's assessment, which showed that the interviewer had rated the applicant highly. Subjects were given the opinions of a "panel of psychiatrists," who, along with other premedical students, were alleged to have also listened to the recording. These materials, which were individually arranged, contradicted almost adjective by adjective the assessment the subjects had originally offered.

The procedures of normal forming were thus rendered inoperative. Three of the 28 subjects resolved the situation by deciding it was all "a joke" or "merely an experiment." But for the majority who were unable to normalize in these ways, the world became "specifically sense-less" (Garfinkel, 1963:189). They were bewildered. They exhibited great anxiety and discomfort. Some wondered if they had "gone crazy." It was as if once the normal forming procedures were rendered unsuccessful, they found themselves with "an amnesia for social structure" (Ibid.).

Garfinkel (Ibid.: 223–226) designed another procedure that illustrates the importance of the interpretive procedure that I have labeled "doing a reciprocity of perspectives" (p. 101 above). This procedure indicates that persons normally act to maintain that they share the same worlds and knowledge. To make this procedure fail:

> students were asked to enter a store, to select a customer, and to treat the customer as a clerk while giving no recognition that the subject was any other person than the experimenter took him to be and without giving any indication that the experimenter's treatment was anything other than perfectly reasonable and legitimate (Ibid.:223).

In Chapter 2, I reproduced one of the cases that resulted from this procedure. The other results offered by Garfinkel display the anomia exhibited there. A physics professor, it will be remembered, becomes the unsuspecting subject of an experimenter, who "mistakes" him for a maître d' and persists in her error despite his attempts to create a reciprocity of perspectives. He tells her afterward "I haven't been so shaken since ——— denounced my theory of ——— in 19—" (Ibid.: 226). These studies indicate that if the reciprocity of perspectives is not accepted by other interactants, social scenes are severely disrupted.

I labeled the third interpretive procedure "employing the et cetera principle" (see p. 101 above). Although this procedure has three subfeatures, the breaching experiment I use as an example seems to explore the importance of only one of them. This feature suggests that normal interactants must permit unclear information to pass while waiting for later clarifying information. Garfinkel (Ibid.:221–223) instructed students to converse without letting any statements pass that they did not immediately feel they understood. Here is one of the cases that resulted from this procedure:

> *Case 4.*   During a conversation (with the *E*'s fiancee) the *E* questioned the meaning of various words used by the subject. For the first minute and a half the subject responded to the questions as if they were legitimate

inquiries. Then she responded with "Why are you asking me these questions?" . . . She became nervous and jittery, her face and hand movements . . . uncontrolled. She appeared bewildered and complained that I was making her nervous and demanded that I "Stop it!"

The fiancee at last covered her face with a magazine and refused to talk. Their orderly relations had been temporarily anomicized by the experimenter's refusal to employ one of the et cetera procedures. His refusal forced the other interactant into simulating schizophrenia.

The Empirical Status of the Breaching Studies

Breaching procedures such as these are not experiments. Instead, Garfinkel (1967a:65) has suggested that they be called *demonstrations,* to emphasize their "results do no more than illustrate what I am talking about" (italics omitted). The linkage between any specific incongruity demonstration and a feature of social knowledge or interpretive procedure is obscure. The logic of the demonstrations does not follow from the theory in any determinate way. One must not look to these breaching studies as a way of building a theory of the reality constructor that will be comparable to the theories of the truly experimental sciences.

The value of such demonstrations is great nonetheless. Deep disruptions of the social order are possible at any moment, in any scene. These demonstrations strongly suggest that ceaseless reality work is necessary for social order to persist.

A serious problem with the breaching procedures is that they became too potent (see Chapter 2). Refinements on several of the techniques I mentioned led to anomia that threatened to linger for days. *Interested persons are strongly advised not to undertake any new breaching studies.* It is immoral to inflict them on others. However, there are ways that one can breach one's own sense of social order. This is not immoral, though it may be foolish. I will mention some of these self-breaching experiments in Chapter 12.

THE REALITY CONSTRUCTOR

Objective and constraining social structures are constructed by social structuring activities. To determine the nature of this reality work, the ethnomethodologist constructs a "model of the actor." The procedures he attributes to the model are descriptions of activities that display the objective and constraining social structures.

Thus the ethnomethodological theory of the reality constructor is about the *procedures* that accomplish reality. It is not about any specific reality. Social scientists often adopt a privileged position about their pursuits. They claim that their findings are about the reality they study. Making connections between social class and occupation, for example, social scientists propose that social class is actually the reason a person has a certain job.

My ethnomethodology makes no such claim. I do not assume a correspondence between my theory and particular realities. The reality constructor is not a picture of actual persons. Jennings (personal communication) once proposed that the ultimate model of the reality constructor would be a machine that could engage in interaction with humans without detection. If the technological problems of such an operation could be overcome, and the ethnomethodologist was actually able to "plug in" the social knowledge and interpretive procedures sufficient for the machine to "pass," there would be no claim that the way the machine engages in interaction is the way a person engages in interaction.[11]

Ethnomethodology is not a method of pursuing the truth about the world. Rather, it examines the many versions, including its own, of the way the world is assembled. Ethnomethodology is not concerned with the truth value of statements about the world except as phenomena. It tries to determine the practices that make any statement true.

To this point we have discussed two kinds of "rules": normative rules (including legal, linguistic, and social science rules; see Chapter 4), and interpretive rules or procedures. Interpretive rules can be used as a theoretical device for understanding normative rule use. Interpretive procedures "fill in" the essential incompleteness of normative rules. Though interpretive procedures can be used in this way, it would be inconsistent to conclude that they are immune from the feature of incompleteness found in normative rules. In fact, each interpretive procedure exhibits the same feature of incompleteness.

The specter of incompleteness neither jeopardizes the enterprise nor spells its end. It is a source of mystery and wonder.

Looked at this way, constructing a list of interpretive procedures, or constructing any finite model is like fashioning a ladder, a tool to carry us upward. At some point, the ladder can be tossed away, as we will no longer depend on it for our climb (Wittgenstein, 1921).

NOTES

1. Ethnomethodologists adopted this research program from Schutz (1962, 1964), who spoke of the construction of "homunculi" and "puppets" as the theorists' solution of theoretical problems. Trading off a more recent metaphor, Crowle (1971) has suggested that the model is analogous to an android, that is, an automated simulated human (cf. Sacks, 1963).

2. Garfinkel has on numerous occasions attempted to codify and systematize Schutz's various discussions of the attitude of everyday life. His first attempt at this synthesis appears in his dissertation (Garfinkel, 1952). In his "Documentary Method" paper (Garfinkel, 1967a:89–94), he speaks in terms of the "findings" of an experiment reported there. In his 1960 paper on the "Rationalities" (1967a:272–279), he offers another summary of the "presuppositions of everyday life." A far more complex listing appears in his "Trust" paper (1963), where 8 presuppositions are listed and described. This list is repeated again as 11 presuppositions in the 1964 "Routine Grounds" paper (1967a:55–56).

Cicourel's treatment of the "interpretive procedures" has a similar history. His first writing (1968, in 1973a:42–73) made a strong analogy to linguistics; six interpretive procedures were "deep" rules to normative "surface rules." A discussion of "role theory" (1970, in 1973a:11–41) distributes the interpretive procedures into three "basic rules." Still another formulation (1969, in 1973a:74–98) produces four interpretive procedures.

3. In this talk, these theorists continually refer to the assumptions that the actor makes in interaction. They do *not* mean that the actor is consciously making choices prior to doing things. Postulating "assumptions" is one way the ethnomethodologist has for talking about the necessary aspects of interaction. There is no necessary commitment to a cognitive formulation. When the ethnomethodologist has been in dialogue with sociologists who employ models of action with mechanistic metaphors (e.g., Chomsky, 1965; Norman, 1969), the fundamentals have been talked about in 'generative' terms (Cicourel, 1973a:42–73). When the ethnomethodologist has been in dialogue with social theorists who use "game" or dramaturgical metaphors (e.g., Goffman, 1959, 1961), analogy has been made to "constitutive *rules*" (Garfinkel, 1963) or "basic *rules*" (Cicourel, 1973a:11–41). Presumably if organic theories were being offered as explanations of action (e.g., Spencer or Freud), the ethnomethodologist would rely on analogy to "basic needs."

In short, the way in which the fundamentals of social interaction are formulated depends on the contrastive theory. The form of the ethnomethodological argument about the construction of action is dialectical. It is dialectical in that any particular formulation cannot be understood without the contrastive theory it opposes.

4. Cicourel's "searching for a normal form" should be compared to Garfinkel's "seeking a scenic source" (1967a:92) and "searching for a pattern" (Ibid.:91).

5. Cicourel's description of the reciprocity of perspectives should be compared to Garfinkel's (1963:212–213; 1967:89).

6. Garfinkel treats the et cetera principle as three procedures: letting unclear information pass (1967a:3, 20–24, 90–91); filling in the ambiguity of indexical expressions (Ibid.:90–91, 92); and the retrospective-prospective dimension (Ibid.:89–90).

7. Crowle (1971:83) has translated these interpretive procedures into simply stated "rules for speakers and hearers." Here are the rules for the speaker, indicating how he should operate upon his social knowledge:

Rule 1.   Talk normally. (Use Rule 2.)

Rule 2.   Assume that the hearer will understand you as meaning the same as he would mean in the same situation.

Here are the hearer's rules:

Rule A.   Assume the speaker is talking normally (Use Rule B.) .

Rule B.   Assume that the speaker means the same as you would mean if you were to say the same thing in the same situation. (Use Rule C.)

Rule C.   If you can see it is relevant, use your (knowledge) of what was said before to interpret the meaning of what is said now.

Rule C₁.   If you still do not understand, use Rule D.

Rule D.   If you do not understand, ask him to clarify what he means. (Use Rule 1.)

Rule E.   Wait and see if what will be said clarifies what has been said.

Rule 1 and Rule A are related to the interpretive procedure, "search for normal forms." Rule 2 and Rule B are related to the reciprocity of perspectives and the et cetera principle. These rules must be operating continuously. Rule C distinguishes between background information and information gained during the course of interaction. Rule D relates to that part of the et cetera principle that relates to "waiting and seeing." Rule E relates to that portion of the et cetera principle that deals with "filling in meaning."

It should be clear that there is no one-to-one correspondence between any of these rules and any interpretive procedure. It represents an attempt by Crowle to codify and simplify Schutz's model, drawing upon the intervening further clarifications attempted by Garfinkel and Cicourel.

8.   I cannot help but reflect on how difficult it is to talk about "meaninglessness." The very words we use to talk about "meaninglessness" are themselves meaningful. The expression "black ooze" does not refer to a meaningless object. Although the expression does not carry a noun as specific as "asphalt," "black ooze" nevertheless is meaningful.

It may in fact be impossible to suspend or "get behind" the meanings provided to us by language and culture to "pure sensation." Layers of meaning may be stripped off (so that "freeway sign" becomes "bright shiny object," then "green flashes"), but each successive account requires a tie to a meaningful category to be processed. As Merleau-Ponty (quoted in Dreyfus and Dreyfus, 1964:xvi) said: "We are condemned to meaning."

9.   Crowle's (1971) dissertation is a possible exception. He uses the model to describe behaviors within a sociological experiment.

10.   Garfinkel (1967a:116–185; see Chapter 7) explored some differences between situated "passing" practices and Goffman's "management" practices in his "Agnes" study (see especially Garfinkel, 1967a:164–185). Garfinkel argues that Goffman's dramaturgical model presupposes a world of constant objects. Goffman does not describe how such objects are ceaselessly created. Garfinkel shows that no amount of "staging" or strategic planning before social scenes was sufficient to account for Agnes's creation of her female sexuality. In Garfinkel's (1960) "Scientific Rationalities" paper (1967a:262–283), he presents this argument against game models on a more general theoretic level.

11.   Anderson and Moore (1966) present a similar argument. They maintain that computers model, but do not explain, human phenomena. One can use models to predict, but not to assert. Assertions, they argue, are the raison d'être of scientific explanation.

CHAPTER SIX

Describably Elegant Knowledge

In Chapter 2, I claimed that every reality possesses a coherent body of knowledge. In Chapter 5, I discussed several general features of social knowledge, features that can be found within every reality, regardless of substantive differences. While the features of social knowledge described in Chapter 5 are general to all realities, the features described in this chapter are particular to a reality.

Sudnow (in Hill and Crittenden, 1968:51) captured the spirit of this ethnomethodological work when he told a group of sociologists:

> The program of ethnomethodology, at least as I see it, is to demonstrate that the member has elegant knowledge in the workings of social structure, *describably elegant knowledge*. The whole enterprise stands or falls in its ability to show the methodical character of the activities of members. . . . It fits with the programmatic task of ethnomethodology to take whatever the member does and deal with it in describably formal ways (italics added).

The call to treat the societal member's "describably elegant knowledge" in "describably formal ways" is not a call to translate that member's knowledge into a system based on formal logic. This would necessarily distort that member's reality. Sudnow is suggesting that ethnomethodology make a task of exploring the intricacies and sophistication of the member's own knowledge. In this chapter, I will report on several studies that implement this program.

TALK AS PERFORMANCE

A concern for the natural order in the use of social knowledge has led some ethnomethodologists to look at the activities that people engage in, and in turn, to look at what people *do* with their language. Turner (1970) locates the ethnomethodological reliance on conversational materials in J. L. Austin's (1961) work on performatives. A performative is conversational material which, by its utterance, accomplishes an act. Saying to another person "I promise" accomplishes promising. Likewise, under the proper circumstances—that is, with the right performers, and at the right place—saying "I do" constitutes marriage, and saying "I'm sorry," accomplishes an apology.

Turner finds Austin's work important because Austin explicitly ties talk (or utterances) to activities. Instead of treating talk as indexing underlying values, attitudes, or beliefs, Austin suggests that talk can be analyzed as the *doing of activities*. Since ethnomethodologists examine the production of talk and not the objects reported by talk, they treat talk as a topic, and not as a resource (Garfinkel, 1967a, 1–4; Zimmerman and Pollner, 1970; cf. Sacks, 1963; Wieder and Zimmerman, 1973). From the ordinary language dictum that activities are done in and by the talk that speakers and hearers use, ethnomethodologists build a parallel claim. A reality is done in and by the use of social knowledge.

An interest in language use, in turn, has focused ethnomethodological attention to talk that occurs naturally. "Naturally occurring talk" is obtained by audio- or videotaping conversations and other speech events when they occur naturally. A transcription of the talk is then made, and analysis is conducted on the transcript. Transcripts of conversations reconstruct talk in a manner similar to the way it occurred. Transcripts have the further advantage of being available for repeated observations; once analyzed, they can be reproduced along with the analysis.[1]

Instances of "naturally occurring talk" have been obtained in a number of ways. Transcripts gathered by others have been examined. To examine "everyday quantification practices," Churchill (n.d.) relied on the previously published interview of a pickpocket, verbatim transcripts of a young married couple, and transcripts from the first five minutes of a therapeutic session between a woman patient and a psychotherapist. Sacks (1966) and Schegloff (1967, 1968) relied on transcripts of telephone calls.

Labov (1969) maintains that talk can be arrayed on a continuum reaching from naturally occurring talk at one end to severely constrained talk at the other. An example of the first would be the talk between husband and wife at the breakfast table. An example of constrained talk would be that between a respondent and a sociologist. This distinction assumes that constrained talk is less real than naturally occurring talk. The ethnomethodologist finds all talk to be equally interesting and equally real, however.

Perhaps the better distinction to be made is in terms of the recoverability of talk. Since they consider talk only as an indicator of underlying structures, sociologists do not normally treat talk as a valuable phenomenon. It is not recorded in any systematic way. At best, field notes of what is said are taken, or forced choice answers are circled. Seldom is the actual talk, with its hesitations, pauses, and interruptions, recorded verbatim by the sociologist.

The ethnomethodological emphasis on "naturally occurring talk" is important, therefore, not because it says that some situations are more natural than others, but because it has elevated talk itself to the status of a phenomenon for study. Sociologists consider respondents' answers as "soft" materials; the numerical summaries of these interviews, experiments, or census surveys are seen as "hard" data. Ethnomethodologists reverse these shibboleths. They treat naturally occurring talk as their hard data, because talk is their phenomenon. They dismiss the numerical representations of reality as "soft," because these data obscure the interactional activities that produced the numerical representations (see Chapter 3; cf. Crowle, 1971; Speier, 1973:76).

What do people do with their language, then? Examination of various works shows that people do things such as describe, identify, categorize, complain, pun, and apologize.[2]

The next question is: *How* do people do what they do with language? Rather than summarize the answers that have been obtained to this question, I will engage you in the procedures by which answers are reached.

THE LOGIC OF EVERYDAY DESCRIPTIONS

Consider for the moment that you are hearing the following string of words spoken in flat tones, each word receiving equal stress and intensity:

the baby cried the mommy picked it up

What sense would you make of that string of words? I would guess that as you read this utterance, you rehearse certain intonations and stresses. You segment the utterance to understand it. The manner in which you break up the string of words into meaningful segments constitutes a "hearing" of the string. Perhaps your hearing resembles one of the following:

(1)　The baby cried. The mommy picked it up.
(2)　"The baby," cried the mommy, "picked it up."
(3)　The baby cried, "The mommy picked it up."[3]
(4)　The baby cried? The mommy picked it up!

In each segmentation of the string there is implicit action and relationship. Sacks, first in his dissertation (1966), then in a series of unpublished lectures (1965–1968), and finally in published articles (1972a, 1972c), provides an analytic framework to account for hearings. Sacks proposes that hearings *constitute descriptions* of the people and the action involved.

Sacks (1966) offers his own observations upon hearing this string of words. Sacks says that he hears two sentences: "The baby cried. The mommy picked it up." Two events are reported: a baby crying, a mommy acting. Each sentence reports an event. The events are not disassociated. They are temporally ordered. One event is followed by another. The order of the events is the same as the order of the utterances: the baby cried, *then* the mommy picked it up.

Furthermore, and most importantly, Sacks says that when he hears this string of utterances, he hears the mommy to be the mommy of the baby. He hears the string that way despite the fact that there is no grammatical reason for this connection. There is no genitive (her) in the second utterance to indicate relationship between the baby and the mommy.

The next stage of Sacks's analysis is the construction of a formal machinery to account for the description he heard, that the mommy is the mommy of the baby. This machinery will describe how descriptions are done. Sacks's notion of explanation is to examine a phenomenon, identify the practices there displayed, and then build an apparatus so that the phenomenon can be reproduced by the apparatus. The goal of the analysis thus seems to be context sensitive. It is a formal description that captures how indexicality is displayed.[4]

Description by Categorization

Sacks reasons that in order for the mommy in the second utterance to be heard as the "mommy of the baby" in the first utterance, these descriptions must go together in some way that does not depend on the grammatical information present in the utterance. Sacks argues that this data, and other material he has analyzed (1965–1968, 1966, 1972c), suggests the construct of a "membership categorization device." A membership categorization device is a collection of categories which may be applied to a population to classify the population. Two rules (at least) govern the application of such devices, the "economy rule" and the "consistency rule." The economy rule says: If a category from a device can be used to categorize another in a referentially adequate way, then the device may be applied to the population being described. The consistency rule says: If a category from a device is used to categorize a member, then that category or other categories from the same device may be used to categorize other members of the population. These rules will become clearer as the analysis unfolds.

For the mommy to be thought of as the mother of the baby, both persons must be classifiable by the same categorization device. To locate the device that contains both the "baby" category and the "mommy" category, Sacks's analysis proceeds as follows:

1.   He examines the first sentence ("The baby cried.") and, adhering to the economy rule, he searches for the devices that include the category "baby." There are at least two such devices: "baby" is a category in the device "family," and "baby" is a category in the device "stage of life." These devices may be represented as follows:

baby, child, adolescent, grown-up, . . .} stage of life
baby, mommy, daddy, sister, brother, . . .} family

2.   Having located devices that describe the people, Sacks attempts to apply them in accordance with the consistency rule. The device "stage

of life" does not apply, because mommy and baby are not both members of that device. The device "family" does apply. Hence, Sacks reasons, he hears the mommy to be the mother of the baby.

The manner in which speaker-hearers employ membership categorization devices does not conform to the canons of formal logic. The relationship between a category and a device is influenced by the context in which the description is accomplished, as analysis of the following reveals:

> Nobody feels any pain
> Tonight as I stand inside the rain
> Ev'rybody knows
> That Baby's got new clothes
> But lately I see her ribbons and her bows
> Have fallen from her curls.
> She takes just like a woman, yes, she does
> She makes love just like a woman, yes, she does
> And she aches just like a woman
> But she breaks just like a little girl.[5]

Applying the economy rule to Dylan's song uncovers the same two membership categorization devices located above. "Baby" is a category in the device "family," and "baby" is a category in the device "stage of life." The possible devices are applied to the other members of the population, in this case, the second mentioning of the same person. In this description of the lover as woman and baby, the device "family" cannot apply, as woman and baby are not members of that device. The device "stage of life" does apply. A contrast is achieved because "woman" and "baby" fit together in a similar categorizaation scheme.

The situational accomplishment of description can be revealed by contrasting these two strings of words. First, they show that the relationship of categories (e.g., mommy, baby) within a given device (e.g., family) is not permanent and stable. The categories that are included in a device on one occasion of description may not be included on another occasion. Categories "baby," and "adolescent" may constitute the device in one display, while "baby" and "woman" may in another.

Second, these examples show that a descriptive category may appear in different devices—the category "baby" appears in the device "stage of life" as well as in the device "family," for example. When the first member of a population is described, many devices apply. Not until the other members of the population are categorized can *the* device appropriate to *all* members of the population be determined.

Thus, the search for an adequate description is not consistent with linear, deductive, logical systems. The first category in a possible description is located. The category indexes possible devices. A second category is searched for, which locks the two categories into one device. If this retrospective linking of subsequent conditions to antecedent ones is a basic feature of commonsense reasoning, then a purely deductive, linear model of explanation will obscure its operation.

IDENTIFICATIONS

The relationship between category and device is not permanent and stable. Rather, it is subject to the influence of the social situation in which the device is used.[6] This situational sense of organization is also apparent in two other speaker-hearer descriptive activities: self-identifications, and location formulations. When people are introducing themselves, it is common to hear an exchange like the following:

A. Hi, my name is Bud Wood, what's yours?
B. Chris Isaac. I'm an engineer.
A. Oh, that's interesting; I'm an alchemist.

Speaker B identifies himself by the use of a category: profession. The next speaker commonly stays within the same device to identify himself, as opposed to choosing a category for a device such as, "I'm from Milwaukee" (Moerman, 1972:184, based on Sacks, 1965–1968). That is, once the relevance of the first category in a collection of identifications is established, the relevance of the second is assured. Yet, the categories in a given device are not constant. They are situational, as the following exchange I overheard at a school demonstrates:

Principal of School A. Are you in charge here?
Principal of School B. Yeah, I'm the enforcer.
Principal of School A. (Laughs.)
Parent of child in School B. Oh, *you're* Mr. Blye?
Principal of School B. Yes, (clearing his throat) I'm the principal here.

A list of the possible identifications of the person in charge of a public school might include "principal," "administrator," perhaps even "leader." But it is unlikely that such a list assembled independently of interactional encounters would place the word "enforcer" in such a categorization device. Categorical selection is situationally accomplished.

This example illustrates another sense of the occasionality of identification assembly. The principal identified himself in two ways in this exchange. Presumably the self-identification was influenced by the different relationships he has with the people involved.

Schegloff (1972) locates a similar feature in the methods used to give directions. Empirically, a location may be correctly referred to by many terms. But, on any actual occasion, not any member of that possible set can be used. To adequately formulate the location of a place, the speaker must select the appropriate category based on an assessment of the person being spoken to. Schegloff uses the example of a nostalgic person in New York City trying to find an abandoned rock and roll concert hall. Approaching someone who appears to be a freak, the person might inquire of "Filmore East"; asking someone who appears to be a businessman, the person might ask for the way to "105 Second Avenue."

Summary

As I argued in previous chapters, the principles of formal logic do not apply to the way everyday members of society employ their social knowledge. Now we have a further way of understanding that charge.

The ethnomethodological interest in the use of social knowledge has led to a study of the ways people talk about one another, categorize one another, and describe things. One of the features of a system built on the principles of formal logic is that the elements of the system are stable. But the ways in which speakers describe persons and things lack such formal stability. The relations among the terms people use in everyday descriptions are decided each time the terms are used. Categorizations are not necessarily consistent across situations. The same categories are not present in a device upon all occasions. The internal structure of a categorization is renewed on each occasion of interaction.

THE ANALYSIS OF CONVERSATIONAL STRUCTURE

Speaker-hearers who are describing, identifying, and formulating place are engaged in interpretive work. As I explained in Chapters 4 and 5, the conduct of such social activities is dependent upon the reflexive operation of social knowledge and interpretive procedures. Some ethnomethodologists have been interested in constructing a general or abstract model of the actor to display these dynamics. In this early phase of conversational analysis, Sacks and his associates were participating in this program, albeit in a novel way. Rather than aiming for a general model of the actor, they constructed numerous specific models. As I see Sacks's work, linguistic expressions were analyzed in order to see the coherence and order displayed by the use of social knowledge.

In more recent work, description of the use of social knowledge has become tangential. Instead of examining conversation in order to describe the speaker-hearer practices that accomplished the conversation, the internal structural arrangement of conversation itself is examined.

This shift in focus raises questions about the place of conversational analysis in ethnomethodology. I return to this issue after I describe this new turn in conversational analysis.

Segmenting Conversation

Conversational analysts locate the components of conversation in a way reminiscent of early abstract linguistics (Brown, 1965:246–349; Chomsky, 1959). Linguistic outputs, such as the sentence, were divided into segments. This "parsing" activity produced supersegmental categories. Thus, for example, the common direct sentence was segmented sequentially into two basic units: a "noun phrase" and a "verb phrase."

Conversational analysis may be understood in a like manner. The conversational analyst looks for categories (or slots) in a conversation that appear independent of the specific conversation. The analyst looks to see if these slots appear in certain parts of the conversation and not others. Certain slots are said to "go together." For example, lingu sts claim that determiners (e.g., the, an, a) go together with nouns (e.g., house, man, wastebasket). Conversational analysis locates similar tying structures.

Unlike abstract linguistic theories, the segmentation of conversations into "slots" has been based on people's actual talk. Sacks (1966) examined more than 500 tape recordings of telephone calls coming into the UCLA Suicide Prevention Center. Schegloff (1968) studied a like number of calls made to the complaint desk of a police department. Telephone calls have been a prime data source for the study of conversational structure, perhaps because they are confined to a single channel of communication, and because the "same" activity recurs, thereby enabling a corpus of materials to be assembled readily. Granted, all communicative exchanges between humans do not occur through a verbal mode. However, when a new program of study is developing, it is convenient to limit the data and phenomena.

An overwhelming number of calls examined by Schegloff (1968) looked like the following (No. 43 in his corpus):

(Phone rings.)	
Police dispatcher.	Police desk. (S p o k e n simultaneously with:)
Caller.	Say, what's all the excitement?
Police dispatcher.	Police desk.
Caller.	Police headquarters?
Police dispatcher.	Yes.
Caller.	What's all the excitement about . . .

A pervasive feature of the organization of these phone calls has been captured under what Schegloff (1968:1076) calls the "distribution rule" for first utterances. The rule may be expressed as: "The answerer speaks first." Schegloff maintains that this rule holds because of the informational resources of the answerer. The caller knows both his own identity, and typically the identity of the intended answerer. The answerer only knows who he is, but does not know specifically who the caller is.

An equally recurrent pattern in the calls analyzed was their adherence to a "sequencing rule": The speakers in telephone conversations speak one at a time, and alternate their speaking in a way that can be expressed as AB, AB, and so on (where A stands for the talk of one speaker, B for the talk of the second speaker).

People do not routinely go about picking up phones to see if someone is waiting to talk to them. When a phone rings, it indicates that a person wants to talk to someone at the place where the phone is located. Schegloff (Ibid.: 1080) treats the phone's ring as a kind of summons. Like other kinds of summonses, such as roll calls, police summonses, and challenges, they "demand" an answer. First utterances are motivated by the summons in the form of the telephone ring. The answering of the phone and the routine greeting will not occur (normally—deviations are discussed below) unless and until the phone has rung.

Paired Utterances

This observation—that people receiving calls speak first, but do so only in response to a "summons" in the form of a ring of the phone—enables the conversational analyst to speak of some utterances as "conversational pairs" (Sacks, 1965–1968; Schegloff, 1968). In order to talk of two utterances, or activities as a sequenced pair, one must speak of their "conditional relevance." One item in a pair is conditionally relevant upon another if, given one item in the pair, the second is expected to occur. Conditional relevance accounts for the response given when the expected second half of the pair is absent. The absence of the second half of a conditionally relevant pair is made accountable.

The summons, in the form of the phone ringing, constitutes the first half of an ordered pair. It "raises the expectation" (Burke, 1931:124) that the summons will be responded to. The answering of the phone constitutes the second half of the pair, it "fulfills the expectation" (Ibid.) raised by the summons.

To this point, the conversational analyst is able to say that telephone conversations have recurrent features: They all begin with a summons; if successful, they all contain an answer to that summons. These "slots" occur at the beginning of each telephone conversation.

The next phase of the analysis turns from a consideration of how a telephone conversation begins to what is said at its beginning. The distribution rule for the first utterance in a phone conversation says that the answerer speaks first. Now the question becomes, are there regularities in what gets said at this juncture? The telephone conversations that Schegloff analyzed typically had a "greeting." Utterances found upon analysis to fit into this slot include "hello," "hi," "howareya," and others. Many of the calls analyzed had appendages added to the greeting. These took the form of some kind of "self-identification." The self-identification slot appeared to have two parts: a "frame" and "terms of identification." By frame is meant such terms as "this is ———," "my name is ———." Terms of identification include, among other utterances, first names, last names, names with titles, and identification of the place being called, such as "police department."

The following diagram schematizes this work. ϕ indicates the sanctioned possibility that the items listed in that category may not appear. That is, items in that category are not obligatory; they can be absent without disrupting the conversation.

Answerer's Greeting Slot[7]

greeting   +   self-identification

$$
\left\{ \begin{array}{c} \phi \\ \text{hello} \\ \text{hi} \\ \text{how are} \\ \text{you today} \\ \text{etc.} \end{array} \right\}
\quad
\begin{array}{c} \text{frame} \\ \left\{ \begin{array}{c} \phi \\ \text{this is} \\ \text{my name is} \end{array} \right\} \end{array}
+
\begin{array}{c} \text{identification terms} \\ \left\{ \begin{array}{c} \phi \\ \text{first name} \\ \text{last name} \\ \text{title and last name} \\ \text{place name} \end{array} \right\} \end{array}
$$

Some additional observations can be made about the internal organization of the greeting slot. Neither the order nor the presence of the two elements is obligatory. Thus, the greeting can appear alone, the self-identification can appear alone, or both can appear together. In addition, the self-identification unit can appear before the greeting, as in "This is Cotton, how are you today?" If a speaker chooses to make a self-identification, however, and uses a "frame," then the speaker must follow the frame with an identification term. The frame cannot stand alone without some accountable reference to its solitary presence being made.

Some of these points can be made clear by looking back at Schegloff's exchange 43 from his police department data. In this instance, the answerer's greeting slot included only an "identification term." Absent are the "greeting" and the "frame" of a self-identification. This greeting, then, would be represented in my scheme as: ϕ, ϕ, place term.

Earlier, I mentioned the presence of paired occurrences in telephone conversations. The presence of a summons was tied to the presence of an "answer." In a similar manner, the presence of an "answerer's greeting slot" is paired with the "caller's greeting slot." The utterance of a greeting by the person answering the phone was usually paired with a greeting offered by the caller.

The structure of the caller's greeting is very similar to that of the answerer's greeting described above. But, the caller does not necessarily provide a *place name* if a self-identification component of the greeting has been chosen. Also, he may add an "identification of the other" request to his greeting, such as "Who's this?" or "Is this Sally's Chic Massage?" This internal structure of the caller's greeting slot may be summarized as follows:

Caller's Greeting Slot

greeting   +   self-identification   +   request for other identification

ϕ
$$\left\{ \begin{matrix} \text{hello} \\ \text{hi} \\ \text{howareya} \\ \text{etc.} \end{matrix} \right\} \quad \begin{matrix} \phi \\ frame \end{matrix} + \begin{matrix} \phi \\ self\text{-}identification \end{matrix} \qquad \begin{matrix} \phi \\ frame \end{matrix} + \begin{matrix} \phi \\ other\ identification \end{matrix}$$

$$\left. \begin{matrix} \phi \\ \text{this is} \\ \text{etc.} \end{matrix} \right\} \left\{ \begin{matrix} \phi \\ \text{first name} \\ \text{last name} \\ \text{title and last name} \\ \text{place name} \\ \text{etc.} \end{matrix} \right\} \qquad \begin{matrix} \phi \end{matrix} \quad \left\{ \begin{matrix} \phi \\ \text{who is this?} \\ \text{is this Sam?} \\ \text{etc.} \end{matrix} \right\}$$

The caller's greeting, like the answerer's greeting, may appear in a different order from the one shown. Or, one or the other units may appear alone, as the following examples illustrate:

(1)   Hi, this is Sid. Is this Curtis?

(2)   Is this Curtis?

(3)   Curtis?

(4)   Hi

(5)   This is Sid.

(6)   This is Sid. Is this Curtis?

(7)   Is this Curtis? This is Sid.

Schegloff's instance 43 is like my hypothetical example 3. The caller to the police station merely states the name of the place he is calling: "Police headquarters?"

To this point I have been treating the occurrence of greetings as if they were all spoken in one turn. Sacks's and Schegloff's data suggest that greeting units can also appear across a number of turns, as follows:

Turn	Utterance	Conversational "Slot"
(1)	(Phone rings.)	summons
(2)	A. Hello?	answer
(3)	B. Hello, this is Sid.	greeting + self-identification
(4)	A. Oh, hi, this is Curtis.	greeting + self-identification
(5)	B. Howareya man?	request for personal state
(6)	A. No complaints.	personal state information
(7)	B. Good. Listen man, I gotta ask you . . .	first topic

The telephone material analyzed by Sacks and Schegloff permit one further observation: The caller provides the first topic of the conversation. This feature is alluded to in turn 7 of this example, and in the last line Schegloff's example 43, where the caller says: "What's all the excitement about?"

The beginnings of telephone conversations can therefore be characterized as a series of paired slots: Summons-answer, and greeting-greeting, followed by the introduction of the "first topic." The units within the greeting slot also appear in pairs. In a separate analysis (Sacks, 1967) has spoken of the subcomponents of a "first greeting" as a "request for personal state information." It is paired with "personal state information," which appears in a return greeting. Personal states include such conditions as one's mood, health, appetite, amount of sleep, and others. Sid, in turn 5 of my hypothetical example above, says, "Howareya man" which is an instance of a "request for personal state information." Curtis (turn 6) responds "no complaints," completing the pair.

The sequence in greeting exchanges can be summarized as follows:

Caller's Greeting Slot

greeting + self-identification + request for other's self-identification + personal state request

Answerer's Greeting Slot

greeting + self-identification + personal state statement

Turn Taking

Segmenting conversations into slots and locating paired occurrences is based on two concepts: utterances and turns. Sacks has defined an utterance as anything and everything that a person says between his own pauses or silence. A turn is all the talk that one speaker says before another person talks. Hence, a turn is more inclusive than an utterance, since it contains one or more utterances. An utterance is more inclusive than the sentence, which is the prime unit of analysis for transformational linguists. The utterance, unlike the linguist's sentence, does work outside its boundaries.

The conversational analyst has not delineated many other conversational slots past these introductory ones. The options for talk beyond initial greetings are diffuse. Rather than pursue these options, attention has been focused on other paired utterances within the body of conversation, such as question-answer pairs and insult pairs. Analysts have also considered speaker selection, topic selection, and conversational closings (Schegloff and Sacks, 1973). Two conversational regularities are that one speaker speaks at a time, and that turn taking occurs smoothly (with "no gaps and no overlaps"). These and other observations suggest that a formal turn taking system operates in conversation (Sacks, Schegloff, and Jefferson, 1974).

Turn taking is described in terms of "speaker selection" rules. There are transition points where current speakers can exit and new speakers can enter the conversation. At these junctures, the current speaker can select the next speaker, he can select himself to continue, or another speaker can select himself as next speaker.

The turn taking techniques by which the current speaker selects the next speaker employ the paired utterances or "adjacency pairs" discussed previously. The question, "What did you think of the pottery sale, Denise?" is an example of an "addressed question." The addressed question is a token of the adjacency pair type of conversational sequence by which "current speaker selects next speaker." You will remember from our earlier discussion of paired utterances that the presence of the first part of an adjacency pair establishes constraints on what should occur in the next turn of conversation. For example, the utterance of certain kinds of questions *should* produce an answer (Churchill, 1972). In a similar manner, Sacks, Schegloff, and Jefferson (1974) suggest that the utterance of this addressed question selects Denise as the next speaker.

In a similar manner, one word questions (e.g., what, how, who) select the last speaker as the next speaker, as in the following example:

(1) *A.* . . . and after that she went to the pottery sale
(2) *B.* Who?
(3) *A.* Denise.

The tag question (e.g., don't you agree, isn't that so, isn't that what you said) operates in a similar manner.

The Accountable Absence of Utterances

Conversationalists act when one item of an expected pair is absent. Relying on Sacks's and Schegloff's work, I have described two utterance pairs in conversations: the summons-answer pair and the greeting-greeting pair. Paired utterances were described as conditionally relevant. The appearance of the first item signals the expected presence of the second item in the pair. When the conditional relevance of conversational pairs is not satisfied, the absence is accounted for.

When one person greets another, and the other does not return the greeting, that absence is noted. Conversationalists may construct "good reasons" for the absence of expected conversational activity. They may say, for example, "He didn't see me," "He must be angry." The following exchange from Schegloff's (1968:1086–1087) materials illustrate this point:

Wife.	Are you mad at me?
Husband.	Why do you think that?
Wife.	You didn't answer when I called you.
Husband.	Oh. No. I didn't hear you.

In Schegloff's data, when considerable time elapsed between the offering of a summons (hello) and the return of an answer, the summons was repeated:

Dispatcher.	Police desk. (Pause.) Police desk. (Pause.) Hello, police desk. (Longer pause.) Hello!
Caller.	Hello.
Dispatcher.	Hello. (Pause.) Police desk.
Caller.	Pardon.
Dispatcher.	Do you want the police desk?

Such repetitions will not go on indefinitely. Nor will they take the same form each time. A child attempting to get his mother's attention may try: "Mom," receive no response, say "Mom" again, then change syntactic forms and emphasis to, perhaps, *"Mother!"* or an emphatic *"Ma!"*

The repeated summons-answer sequence in Schegloff's exchange 43 can be understood in this way. By speaking immediately, the caller violated the distribution rule for first telephone utterances: The answerer could not speak first. Because the anticipated answer to the summons was not allowed to occur, the summons-answer sequence had to be repeated to maintain the structure of the conversation.

An "official absence" of an expected conversational utterance leads to an account of the absence of the answer or other activity. When one rings the doorbell and receives no answer, one infers that "no one is home." One also infers that the fact that "no one is home" *accounts for* the fact of no answer. The absence is thus accountable.

> A husband and wife are in an upstairs room when a knock on the door occurs; the wife goes to answer it; after several minutes the husband comes to the head of the stairs and calls the wife's name; there is no answer and the husband runs down the stairs (Schegloff, 1968:1087).

The husband goes down the stairs to find out what would provide an account of the absence of the wife's answer. Accounting for the absence of an expected feature of interaction becomes a test for the reality of a rule. An accountable absence displays its normally unnoticed presence (cf. Garfinkel, 1967a:3–24).

THE ELEGANCE OF MEMBERS' KNOWLEDGE

Here, then, is a look at a research program that began as an attempt "to demonstrate that the member has elegant knowledge in the workings of social structure" (Sudnow, in Hill and Crittenden, 1968:51), and developed into a study of the structure of conversation.

Because conversational analysis differs from other ethnomethodological studies, the question is often raised if it is ethnomethodology at all. There are at least four answers to this question.

One answer derives from Sacks's (1963) first published paper. Sacks criticized social science for treating talk as if it stood for something else. Rather than accepting the facticity of talk, Sacks said that the first task of sociology should be the investigation of how talk itself is organized. Social phenomena are displayed in talk. Therefore, Sacks recommended, talk should be social science's primary phenomenon.

If conversational analysis is seen as growing out of this early statement of Sacks, its purposes are like those of other ethnomethodological studies. Categorization practices, greeting practices, and descriptive practices constitute a description of the members' "elegant knowledge in the working of social structure."

It is easier to give this understanding to the earlier studies in conversational analysis than to the later studies. These later studies suggest a second understanding of the work. As a search for turn taking structures, adjacency pairs, and so forth, conversational analysis closely resembles abstract linguistics. For example, Sacks, Schegloff, and Jefferson (1974:702) describe the turn taking apparatus of conversation as "two components and a set of rules." This comment and the tone of the Sacks, Schegloff, and Jefferson paper recalls Chomsky's (1965:8, 17) descriptions of a generative grammar as a system of syntactic, phonological, and semantic rules that assign structural descriptions to sentences. Viewed this way, conversational analysis is a search for structures. Like abstract linguistics, it makes no reference to structuring activities.

This omission of a structuring level constituting structures has led Cicourel (1973a:68–71) to a third interpretation of conversational analysis. Cicourel maintains that conversational analysts implicitly rely on the model of the structuring actor I reviewed in Chapter 5. For example, for turn taking to occur, the speaker-hearer must interpret the situation, employ an appropriate speaker selection rule, and recognize the speaker change transition points in the conversation. Such complex judgmental work is not explicit in conversational analysis.

If turn taking structures are examined for the conversational practices that produced them, a fourth version of the work can be constructed. Then, both the early and the later work can be seen as descriptive of situationally bound practices. The conversational structures can be studied for the social knowledge and interpretive procedures that speaker-hearers selectively use to construct conversations.

Transforming conversational analysis into a study of scenic practices in this way makes their findings situationally specific. These findings would not have the same status as interpretive procedures in the model of the actor. The conversational practices are scene specific.

The conversational practices described in this chapter and the other scenic practices studied by ethnomethodologists (see Chapter 7) do not exhaust the list of possible practices used to accomplish reality. As new scenes are continually being created, the enterprise of assembling scenic practices seems endless.

A list of practices that constitute various scenes can be examined for their common properties. Some properties of such practices are suggested in Garfinkel (1967a) and Garfinkel and Sacks (1970) and are described in Chapter 9. For now I want to point out that locating properties of practices would provide the basis for a general theory of social structure and social structuring. When the enterprise is viewed as the search for the properties of practices, conversational analysis contributes to the compilation of the list of practices. This fourth interpretation would include conversational analysis within the purview of this general theory.

As this discussion reveals, the place of conversational analysis within ethnomethodology is highly controversial. No single interpretation captures its place.

Conversational analysis is especially provocative for ethnomethodologists because of its radical position on the reflexivity of reflexivity. Conversational analysts have been willing to ignore the indexical relations between talk and its context. They have treated talk as possessing finite meanings. In so doing, conversational analysts have suspended consideration of the consequences of reflexivity that other researchers have treated as ethnomethodology's essential phenomenon (see Chapters 7, 8, and 10).

In order for any ethnomethodological research to be conducted, reflexivity must be ignored at some point. Otherwise the research becomes solipsistic. Conversational analysis differs from other ethnomethodologies in that it does not treat reflexivity as a phenomenon at any point.

NOTES

1. This statement of methodological rigor should be compared to Cicourel's (1968:2) call for sociological investigators to display their materials, locate their conclusions in the materials, and then demonstrate *how* the conclusions were located in the materials (cf. Mehan, 1973:328).

2. See the works of Churchill (n.d.), Sacks (1965–1968, 1966, 1972a, 1972c, 1973), Schegloff (1968, 1972), Schenkein (1972), Speier (1973), and Turner (1970).

3. Readings (2) and (3) are courtesy of Howard Schwartz (1971:185)

4. For detailed descriptions of indexicality, see Chapters 4 and 10.

5. The lyrics are from Bob Dylan's "Just Like a Woman," courtesy of Dwarf Records.

6. This finding is consistent with the recommendation made by Zimmerman and Pollner (1970:80–108) that the features of a particular setting are not a stable corpus. Rather, the organizational scheme that assembles a setting's features is established on the occasion of the description. Jules-Rosette (1973:163) locates this occasioned selection in the way in which Biblical passages were selected to convey basic teachings in the Apostolic churches she studied in Africa: "All passages had a moral and instructional intent, but specific instructions were relevant to the situation at different times."

7. These diagrams of conversational structure are constructed from the available texts, as supplemented by Ervin-Tripp's (1973:304ff.) discussion of "American address terms." Churchill (1972) displays the organization of conversational slots in a "tree structure."

CHAPTER SEVEN

The
Reality
of
Reflexivity

Most ethnomethodologists agree that reflexivity is fundamental to ethnomethodology. Nonetheless, there is deep disagreement concerning its meaning. Some treat reflexivity as a phenomenon, some as a theory. Still others claim that reflexivity is a method, or call it a theology. I focus on these differences in the next four chapters. In this chapter, I describe four disparate programs that treat reflexivity as a phenomenon. In Chapter 8, I review some ontological problems associated with research into reflexivity. In Chapter 9 and 10, I place the concept of reflexivity in a more inclusive theoretical frame.

THE REALITY OF A HALFWAY HOUSE

Wieder provides a description of reflexivity. The scene of Wieder's work was a halfway house for paroled ex-convicts. Wieder (1973:43) first did traditional ethnography and then turned his attention:

> to the production of that ethnography as an accomplishment. . . . The ethnographer's experience *as such,* as an "object in a social world," then becomes a primary source of data (cf. Ibid.:183–214).

The reality Wieder wished to investigate was staff and resident interaction. He first offers a description of the staff and resident knowledge
systems. From the perspective of the staff at the house, this system con-
sisted of two separate subsystems. One included the official history of
the house and the responsibilities, ideals, and hopes of the staff
(Ibid.:46–72). The second subsystem was the "convict code." This code
was shared with the inmates. Wieder concentrated his research on it.

Both staff and residents repeatedly told him that there was *a* code
and that every resident in the house knew it. The residents had learned
it, Wieder was instructed, when they had been in the "joint."

> The code was also employed by staff in talking to the residents. It went
> full circle, being mostly employed by residents in explaining themselves
> to staff, then in staff's explaining residents to other staff, and finally, on
> some occasions, staff's actively promoting the story of the code to the resi-
> dents (Ibid.:162).

The code instructed residents how to behave toward one another and
toward officials of the penal system. It constituted a system of rules,
and dictated a moral order. Not living up to the code was a sanctionable
offense. As ex-convicts and ex-drug addicts, all the residents expected
to be someday returned to prison. Beatings were administered there
to those who broke the code. Knowing the code and following it was
thus a matter of life and death.

Wieder heard these and other things about the code in bits and pieces.
He was able to provide the following coherence to these bits. They represent maxims of proper conduct for residents.

1.   Above all else, do not snitch.
2.   Do not cop out.
3.   Do not take advantage of other residents.
4.   Share what you have.
5.   Help other residents.
6.   Do not mess with other residents' interests.
7.   Do not trust staff—staff is heat.
8.   Show your loyalty to the residents (Ibid.: 115–118).

Like Castaneda's (1968) codification of Don Juan's knowledge (see
Chapter 2), Wieder's presentation is a translation of the vernacular. No
resident knows the list in this form. Like the policeman's knowledge

of the law described in Chapter 4, the code cannot be exhaustively described. Its relevant aspects emerge situationally.

Wieder's early presentation of the code is like the presentations sociologists often make to document the existence of "informal rules" in "deviant subcultures" (Wieder, 1973:120–125). Wieder shows how the code can be used to explain deviance.

In the second part of the study, Wieder begins to detail the reflexive use of this code. He focuses on the reflexive and the interactional features of realities (see Chapter 2). To introduce these two additional features, he compares hearing the talk accompanying a travelogue, where:

> one encounters the story shown on the screen and the identifications, explanations, and descriptions of the narrative heard over a loud speaker as discreet occurrences—narrative and picture. . . . Typically, explanations are temporally juxtaposed to the scenic occurrences they explain. . . . one listens to the narration and sees the film passively as a depicted scene for one's enjoyment or edification, not as an object that one must necessarily actively encounter and immediately deal with. Coupled with the feature of the passive audience, the narrator speaks for whoever listens. The parties hearing him are unknown to him, do not act upon his fate, and indeed have no involvement with him beyond their listening (Ibid.:165–166).

Social knowledge systems such as the convict code are traditionally treated like this within social science. But Wieder says that this is not the way the code is used within its own settings. It "was not simply or merely a description of life in a halfway house." The code "was told within that scene as a continuous, connected part of that scene by being manifested as an active consequential act within it" (Ibid.:166).

Actual use of the code differs from mere description in two analytically separate ways. One of these Wieder sometimes labels "formulating many aspects of the scene," and sometimes "persuading" by telling the code. The other feature is the "consequentiality" of telling the code. Wieder (Ibid.:167) says that these are "the two aspects of what ethnomethodologists call the reflexive operations of natural language accounts" (cf. Ibid.:130, 216). In the terminology of Chapter 2, Wieder's consequentiality is the reflexive feature of realities. His persuasive or formulating aspects of telling the code correspond to the interactional feature of realities.

Wieder offers many examples of these two features. To display the reflexive and interactional use of the code, I will focus only on that element of the knowledge system which says, "Do not snitch."

The maxim, "Do not snitch," means that good residents do not supply information to staff concerning the activities of other residents. But defining the maxim in this *one* way necessarily glosses the multiple meanings it has in interaction. When "I don't snitch" or "Cons don't snitch" is said in the house, it is seldom offered as an abstract statement describing a part of the convict code. When staff or residents refer to this or any element of the convict code during the ongoing life of the house, they say it within a web of practical circumstances. The saying is offered as an index of those circumstances. It is a call for the hearer to organize the ongoing interaction in accordance with that part of the convict code which exhorts residents not to tell on each other.

Wieder (Ibid.:168) writes that "When talking with residents, staff and I often had a relatively friendly line of conversation terminated by a resident's saying, 'You know I won't snitch.' " Such sayings were not offered as a *description* of the code. Rather, they indexed what the resident felt had just happened in the conversation. By saying, "I won't snitch," he reported his understanding that he had just been asked to snitch. He also formulated the fact that the speaker was one kind of person, a resident, and that the hearer was another, a staff member. The saying indexed these implicit "facts," making the implicit explicit. The saying answered the staff member's question by saying that it would not be answered. It supplied a reason for not answering—"I'm not answering in order to avoid snitching." One saying could do all these things because the speaker was a part of the same scene his talk was indexing. Actual talk does not occur like a travelogue, with the scene and the narration separate. In everyday life, scene and action are not discrete but "mutually determinative" (Ibid.:216).

If rules do not appear independently of their particular ongoing invocations, how is it possible for the staff and residents to treat them so? Wieder suggests an answer. Formulations not only index, they have real consequences within scenes. They create new practical circumstances, and these new circumstances show them to be "true."

In Chapter 4, I discussed several studies illustrating the "essential incompleteness of rules." Wieder's work illuminates this phenomenon from the obverse side. Those earlier studies began with rules and situations. They demonstrated that rule use depended upon particular circumstances within situations. Wieder began with the convict code and

demonstrated that these rules create social situations. Wieder's work illustrates that such rules are never invoked by residents for abstract or
merely descriptive reasons. Rather, they do work. They are offered as
means for particular interactants at particular times to do particular
things. To say, "You know I won't snitch," accomplishes different things
within different scenes. Said to a staff member the ex-convict hates it
can be a shout of defiance. Said to one that he feels is his friend, it
can be an apology for an impossible situation. But in all cases, the power
of the saying comes from the sense that not "just anything" has been
said. The saying demonstrates that the code stands independent of the
particular scene in which it is invoked. This is accomplished by every
saying of the code.

Wieder discusses this reflexive use of the code at two analytically separate levels. The first level, which he calls "the consequentiality of telling
the code," can be illustrated by that same example of a resident saying,
"You know I won't snitch." In addition to indexing, such an utterance
changes the very practical circumstances for which it now stands as a
description. By invoking the code's axiom on snitching, a resident re-
buffed the staff member and "called for and almost always obtained
a cessation of that line of conversation" (Ibid.:169). This left the staff
member ignorant of what he would have learned had the resident answered differently. The resident's answer further warned that the conversation would become unpleasant if the resident did not accept the
ex-convict's answer of not answering. The resident was appealing to the
"fact" that if he snitched instead of answering as he did, "the potential
consequences for him could include beatings and even death"
(Ibid.:169–170).

At the second level, Wieder (Ibid.:203, cf. 131) concludes that the
convict code "consists of a collection of embedded instructions for perception." Once one becomes an insider, one does not merely speak and
hear the code. One learns to *see* it.

A newcomer, whether a staff member associating with convicts or a
man entering a society of captives for the first time, is taught to perceive
scenes in terms of the code. "The persuasive talk of 'old hands' becomes
embedded instructions for the novice, which he uses as a schema of
interpretation in his active, interpretive search for structure and meaning" (Ibid.:209).

Early in his work, Wieder observed behavior manifestly deviant from
the stated aims of the house. Like Goffman, he described this behavior

as "doing distance," "doing disinterest," "doing disrespect," "doing un-reliability," "doing violations" (Ibid.:73–112). These stable patterns of behavior appeared across various cohorts of residents without fail for 18 months. Once Wieder learned the code he could explain deviant patterns in terms of it (Ibid.:118–120). But Wieder, like all residents and staff, had to be taught to see this way, through numerous instances of hearing the code mentioned and alluded to in "bits and pieces." Every telling of the code taught the code's reality again. Residents invoked the code as a way of structuring their mutual perceptions of the swarm of behavior surrounding them.

Wieder is not arguing that the convict code is unreal. It exists as an objective and external constraint within the reality of the halfway house. But it obtains its facticity only from a ceaseless body of reality work. Thus, as Wieder writes: "it is much more appropriate to think of the code as a continuous, ongoing process, rather than as a set of stable elements of culture which endure through time" (Ibid.:186). Wieder demonstrates that realities can be shown to contain coherent knowledge systems. These systems are constituted and sustained by in-dexical interactions. Wieder's work shows too that such indexical use of knowledge reflexively informs later scenes. It structures them such that those indexes are perceived as more "correct" than when they were first uttered.[1]

SCENIC PRACTICES

Garfinkel (1967a, 1967b; Garfinkel and Sacks, 1970) suggests studying the interactional work that accomplishes reflexivity. He recommends viewing this work as sets of scenic practices. Scenic practices accomplish the particularity of particular situations. Their presence is restricted to the substantive scenes in which they occur. Such practices differ from the interpretive procedures of Chapter 5, and from the language prac-tices of Chapter 6.

Interpretive procedures are general practices. They are assumed to be present in all social scenes. Scenic practices are scene specific. They are more like the language practices studied by conversational analysts (see Chapter 6). Neither scenic nor language practices are claimed to be present in all interactions. Nevertheless, the two practices differ in obvious ways. Language practices are descriptions of language use. Scen-ic practices are descriptions of phenomena that language and other symbolic behaviors combine to display. All three practices describe reflexive work. They differ from one another in the descriptive level of analysis each assumes.

Unlike interpretive procedures, scenic practices "exist in empirical multitude" (Garfinkel and Sacks, 1970:343).

> Their multitude is indicated in the endless ways that persons speak. Some indication of their character and their differences occurs in the socially available glosses of a multitude of sign functions as when we take note of marking, labeling, symbolizing, emblemizing, cryptograms, analogies, anagrams, indicating, miniaturizing, imitating, mocking-up, simulating (Garfinkel, 1967a:31). ·

Garfinkel sometimes speaks of "glossing practices" and sometimes of "scenic practices." I have collapsed the two into the single concept of scenic practices (cf. Garfinkel, 1967a:1–34; Garfinkel and Sacks, 1970).

Garfinkel's research has uncovered scenic practices in numerous settings. Most of this work is unpublished. In print, Garfinkel has offered examples of degradation practices (1956a), juror practices (1967a:104–115), sexual practices (1967a:116–185, 285–288), documenting practices (1959:57–59; 1967a:76–103), psychiatric clinic personnel practices (1967a:186–207; see Chapter 3, above), accounting practices (1967a:3–4), suicide prevention center practices (1967a:11–18; 1967b), coding practices (1967a:18–24) and scientific theorizing practices (1960, in 1967a:262–283). Several of these studies merely suggest the possibility of describing particular practices; they do not actually describe them. Garfinkel's discussions of the sexual and of the documenting practices are more complete.

Sexual Practices

Like all objective facts, "male" and "female" are reflexive accomplishments. Garfinkel (1967a:116–185, 285–288) documents this claim by examining the woman's work that accomplishes womanness. He uncovered these practices through discussions with a 19-year-old woman named Agnes. Garfinkel met Agnes in 1958. She had prototypical 1950s measurements: 38-25-38. She was pretty, with "a peaches and cream complexion, no facial hair, subtly plucked eyebrows, and no make-up except for lipstick" (Ibid.:119). She was obviously a woman.

But Agnes had not always been a woman. For the first 16 years of her life, she had been a boy. Her birth certificate listed her sex as male. Her mother, siblings, relatives, and playmates had all treated her as a male. Nonetheless, Agnes told Garfinkel that she had known all along she was a girl. At the age of 16 she ran away from home and donned feminine clothing. Since looking like a woman was not enough, Agnes had to learn the practices women use to be accepted as real women.

Garfinkel (Ibid.:136–137) reports that almost every situation Agnes faced had the feature "of an actual or potential character and fitness test. It would be less than accurate to say of her that she passed than that she was continually engaged in the work of passing." Different scenes required different passing practices. Agnes discovered that a sexual category is not a "status" in social structures. Rather, she found that being a woman required a ceaseless process of social structuring. This work manufactures the appearance of static sexual categories. Most females learn these passing practices in their youth, and thus do them unknowingly. Agnes had had no such training, and so had to learn by doing. For example, cooking is a common feminine activity in American society at midcentury. Agnes did not know how to cook. At one time, she was engaged to be married. She seized an opportunity to learn from her mother-in-law-to-be how to prepare the exotic dishes her fiancé liked to eat. In her kitchen, Agnes learned not only how to cook these dishes, she learned simultaneously how to cook at all. While being taught the intricacies of cooking curry, she learned to pass as a person who could do the more routine feminine practices: she learned to measure and combine ingredients, to heat an oven and scour sinks, and so forth.

Dating was another set of practices Agnes did not know. She found passing as a normal woman in these situations immensely complicated. Her friends and roommates enjoyed telling stories about their previous dates. Agnes listened to these tales to learn correct dating practices. However, no amount of listening was ever able to equip her fully for a competent performance. She had to learn within the practical circumstances of any date what she had to do to be seen as a real woman.

One of Agnes's most persistent difficulties was learning to speak as a normal woman speaks. Garfinkel (1967a:168) writes that to learn the proper practices within particular scenes:

> A favorite device was to permit other persons, and in many of our conversations, me, to take the lead so as to see which way the wind was blowing before offering a reply. She had a way of permitting the environment to

teach her the answers that it expected to its own questions. Occasionally Agnes would give the device away by asking me, after an exchange, whether I thought she had given a normal answer.

This passage illustrates why some practices are called *scenic*. Scenic practices are activities that appear within specific scenes as a "normal" possibility of those scenes. To be competent in a scene means to enact some of the possible normal practices. Anytime one enters an unfamiliar scene one becomes self-conscious of these practices. One feels alert and carefully watches others to determine what is expected. Agnes was a unique resource for displaying this work. She was a stranger to scenic practices that few of us past adolescence ever experience as problematic. Agnes was uniquely "equipped to teach normals how normals make sexuality happen" (Ibid.: 188).

The everyday view is that sexuality consists of biological characteristics. Garfinkel demonstrates that sexuality consists of passing practices. I have purposefully refrained from reporting that Agnes had a normal-sized penis and scrotum. Scientifically she was properly classifiable as a male. But she learned *to be* a woman. Social being is distinct from scientific methodologies. One is a man or a woman within the social order because of the practices one employs. These practices reflexively produce the "social structures of everyday activities" (Ibid.: 185), of which sexual "facts" are but one of an almost infinite number.

Documenting Practices

Garfinkel used Agnes to emphasize the fact of scenic practices. He did not attempt to exhaustively describe the activities that constitute scenic sexuality. In another study, Garfinkel (1962, in 1967a: 76–103) offered such an exhaustive description. Adapting some of Mannheim's (1952) work, Garfinkel gave these practices the general title of "the documentary method of interpretation." These practices describe the way persons impute "biography and prospects to . . . appearances" (Ibid.: 77). The studies reviewed in Chapter 5 inform us of the *general* way this is done. In his work with the documentary method, Garfinkel examined a particular scenic aspect of this process.

The species of "scene" to be examined is any situation where some observed occurrences must be matched with an unseen occurrence. Prototypical unseen occurrences are "motives" and "intentions." Garfinkel (Ibid.:78–79, 94–103) emphasizes that such documenting work, which is pervasive in social science, is a common practice within everyday life as well. He offers the following general characterization of the documentary method:

> The method consists of treating an actual appearance as "the document of," as "pointing to," as "standing on behalf of" a pre-supposed underlying pattern. Not only is the underlying pattern derived from its individual documentary evidences, but the individual documentary evidences, in their turn, are interpreted on the basis of "what is known" about the underlying pattern. Each is used to elaborate the other (Ibid.:78).

Garfinkel (Ibid.:79) designed a demonstration scene in an effort "to exaggerate the features of this method in use and to catch the work of 'fact production' in flight."[2] He told subjects that research was being undertaken by the Department of Psychiatry in an effort to explore alternative means of personal counseling. Each subject met a person falsely represented as a counselor in training. Subjects were placed in a room by themselves and told to formulate a series of yes and no questions about a problem that was then deeply concerning them. There was a microphone for communicating with the counselor. Between each question the subject disconnected the microphone and, in private, tape-recorded his comments on the exchange. Once he exhausted himself and arrived at a next question, he turned the microphone on again, asked his question, and received another no or yes.

The answers the subjects heard were predetermined and random. Though the observed occurrences were "really" random, the subjects heard them as patterned. Garfinkel offers sample transcripts from two of the subjects, then a list of scenic practices which describe the work that constitutes the documentary method. This is a short section from one of the transcripts Garfinkel (Ibid.:83–84) reproduces:

S.   Do you feel that it would be a better situation if we were to get married and neither one of us were willing to talk about the religious difference or to give in on either one side, that we bring our children up in a neutral religion other than the two that we believe in?

E.   My answer is yes.

S.   Well perhaps this would be a solution. If we could find a religion that would incorporate our two beliefs to a certain extent. I realize that perhaps this might be literally impossible to do. Perhaps in a sense this neutral religion might be something almost made up by ourselves because honestly I feel that religious training, no matter which belief it is if not carried to extremes is good, for everyone should have a certain amount of religious training along the lines. Perhaps this might be a solution to the problem. I guess I should follow this along a little bit further and see exactly what happens. I am ready for number eight.

If we were to get married would it be best for us to live in a new community where we will not be in contact with our parents if we were getting a lot of family pressure over religious differences?

E. My answer is no.

S. Well, I kinda tend to agree with this answer. I feel that you wouldn't be accomplishing too much by running away from the issue and that perhaps it would be one of those things in life that eventually you would just be willing to accept it and that the families and we would get along harmoniously together. At least I hope it would work out if that situation comes about. I think it would be best for both families together that we are not going to work it out if we run away from our problem. So we best remain there and try and work it out. I am ready for number nine.

If we did get married and were to raise our children do you think that we should explain and tell our children that we once had this religious difference or would we just bring them up in this new religion, that is, their religion, that we talked about, and let them believe that that is what we originally believed in?

E. My answer is no.

S. Once again I kinda agree with this. I think they should be told because undoubtedly they will find out. And if they did find out that there was this difference that we once had they would feel that we were sneaking or trying to hide something from them and this would not be the best situation either. So I believe this would be the best situation. I am ready for number ten.

Do you feel that our children, if there were any, would have any religious problems themselves because of us the parents and our difficulties?

E. My answer is no.

S. Well I really don't know if I agree with that or not. Perhaps they would have trouble if confusion set in and they were to feel that they did not know which is right and which is wrong or what side to pick if they did not want to stick with their religion. But I kinda feel that if their religion was a wholesome one which supplied the needs of a religion and that which a religion does supply that there would not be any problems with them. But I suppose that only time will tell if such problems would come about. I am finished with my comments now.

E.   Okay, I will be right in.

Garfinkel (Ibid.:89–94) follows the transcripts with a list of scenic practices. These practices describe how subjects did the work of treating random answers as documents of a motivated underlying pattern. To summarize some of these documenting practices:

1.   Subjects heard the yes-no answers as answers to their questions.

2.   When subjects could not immediately understand an answer as an answer to their qeustion, they searched for such an understanding.

3.   Subjects used present answers to alter their understandings of previous exchanges. They changed their understandings as they went along.

4.   Subjects used their present understandings or absence of understandings as a guide for formulating present questions. No subject administered a preprogrammed set of questions.

5.   Once an answer was heard, subjects were willing to change their interpretation of their own question in order to hear the answer as an answer to their question.

6.   No answer was so inappropriate or so contradictory that subjects could not see its reasoned intent. Inappropriateness and contradictioriness could themselves be used as guides to that meaning.

7.   From the first answer until the end, subjects found a pattern in the counselor's responses. This pattern constituted the counselor's "advice." Some subjects sometimes understood the pattern to be "deceit."

8.   There was vagueness built into the subject's imputation of pattern.

9.   Subjects assumed a body of social knowledge in common with the counselor. The relevant parts of this corpus shifted according to the subject's present needs. The subject invoked what was required at any moment to document the counselor as a motivated person of good character.

In this way then, Garfinkel sketches the specific work that is used to treat "an actual appearance as 'the document of,' as 'pointing to,' as 'standing on behalf of' a presupposed underlying pattern" (Ibid.:78).

Documenting is only one of many scenes where particular practices may be sought and described. As mentioned above, Garfinkel has examined eight other types of scenic practices in his published work. His goal is not to devise lists of practices; rather, it is to find a method for examining reflexivity at close range. An "empirical multitude" of scenic practices can be found. The "crux" of recommending their study, Garfinkel says, is that they are "reflexive" or "incarnate." That is:

> such practices consist of an endless, ongoing, contingent accomplishment; that they are carried on under the auspices of, and are made to happen as events in, the same ordinary affairs that in organizing they describe . . . (Ibid.:1).

For Garfinkel, the total conglomeration of scenic practices constitute the social order. The practices do not simply illustrate reflexivity, they constitute that phenomenon.

EXPERIMENTAL ETHNOMETHODOLOGY

Theory and method intertwine.[3] How one conceives of reflexivity determines how one can properly conceive of it. Most research within ethnomethodology denies the relevance of the canons and logic of natural science. It seeks to build a new perspective on the old problems of reliability and validity. But rather than abandon the logico-empiricist perspective, some ethnomethodologists have attempted to develop an improved empirical social science. The most recent[4] such program is contained in Zimmerman and Wilson (1973).[5]

Zimmerman and Wilson express discontent with ethnograpaic studies of indexicality and reflexivity. They realize that data are reflexively related to the methods of investigation. Zimmerman and Wilson attempt to circumvent this problem by having experimental subjects segment meaningful displays into "natural units." The goal of this research is to uncover universal empirical laws.

This work begins with an explicit acceptance of the ethnomethodological theory of meaning. Garfinkel (1967a:185–186) has described the consequences of looking at the world with this theory:

> The work of doing water witching, mathematics, chemistry, and sociology ... whether done by lay persons or professionals, would be addressed according to the policy that every feature of sense, of fact, and of method for every particular inquiry is the managed accomplishment of organized settings of practical actions; further, that particular determinations in members' practices of consistency, planfulness, relevance, or reproducibility of their practices and results are acquired and assured only through particular, located organizations of artful practices.

Schwartz (1971:210) has argued that this theory of meaning amounts to "a set of descriptive procedures to turn the whole world into collections of social practices." He contrasts this theory with the theory undergirding science:

> From the theory of models from logic one gets the image of meaning as stable relations between objects, sets, and structures on the one hand, and symbols tightly tied to them on the other. Here, in ethnomethodology, the image of meaning is that of a transient collage which is put together, torn down, added to, subtracted from, changed around, from occasion to occasion (Ibid.).

Zimmerman and Wilson employ the logical theory of meaning to learn about the ethnomethodological theory.

The logico-empiricist theory is fruitful, they maintain, only if applied to phenomena that have no substantive meanings. It is therefore not a fruitful methodology for the study of social action as traditionally conceived within sociology (cf. Wilson, 1970). Zimmerman and Wilson thus eschew any interest in the phenomenal experiences of actual parties to actual scenes, as these are not amenable to the logico-empiricist methodology.

The phenomena Zimmerman and Wilson say they will measure are the same phenomena ethnomethodologists have referred to as "indexicality" and "reflexivity." They will be able to apply logico-empiricist methods to these phenomena because they will not be interested in the meaningfulness of these phenomena.

Ethnomethodologists agree that methods borrowed from natural science are inappropriate for the study of meaningful phenomena. Most ethnomethodologists have attempted to change the methods to fit the phenomena. Zimmerman and Wilson change the phenomena to fit the methods of natural science.

There are two parts to what Zimmerman and Wilson mean by logico-empiricist inquiry. Both depend on the logical theory of meaning Schwartz characterized above. The first of these is literal measurement. The second is invariant empirical laws.

Literal measurement specifies a category or class, and identifies the properties that objects must possess in order to be included in that class (Cicourel, 1964; Wilson, 1970). In literal measurement, phenomena "are treated without reference to their intrinsic meanings since they have none save that assigned within the natural scientists's theory" (Zimmerman and Wilson, 1973:6). Numerals can be assigned and manipulated without distorting the meaning of the phenomena being studied as those phenomena are not assumed to possess any meaning independent of the scientist's measurement practices. In their paper, Zimmerman and Wilson offer such a phenomenon and suggest how it could be literally described.

They argue that this procedure could lead to the discovery of *invariant empirical laws*. These invariants are not to be confused with the essential and/or invariant features discussed in phenomenology (e.g., Gurwitsch, 1964; Husserl, 1913) and recently adopted by some sociologists (e.g., Psathas, 1973; Psathas and Waksler, 1973; Wieder, 1973). Phenomenological invariants do not permit the construction of laws stated in formal symbolic languages. But these are the statements that Zimmerman and Wilson seek. They are not to be invariants of any substantive phenomenal display, but rather statements of *relations* among rigorously defined and measured concepts.

A description of the actual experimental procedures that Zimmerman and Wilson are using is premature. Their work has just begun. It is the version of ethnomethodology they present that is of interest here. They argue that their rigorous experimental approach to the phenomena of ethnomethodology will eventually be able to be "articulated" with other methodological approaches, especially what they call the "phenomenological approach" of Bittner (1973) and, to a lesser extent, of Wieder (1973). They suggest that these less rigorous methods can deal with substantive meanings. Their experimental method ignores such meaning. Articulated, the two methods will shed light on the same phenomena from two methodological directions.

I began this section by repeating the claim discussed in Chapter 3, that one's theory and method are inextricably intertwined. Can an experimental method measure the "same" phenomenon as a phenomenological method? When Wieder discovers reflexivity in his and others' talk in an actual halfway house on a particular day at a particular moment, is this the "same" reflexivity that Zimmerman and Wilson propose to measure literally and define within a theory of symbolic relations? I think the answer *can be* yes, but the issue turns on the commonsense model that is guiding the research.

Zimmerman and Wilson (1973:12) anticipate this issue. They emphasize that they have not adopted logical empiricism as "a philosophy of science, much less [as] an adequate world view." It is only a "methodological attitude," a codification of some rules and principles for the undertaking of one kind of inquiry. They make clear that their image of man is broader than the logico-empiricist image. The commonsense model that undergirds their concerns informs them that a phenomenon measured experimentally is "really the same" as that phenomenon measured in field studies.[6]

Zimmerman and Wilson's sense of reflexivity is not shared by all ethnomethodologists. This, of course, does not mean that Zimmerman and Wilson's work is uninteresting. Its audacity should arrest the attention of ethnomethodologists and sociologists alike.

The possible articulation of Zimmerman and Wilson's findings with other ethnomethodologies is a red herring. It is only from within their perspective that it is important, for they are committed to deductive theory. As I conceive of it, ethnomethodology has room for both deductive theory-building and more anarchical activities. In the next section, I discuss a call for an ethnomethodology that avoids all theorizing, reporting, describing, and analysis. Once I have described this program I will state why I think such disagreement should not be seen as troublesome. No unifying resolution of these disparate "theories" and "methods" need be attempted.

ETHNOMETHODOLOGY AS PARANOIA

Schwartz (1971, n.d.) has offered several arguments against the above research programs. He maintains that reflexivity points to a subjective phenomenon that connot be described by ethnographies, practices, or literal measurement. In a related argument, he suggests that reflexivity has been accorded such a broad status that it is not an informative idea. Schwartz offers these criticisms as a precis for a new approach to the study of reflexivity. I will review his critique, then summarize his alternative program.

To understand what rankles Schwartz, recall how reflexivity has usually been defined. For example, Garfinkel (1967a:1) begins his *Studies in Ethnomethodology* by claiming that the "central recommendation" of ethnomethodology is:

> that the activities whereby members produce and manage settings of organized everyday affairs are *identical* with members' procedures for making those setings "account-able." The "reflexive" or "incarnate" character of accounting practices makes up the crux of that recommendation. When I speak of accountable my interests are directed to such matters as the following. ... that they are carried on under the auspices of, and are made to happen as events in, the same ordinary affairs that in organizing they describe ... (italics added).

The work of Garfinkel, Zimmerman, and Wilson reviewed above explicate this exhortation. They each claim that members' procedures are *identical* with the events or structures they describe. Symbolic activities both describe and organize the thing described. Schwartz offers several reasons why such a conception of reflexivity should be abandoned.

Schwartz concentrates first on the issue of "identity." He (1971:1–155) details some insoluble logical problems entailed in this concept (see Chapter 3). Schwartz turns this discussion of identity on the claim that members' methods reflexively create and are identical with social structures. This claim has typically been used to turn the problem of social structures into a problem of members' methods. But to maintain that the two are identical implies that the opposite formula could be used as well. The problem of members' methods could be subsumed under the problem of social structures. If they are identical, to study one necessarily illuminates the other. Sociologists interested in social structures and ignorant of members' methods thus become ethnomethodologists.

Schwartz explores a host of similar problems involved in calling any "two" phenomena identical. Schwartz's first critique is directed at the meaning of the theoretical talk undergirding ethnomethodology. He offers a second critique that is methodological. However reflexivity may be conceived, it is a subjective phenomenon. *Analysis* of subjective phenomena necessarily relies upon ideas of "error" and/or "mistake"

(Ibid.:156–178). Ironic contrasts are made between what the person acknowledges and what the analyst's analysis reveals. Matters such as fact or truth or empirical law become relevant. One must ask if the analysis is accurate. These issues are clearly relevant in the Wieder, Garfinkel, and Zimmerman-Wilson approaches to reflexivity. Schwartz argues that to analyze subjective phenomena necessarily distorts such phenomena. He says that subjective phenomena should be displayed. Displays of subjective phenomena such as reflexivity pose "an issue of faithfulness rather than correctness" (Ibid.:263). In this work, "the notion of phenomenon becomes logically prior to the notion of truth" (Ibid.:266;see also Ibid.:269; n.d.:18–20).

Before I display Schwartz's alternative methodology, the reader should understand the irony of Schwartz's second reflection. He argues against previous ethnomethodologies much as ethnomethodology once argued against traditional sociology (see Chapter 3 above). He maintains that ethnomethodology has distorted its phenomenon by describing it. This distortion has been unrecognized or, at least, unacknowledged.

A third critique focuses on the *ontological* status of reflexive phenomena. Schwartz argues that reflexivity is not a "deep" phenomenon. He maintains that it is not an omnipresent fact of language use. Schwartz offers a novel reading of Garfinkel's breaching studies (see Chapters 2 and 5 above) to support his claim. Typically these demonstrations are claimed to illustrate that an unnoticed but ceaseless body of reality work exists beneath all stable social structures. Schwartz claims that these demonstrations illustrate an alternative phenomenon; they reveal that:

> a clear alteration of natural approaches [is necessary] in order to see common-place actions as rule governed, norm-relevant—as theoretical structures and in particular as theoretical descriptions. They do not usually look like that (1971:245).

Schwartz's discussion implies that the ethnomethodologist's experience is no deeper than the experience of persons who know nothing of such loops.

In other words, Schwartz is arguing that reflexivity is a horizontal and not a vertical phenomenon. It does not exist someplace below the mere appearances of everyday life. It is an experience that sometimes occurs and sometimes does not along the temporal horizons of persons as they meet their lives. This is not to say that Schwartz thinks that

ethnomethodologists have "merely" created reflexivity. It is a phenomenon that others beside ethnomethodologists produce. But Schwartz
warns against generalizing from these occasional experiences to claims
about the constitution of all social structures and all social scenes.

The purpose of Schwartz's work is to outline a new program for exploring reflexive phenomena that are immune to the three faults I have
just reviewed. He offers a definition of reflexivity that avoids the identity
problem: "It may be briefly stated thusly: The reflexivity of descriptions
consists in the innumerable ways in which they are part of what they
describe" (n.d.:21). Schwartz (1971) says that there are recurrent phenomena in everyday life where such reflexive phenomena appear, and
offers this example from his notes on a mental hospital ward. A staff
member says to a patient: "Did we tell you Doctor Glick will be gone
for two weeks?" (1971:231). This is the kind of example that Wieder
uses so extensively to build his claim that all talk is reflexive. The staff
member in Schwartz's example is clearly telling something and simultaneously telling about the telling. He is talking about the doing and doing
the doing at the same time. The talk is, in Wieder's terms, multiformula-
tive and multiconsequential. Schwartz acknowledges this but says that
such examples "are merely academic oddities, there being no reason
to suppose such a self referential reflexivity is in any sense a recognized
one and many reasons to think the contrary" (Ibid.:231–232). The ethnomethodologist may say that such examples exhibit reflexivity, but in
so doing he distorts the way the talk has been experienced by the participants to the talk.[7]

This procedure also makes reflexivity refer to everything and so to
nothing. It does not discriminate and so does not inform. Schwartz recommends saving the concept of reflexivity for those occasions where
people recognize and display it.

Reflexivity is frequently recognized by persons diagnosed as paranoid
schizophrenic. Schwartz found that "if a person was crazy in a certain
way, phenomena in social scenes which interested ethnomethodologists
were noticed by him in an explicit way" (Ibid.:250). In such cases, the
persons experienced his or others' descriptions "as a part of what they
described" (Ibid.:233).

> For him certain of what has been termed the omnipresent features of his
> interpretive processes become visible and attended to as noticeable charac-
> teristics of his world. This they are not for the normal individual under
> the natural attitude (Ibid.:251).

Psychiatrists attempt to treat such phenomena as "projection errors" (Ibid.:232–233; Schwartz, n.d.).[8] Philosophers have conceived of the problem as "self-referential statements." Some examples of this philosophical concern are the Cretan's report that all Cretans are liars, the claim that all generalizations are false, and the statement that you can never get out of your own paradigm of thought (Schwartz, 1971:267–268).

Among schizophrenics, such projection errors occur when the "thing" and "thing described" are seen reflexively. This is reflexivity as the ethnomethodologist has traditionally conceived it.[9] But reflexivity defies description. It requires a new methodology. Schwartz (Ibid.:178–179) summarizes the difficulties such a new approach must face:

> But how does one examine a few major abilities persons seem to have where (1) it is counter-indicated to overdescribe these in analytic detail; (2) their principle significance is in the possibility of doing them, not understanding them: (3) the phenomena they make available are specifically unavailable via the widely used methods of reportage which academic training prepares one to understand and use?

Schwartz's (Ibid.:270) solution is to seek a social science methodology where "the notion of success replaces truth as the criteria of validity." He argues that rather than analyzing phenomena such as projection errors (nee paranoid reflexivity) the researcher should *learn to do it*. For example, to know about the experience of persecution, Schwartz (Ibid.:283) suggests "going around the world noticing what negative events seemed to happen when you were around, events that need not usually happen in terms of common sense reasoning about plausibility."

Much learning is required to come to experience in a paranoid manner. On the psychiatric ward Schwartz studied (Ibid.:284), a man heard every use of the pronoun "it" as standing for his penis. He had to work hard to hear every "it" in that way. Schwartz argues that researchers should not erect analyses about such phenomena. They should learn to experience this way. Analysis from without will not penetrate such phenomena.[10]

The first task of Schwartz's new approach to social phenomena is to learn how to experience in a new way. He tests his competence against natives' experience. The next task is to return to one's colleagues and display the phenomenon. A display is not a report or description. It is not about the subject phenomenon, it is more a demonstration of it. Schwartz recommends these demonstrations with the metaphor of a theatrical play:

> The idea is to try to display certain things to the audience by a performance that evokes certain reactions and reflections. To that end the correspondence of the dialogue with actual events and discourse which occurred at some other time and place is not at issue because the phenomena is not something else for which the play is a representative; it is what happens to those who witness the performance (Schwartz, 1971:180).[11]

Schwartz's dissertation is a theoretical preparation for future performances. Nonetheless, it contains several displays and I will summarize one. To borrow Schwartz's metaphor, my next paragraphs are like a plot summary of *Hamlet*. They do not exhibit the phenomenon Schwartz displays. Nevertheless, they forebode what Schwartz's display achieves.

One of Schwartz's plays exhibits persons who experience "descriptions" and "things described" reflexively. Schwartz (Ibid.: 246–247) discusses two persons diagnosed as schizophrenics. He shows that they made a creative leap from a paranoid to a reflexive vision. In the first mode there was much anxiety, in the second much relief. In the first mode the objects came to the persons with a malevolent cast. In the second mode these objects appeared similarly, but the persons simultaneously saw these objects as part of a paranoid process. Schwartz calls this leap "non-discursive reasoning."

Schwartz (Ibid.:247–248) introduces a third character, a woman with paranoid "delusions of reference." She experiences a world pregnant with messages directed solely at her. They come from supernatural beings who are interfering with the world in order to tell her secret and frightening facts about her character and future. She is in terror and misery. The most trivial occurrences signal the presence of an omniscient being, who announces that this woman is an evil being, with a terrible fate ahead of her.

Schwartz himself now joins the cast of his display. He penetrated this woman's reality. He told her that her horrible thoughts should be taken one step further. She should begin treating the appearance of each of the messenger spirits with suspicion as well. Perhaps their presence was merely a thought being planted within her world by yet more malevolent beings. Schwartz describes his "plan" as follows:

> The very process producing the terror was to be used to kill itself by bring-
> ing the terror itself under the same suspicion. At some point, she needed
> to simply *start* addressing everything whatsoever with her suspicion, with
> no jumping off preparation, no diving board. After that there would be
> no way to be sure about your desperate situation and the anxiety should
> subside. This was indeed what happened (Ibid.:248).

The woman made the creative leap and her anxiety subsided.

There is a trick in this display. When Schwartz encouraged the woman
to "simply *start* addressing everything whatsoever with her suspicion,"
why did she not apply this to Schwartz's advice as well? Why did she
not see that he too was trying to make her suffer by making the evil
suggestion that her spirits should be mistrusted? These possibilities were
avoided because Schwartz was "inside" her experience. His purpose was
not to analyze the phenomenon "but to do it" (Ibid.:266). His success
with this woman shows that he learned to do paranoia. He did it so
well that he could help another out of it.

Schwartz (Ibid.:271–285) uses his knowledge to present a novel picture of the paranoid process. Paranoids have the same discursive skills
as nonparanoids. Their "interpretive processes" and "commonsense reasoning" are unimpaired. Only their nondiscursive reasoning is affected.
In their everyday experiences they see God, spirits, feel the ether wind,
hear the dead, and so forth. In many cases a paranoid's "cure" will
consist of learning to talk and describe normally the everyday "world
which he is no longer in" (Ibid.:274). The creative leap described above
is perhaps the paranoid's first recognition as to how this might be done.
It involves becoming an ethnomethodologist—learning that one can treat
the world as if it consists of members' methods. So aware, one can begin
to pass as normal.

In summary, Schwartz's program grows from his critique of earlier
ethnomethodological research. I divided this critique into three parts.
One part was theoretical and criticized earlier conceptions of reflexivity
as formal nonsense. A second part was methodological and argued that
subjective phenomena such as reflexivity could not be described without
distortion. A third part of Schwartz's reflections concerned the ontological status of reflexivity. He maintained that earlier ethnomethodologists
erred in treating reflexivity as an omnipresent phenomenon. Schwartz's
alternative program avoids this ontological problem, does not describe,
and eschews formal logic theory.

THE FAMILY OF REFLEXIVITY

In this chapter I have reviewed four approaches to reflexivity. In Chapter 2, I offered a fifth. These do not exhaust the studies of reflexivity (e.g., Cicourel, 1973a). In Chapters 8 and 10 I offer further analyses of the idea. Like any of the other views, they can be read as *the* general statement defining reflexivity; but this would be an incorrect way to look at any particular exegesis of reflexivity.

Within my perspective on ethnomethodology, it is not useful to decide once and for all whether reflexivity can be studied experimentally, ethnographically, or phenomenologically, or whether reflexivity can be reported, displayed, or analyzed. Reflexivity proves itself by the variety of programs that have been created in its name.

These programs share a "family resemblance" (Wittgenstein, 1953). Reflexivity is that "something" that they have in common. The resemblance that is the reflexive mien may be recognized if these programs are viewed one after the other. But one cannot predict what the next member of the family will look like by looking at the existing members.

I think that Pollner (1970) is correct when he indicates that reflexivity is ultimately an occult phenomenon. Eglin (1973) has convincingly traced its history to medieval alchemy. There could be infinite sayings about reflexivity, and still reflexivity would not be captured. Reflexivity will exhaust us long before we exhaust it.

NOTES

1. I have used the five features of reality described in Chapter 2 as a way of organizing Wieder's report, since Wieder (e.g., 1973:132) claims " 'telling the code' . . . was productive of *a* social reality" (italics added). I have shown how easily this discussion can be used to illustrate the reflexivity, knowledge, interactional, and permeability features of reality. The fragility feature is less prominent in Wieder's report. However, he makes implicit reference to this feature when discussing the untoward consequences that arose when the code was ignored and/or not accepted as a fact. By viewing Wieder's work in this way, I hope to have illustrated the efficacy of the five features, even though they are not an explicit theoretical frame in Wieder's writing.

2. McHugh (1968) used a similar quasi-experimental procedure. His findings contrast interestingly with Garfinkel's, as he depends not on Schutz's perspective, but on Mead's (1934, 1959).

3. The argument that theory and method are inseparably intertwined is elaborated in Cicourel's *Method and Measurement in Sociology* (1964). He argues that sociology's theory

(its "model of the actor") is incompatible with sociology's methods, and that therein lies the social sciences' persistent flaw and source of frustration (see Chapter 3 above).

4. Mehan and Wood (1969) and Wood (1969b) earlier offered an argument for experimental studies in ethnomethodology like Zimmerman and Wilson's. They too argued that such a rigorous inquiry could be done only once an interest in meaning was eschewed. Their experimental procedures were designed to produce literal measurement and invariant laws but, due to a lack of equipment, will, and interest, were never translated from theory into practice.

5. Zimmerman and Wilson (1973) trace ethnomethodology's interest in experiments to Garfinkel (e.g., 1952, 1963, 1967a). However, in Garfinkel's reports there never appears an interest in doing experiments "better" than social scientists have already done them. In fact, he seems reluctant even to use the term "experiment," preferring to call his studies "demonstrations." I believe that the attempt to conduct rigorous experiments is peculiar to some of those ethnomethodologists associated at some time in their careers with the University of California, Santa Barbara. Three dissertations (Crowle, 1971; W. Handel, 1973; and Jennings, 1972) completed there call for such work, though each seems to offer separate justifications for the faith such "real" experimentation can be done. The papers mentioned in note 4 were also Santa Barbara papers. I believe that Jennings and Wilson were especially influential in creating a climate where such thoughts could be unhesitatingly entertained. Zimmerman and Wilson's "mistake" in attributing this program to Garfinkel may be due to Wilson's modesty.

6. In referring to the "commonsense" image directing one's research, I am indexing the "new" philosophy of science that has replaced the hegemony of logico-empiricism. This new image of science claims that scientific theories exist only within an unarticulated and ascientific *weltanschauung* (see Feyerabend, 1965a, 1965b; Pepper, 1942; Polanyi, 1958, 1969). I am proposing that some ethnomethodologists may have a world view that will allow them to see experimental laws and field method findings as the same, while others will not. It is clearly an extralogical issue. I find these points built into Zimmerman and Wilson's paper. This seems to be the reason they refuse to treat logico-empiricism as it is usually treated, that is, as a philosophy of science. See note four, page 72 above.

7. See Schwartz (1971:244): "The experience the analyst has of social scenes, looking in from the outside and having abstract concerns such as locating things called descriptions, is special. Most of the things he experiences as either descriptions or described . . . never look like that from the inside . . . where in some sense neither of these features are relevant." See also Schwartz (n.d.:10) and Bittner (1973).

8. See Schwartz (1971:195–196): "The protypical one (projection error) may be outlined thusly: One starts as the witness, experiencing "this-definite-objective-phenomenon-which occurs." Next one experiences "the-self-same-phenomenon-is-actually-my-interpretation" where this last is in some way in error in its correspondence to the real phenomenon, which consists now of some real-phenomenon-as-described, experienced in the present setting." For a more detailed discussion of this process, see Schwartz (n.d.:17ff.).

9. Because these experiences of reflexivity appear among paranoid schizophrenics, Schwartz (personal communication) has suggested that paranoia is a prerequisite for a competent ethnomethodologist.

10. I explore this research program in greater detail in Chapter 12, where I label it a method of "becoming the phenomenon." Schwartz's dissertation was one of the central documents in the development of this program.

11. Schwartz offers several other ways to understanding the character of his writing.

He points out, for example, that in teaching dance it was "sometimes best to give a symbolic description of a movement which was *flat wrong* rather than a descriptively correct one," (1971:71). In trying to follow the incorrect notation, the correct movement is "more easily and naturally arrived at." The same is true for teaching some games to beginners (Ibid.: 171). Some card tricks may not have *any* correct description, but can only be learned in the doing. Schwartz also writes: "If it is the acoustic properties of the music that is the contended phenomena, it will not do to be given just the score; you will need to hear to decide" (Ibid.:201).

CHAPTER EIGHT

The
Reflexivity
of
Reflexivity

Reflexivity has been more than a phenomenon for ethnomethodology. It has indexed a personal trouble. The finding that all realities justify themselves only reflexively casts doubt on the reality of reflexivity. What kind of ontological claim can be made for ethnomethodological studies if their discoveries arise only upon analysis? In traditional social science terminology, this is the problem of validity. Wallace (1972) illustrates the havoc that reflexivity plays on this problem.

VALIDATION OF A THEORY

Wallace, a research assistant in the drug research briefly discussed in Chapter 2, uncovered a recurrent phenomenon in the interviews, diaries, and field work reports that Zimmerman and Wieder had amassed. Dopers seemed to agree about the nature of marijuana. They called it a "mind expanding drug" and reported that similar experiences occurred upon inhalation of the herb. Wallace summarized the folk belief about marijuana as follows:

> As a mind drug, it is thought to "do things to your head"; it is understood to alter the user's experience in the world by increasing or heightening his "sensitivity." According to common belief, smoking marijuana causes

the user to be more aware of his body states, moods, or emotions, and his social and environmental situation. A heightened sensitivity is also understood to consist of the commonly known effect of "being able to get into things more," which is to say that when the user is stoned, he is likely to become significantly more engrossed in mundane activities, whether they be talking, watching television, making love, or whatever (1972:7–8).

Within the paradigm of contemporary social science, Wallace's summary of the doper's belief is valid. Having discovered the folk theory in the interview data, he searched the diaries and field notes to see if they falsified the theory. They did not. Nonetheless, Wallace decided to validate his analysis further by asking dopers informally if smoking marijuana increased sensitivity. Wallace reports: "On virtually all occasions the replies were positive, but the sense of most replies was one of realization, like: 'Yea, that's a good way of talking about it,' " (Ibid.: 14). It was as if they had not thought of it before, but thought it was true once he mentioned it.

I had the feeling that the validation procedure was not establishing the objectivity of the theory but actually teaching them a way to articulate their drug experiences. I had the feeling that I was actually teaching them how to recognize what I wanted them to demonstrate that they already knew. I was pleased that they were able to use the theory, but I was really trying to show that it is something they already "possessed" before I asked them about it. This became a paradoxical task because it required that I ask them if the theory is right without telling them the theory (Ibid.).

Wallace did three more interviews. He did not ask directly about "heightened sensitivity," but rather posed questions like: "When you smoke dope, what happens, what does it do to you?" He presents representative portions of each of these transcripts. Though none explicitly mention the words "heightened" or "sensivitity," a synonymously common belief is there upon analysis. As Wallace says, "It is there, *if you look for it*" (Ibid.:34).

This realization led Wallace to conclude:

It seems that the only thing of which we can now be sure is that *I have* a theory of sensitivity, its existence being relative to my methodic perception of it, and that I have the ability to address myself with a cultural concern to talk about getting stoned and to reify structure thereby apparent in that talk (Ibid.:35).

Problems of validity thus become problems of ontology. Wallace's work raises a deeper question than whether dopers have *a* common belief. It reveals the peculiarity of claiming that others have *any* beliefs. This raises the question for the social scientist of how he can claim that attitudes, norms, expectations, and so forth exist independent of his methods of describing them.

Though the ethnomethodologist avoids a theory of common beliefs, he too faces this ontological problem. How can he claim that interpretive procedures, or indexicality, or reflexivity exist independent of his methods of describing them?

Wallace did everything he could to resolve this problem of validity. After he had reached the impasse described above, he decided to bring together the three persons he had interviewed. He hoped to let them talk on their own about dope and see if they would come to agree. Wallace quickly found that "nothing could happen until I at least hinted as to the nature of the game (Ibid.:41)."

Wallace had to construct a frame in which his invitation to come together to talk would make sense. Otherwise the three could not proceed at all. So Wallace told them he had found contradictions in their descriptions of getting stoned, and asked them to discuss these contradictions. He found that the dopers treated what he said were contradictions as agreements. They seemed to begin with the assumption that "getting stoned" was the same entity for all. Therefore, everything anyone said about it necessarily expressed agreement. It was as if they had agreed to agree. Here is part of the transcript he presents:

Interviewer.	OK, there was an apparent problem here between what you told me, number 3, and what number 1 told me. You told me that your mind tends to wander when you are stoned, is that right?
Doper 3.	Yea.
Interviewer.	But number 1 was telling me how it seems that when you are in a conversation you could get so into the conversation that you would carry it to ultimate conclusions.
Doper 3.	But that is wandering, isn't it?
Doper 1.	Yea, it is.
Doper 3.	You don't generally approach things that way. You can wander off in different directions. Something

	strikes you and you can follow a different chain of events.

Doper 1.   Well I am thinking, ah, it happens on good dope, that you just get really, ah, you have one general idea with you, and it is not that things are leading you on, you have a general idea about what you want to get across and then in a conversation with someone else you carry it, you can just go on and on into it.

Doper 3.   I think I find the same thing as you do, but for me it is more moving from conclusion to conclusion, I mean, when you are talking to somebody and you get into it you bring up something and you talk about it for awhile and it goes off into something else, you know.

Doper 1.   Yea, ah, this is good because this is clarifying what I was saying, what I wanted to say before, and that is, ah, every once and awhile I feel I can focus in on something really well when I am stoned.

Doper 3.   Oh yea, for sure.

Such seemingly disparate activities as "wandering" and "carrying a conversation to ultimate conclusions" are claimed to express similar states of "increased sensitivity." They are accepted as one state, being stoned.

In another example from this session, Wallace describes one doper who claims that different types of marijuana have different effects. This person further maintains that this is the "same" belief held by another, who says that the drug has no determinate effects itself, but that effects are entirely dependent upon the "set and setting" of the doper. Not only does the first doper claim that his belief agrees with the second, he uses the vocabulary of the second to demonstrate that agreement, and the second doper finds his explanation "right." The dopers used Wallace's preliminary instructions as a guide for what they then did. Wallace had said that the problem was "disagreement," so they proceeded to demonstrate that there was only agreement.

But there was disagreement, for Wallace at least. Here is how he experienced the session:

their concern with demonstrating agreement did not "come out of the blue," or occur simply because they are cultural colleagues, but because

I suggested in the introduction that the demonstration would make sense if they agreed. I provided them with a method for finding the sensible character of interaction in the setting and they actually created that sense by reflexively employing the "we are agreeing" formulation. It is as if I defined a game for them to play (Ibid.:47).

Although at one point in the demonstration the informants negotiated a theory that was very similar to my theory of sensitivity, I am still constrained to see the production of that theory as relative to the cultural concern I created in them. I did not demonstrate that they really have such a theory, but that they, just as I can, through a cultural concern, creatively accomplish a folk theory about the nature of getting stoned (Ibid.:48).

Wallace began with a discovery in his data, the belief in heightened sensitivity. The more he attempted to validate that theory, the more he came to experience that analytic constructions about realities may be both correct *and* external to them. That people can recognize such constructions is no guarantee that they have them independently. It may illustrate only that they have the ability to "play the social science game."

THE REFLEXIVITY OF REFLEXIVITY AS A PERSONAL PROBLEM

The ontological problem raised by Wallace's materials has been called "the infinite regress problem" by ethnomethodologists. I think that "the reflexivity of reflexivity" is more appropriate; the regress terminology summons up a mathematical and philosophical tradition only tangentially related to the dilemma ethnomethodologists face. Wilson (1971:7) has provided a general formulation of the problem:

imagine an ethnomethodologist studying the properties of the documentary method of interpretation [see Chapter 7] in some situation he has observed. In the midst of his analysis, he is reminded that his analysis itself involves the use of the documentary method of interpretation and he ought, therefore, to subject his own use of the documentary method to analysis. However, shortly after undertaking this second level of analysis, it occurs to him that he is again using the documentary method, so he begins to subject this to analysis. But he soon realizes that his third level of analysis again involves the documentary method, so . . .

Substituting any other ethnomethodological concept or finding for "documentary method" leaves the problem unchanged.

Opponents have sometimes called ethnomethodology a "cult." Insofar as this label applies, it does so because of the reflexivity of reflexivity. Students of ethnomethodology sooner or later pay blood dues over the problem. Those who have never been caught in the reflexive regress can only superficially understand the energy that drives ethnomethodologists. The reflexivity of reflexivity lies behind Garfinkel's (in Hill and Crittenden, 1968:3) statement that ethnomethodologists know *Tsoris*. Ethnomethodology is only "for whoever has the nervous system to withstand it . . . for whoever can take it" (Ibid.:130).

Though they are rarely written this way, every ethnomethodological study speaks to the spectre of the reflexivity of reflexivity. Garfinkel (Ibid.:143) says that "there is a kind of agreement in the work that we find our own ways." This suggests that once an ethnomethodologist has encountered the reflexivity of reflexivity, he knows nothing. This experience is only initiatory. Each ethnomethodologist must go beyond that spectre to find his own unique way.

In Chapter 2, I offered a partial description of my own solution to the reflexivity of reflexivity. In the final four chapters I explore my perspective further. In these middle six chapters I have offered an interpretation of the solutions of others. Every program I have reviewed shares a common prejudice. Each asserts that despite the reflexivity of reflexivity, valid claims can be made about the nature of the concrete world. Claims are of course tempered, equivocated, and relativized in various ways, but they nevertheless remain assertions about some *thing*. They retain a commitment to empirical work, albeit of novel kinds.

Blum (1970a, 1970b) and McHugh (1970; McHugh et al., 1974) have argued that empirical ethnomethodology lacks "analytical nerve." They maintain that the reflexivity of reflexivity dictates the complete repudiation of *all* empirical rhetoric and paraphernalia. A small group of ethnomethodologists has been voicing this claim since the inception of ethnomethodology. But these individuals typically quit ethnomethodology and the academy in search of some other way of life. Blum and McHugh and their colleagues (Foss and Raffel; and Filmer et al., 1973) repudiate this group as "nihilistic." Blum and McHugh's work counterposes my review of the empirical studies in ethnomethodology.

REFLEXIVITY AS A FORM OF LIFE

Building on earlier work of Blum (1970a, 1970b) and McHugh (1970), McHugh, Raffel, Foss, and Blum (1974) argue that the reflexivity of reflexivity destroys the warrant for social science. McHugh et al. (Ibid.:22-23) turn this argument against ethnomethodology as well. They maintain that the various programs I have described in this book are like social science in that they continue to cling to a "descriptivist form of life." McHugh et al. offer an alternative method that does not assume that language describes any phenomena beyond itself. They set this method in opposition not only to social science and ethnomethodology, but to nihilism as well. Their method is offered as an alternative to both social scientific inquiry and no inquiry.

McHugh et al.'s book consists of an introductory statement of their method and six "exemplifications" of that method. The topics of the exemplifications are drawn from everyday life. However, the authors are not interested in those topics per se or in the phenomenon of everyday life itself. Substantive topics are for them but "a point of departure," which "provides the practical and concrete incentive for reflexive inquiry" (Ibid.:11).

Reflexive inquiry is both their method and their goal. It is about no particular thing, but rather about the possibility of things, in particular about the possibility of itself. No-thing constitutes "the foundations that make what is said possible, sensible, conceivable" (Ibid.:2). These foundations are variously referred to as "grounds," "auspices," "grammar," and "deep structure." The latter two terms should not be confused with linguistic concepts of the same name. They mean for McHugh and his associates what Wittgenstein (1953) meant by grammar. Foundations are the no-thing out of which particular things arise. Their method attempts to make the presence of these foundations available.

Their method treats speaking and writing as similar activities. To do either is to face away from the fundamental grounds upon which utterances arise. Their method thus relies on a collaborator who "reminds us of that which we have to forget in order to speak" (Ibid.:4).

A topic is chosen. One analyst writes a first saying about that topic. This analysis is then shared with one or more collaborators. These collaborators write a second analysis detailing the grounds that made the first analysis possible. One complete analysis requires at least these two steps. Any second analysis can be followed by a third revealing the grounds of the second. A third analysis can be followed by a fourth, ad infinitum.

Response papers are not related to each other like conversational utterances. A response rises upon the hidden grounds of the paper to which it speaks. A requirement of any legitimate second analysis is that it be in dialectic dialogue with the original.

In brief, this method differs from those used by social scientists and most ethnomethodologists in two ways. It makes no claim to be about any *thing*. McHugh and his associates distinguish rigorously between reporting and analyzing. They even maintain that their description of their method should not be treated as a report. The second distinctive feature of their method is its dependence on collaborators. Analysts must collaborate with at least one other person or with an intellectual tradition serving as an other.

These features will be clearer as I review their substantive chapters.

Exemplifications of the Method.

McHugh et al. (Ibid.: 21–46) analyze "motives." They maintain that everyday persons treat motives as if they cannot be analyzed. They detail the grounds of this belief. In so doing they exhibit its myopia. Their analysis of people's use of the concept motive displays that such analysis is possible.

McHugh et al. (Ibid.: 109–136) also analyze people's view of "snubs," in a chapter that begins with another precis of their method. It is related to Socrates, who is credited with introducing "the analytic tactic of examining near-at-hand mundane examples in order to fasten the mind on the essential feature of a problem which the example covers over" (Ibid.: 109). This reminds us that the authors are not interested in snubs, but are using them to point toward "deeper" features.

Their first analysis of snubs reveals that people ordinarily experience them as a denial of recognition. McHugh et al.'s second analysis discloses, however, that snubs are really an exhibition of people's lack of analytic nerve. McHugh et al. see snubs as a refusal to do analysis in everyday life, even when the opportunity is offered.

The authors also build first analyses from two topics drawn from the sciences, bias and evaluation. They observe that scientists treat bias as a *thing*, and analyze the grounds for such a seeing. They maintain that science assumes that there are two separate modes of speech. One mode expresses context-bound characteristics of a speaker. The second mode sees language as a message from nature. In this mode, the messenger per se is irrelevant. The messenger merely presents the world with a copy of natural things through the medium of one other thing, speech. Bias is a charge that the first mode of speech has been offered when the second mode was expected.

McHugh et al. argue that science's assumption that two such modes of speech exist *creates* the problem of bias. They maintain that their own form of life assumes no such dichotomy, and thus exhibits none of the methodological difficulties inherent in science. Again, their purpose is not to attack science but rather to exhibit its grounds.

> In this sense, we have asked whether such a life [i.e., the scientific] is worth living, whether such a world is worth our commitment, and we have brought an alternative world to view (Ibid.:75).

It is evident that McHugh et al. are building a moral argument. As I mentioned above, they are concerned not only with differentiating themselves from science, but also with recommending a program that is not nihilistic. This program is built on questioning the "worth" of commitments and exhibiting an alternative commitment that seems worthy of rational people. This moral tone emerges yet more strongly in their analysis of "evaluation" in science (Ibid.:76–108).

Their first level analysis of this topic reveals that scientists view evaluation as merely a "descriptivist" problem. Judgments are alleged to be derived from rule use, not from personal decision. As an example, the authors draw upon rejection letters written by anonymous referees for a natural science journal. These letters present themselves as reports of the decision making of the referees. Referees invoke criteria supplied to them by the editors of the journal. McHugh et al. argue that these criteria constitute an ad hoc list of rules and are essentially incomplete. Referee rejection letters gloss the practical circumstances that lead them to invoke certain rules while ignoring others.

McHugh et al. thus ask: "Why does science lie? . . . why does science require itself to transform its moral judgments into descriptive statements?" (Ibid.:95). They answer this question by offering a second analysis of evaluations. They display the grounds or auspices of science's lie. They conclude that if science did not treat its evaluations as merely descriptivist problems, it "would have to admit that there is no reason internal to science for rationally grounding what it does" (Ibid.).

Science cannot admit that it justifies itself only reflexively and remain science. Science begins with the faith that all things in the world can be objectively described. If it did not treat its own decision-making process as such a descriptivist phenomenon, science "would have to conclude that the grounds of its authority cannot be addressed by its method" (Ibid.:95; see Chapters 2 and 3 above).

McHugh et al.'s "complaint" is not that science is committed to treating its moral judgments as merely descriptive problems, but rather that science does not recognize this commitment as *a* commitment. McHugh et al. analyze the scientists' commitments to exhibit their own alternative commitment. This difference in perspective is especially clear in an appendix they offer to their evaluations chapter. They submitted this chapter to a social science journal and received evaluations from three anonymous referees. They reprint each of these evaluations and treat them as a first analysis to which they provide a dialectical response.

Referee B complains that McHugh et al.'s paper does not accurately *describe* the phenomenon of evaluation. McHugh et al. point out that description was not their purpose. Referee B's evaluation "shows how he forgets the committed character of speech through his treatment of his talk as the only possible talk" (Ibid.:101). Referee B is so deeply committed to descriptivist talk that he is not aware that this represents *a* commitment. He thus fails to see that McHugh et al. have a different commitment; they are not seeking to describe commitments, but rather are seeking to display them.

Speech that attempts to display differs radically from speech that attempts to describe. The grounds of display are strange to those of us habituated to treat words as things. This radical shift is evident in the following passage:

> our speech has shown what it means, that is, *it is what it is.* Our speech shows what it is as a representation of that which grounds our words, rather than as . . . arrangements whereby words explicate other words. To ground words in language is to shift the burden from words-as-usage to the dialectic speech of which words are only a display (Ibid.; italics added).

McHugh et al. further exhibit this novel approach to writing in their analyses of "travel" (Ibid.:137–153) and "art" (Ibid.:154–182). I refer to their analysis of travel later in this chapter.

As art is not grounded in something besides itself, it is radically unlike any other topic. They contrast their approach with art history and the sociology of art. Both of these transform art and so lose art's essence.

The sociology of art is sociology, not art, just as "art history as it is conventionally practiced, takes the art out of history" (Ibid.:159). Such analyses treat the artifacts as caused effects of analytic concepts. But art as art is not caused. To see something as art is to "see *it*, not what it represents" (Ibid.:158). When art is related to either history or artists, it is no longer art. Art is exhaustively concrete, essentially and completely itself.

For McHugh et al., art is of interest because it "produces first of all a version of how it is possible *not* to do an analysis" (Ibid.:174). The authors nonetheless analyze art, but their analysis respects art's otherness. They use art as a further means for illustrating their own form of life. They find in art "a deep distinction between it and ourselves" (Ibid.:180). While McHugh and his associates are committed to searching for grounds, "the rule of art instructs us to look at the thing itself, not to provide for it, not to see it in terms of a set of grounds" (Ibid.:126). They emphasize that this finding about the rule of art is not *about* art. It is an illustration of what they wish to display about the form of life that is analysis. They write: "This point, like all points in this book, is not a concrete truth but a way of making reference to analysis" (Ibid.:176). They are no more interested in art than in any other concrete topic. Their abiding interest is in analysis.

McHugh et al. are also interested in encouraging others to undertake analysis. Such additional engagements are an essential part of their method: "Readers are asked to treat our papers reflexively. They are asked to become our collaborators. This is our version of how to read" (Ibid.:8). By taking the dialectic role of alter to their written ego, you, the readers are asked "to formulate the auspices that lead you to see how it is *possible* that they come to look like whatever they look like [to you]" (Ibid.:9). I follow this advice for reading in the following pages.

The Method Applied to the Method

I will use McHugh et al.'s method of analysis to search for the grounds of that method. One can be committed to their technique of analysis without simultaneously embracing the metaphysical grounds they adduce for their method.

McHugh et al.'s work grows out of a dualism that should be familiar to readers of this book. They repeatedly stipulate that analysts must differentiate between the "theoretic-analytic" and the "concrete," that is, between "the grounds or auspices of phenomena" and "the phenomena themselves" (Ibid.:2–3). In Chapter 4, I reviewed this distinction under the name of "essential incompleteness" and "essential indexicality." Briefly, this is the principle that phenomena themselves can not be exhaustively described or explained by analysis. Ethnomethodologists have used this both as a theoretic device directing their research and as a concrete phenomenon to be investigated.

I reviewed the irony in this program at the close of Chapter 5. The ethnomethodologists' own analysis of essential incompleteness must forever remain incomplete. The ethnomethodologist cannot solve the problem of indexicality. Every description of incompleteness exhibits the incompleteness once more. Such looping mainifests the reflexivity of reflexivity. McHugh and his associate's work begins with this loop. They differ radically from other ethnomethodologists in what they do in the face of it.

McHugh et al. write that their method is a way "to grasp the *reason* for the essential incompleteness" (Ibid.:10; italics added). They do not want to describe it, or even to display it as Schwartz proposes (see Chapter 7). They claim instead that their method reveals its *reason*.

Like other ethnomethodologists, the authors begin with the distinction between descriptions and things described. But they go beyond this distinction; they arrange these twin phenomena in a hierarchy. Analysis, they maintain, is superior to concrete phenomena, because analysis is closer to that entity which is beyond them both. This entity is Being.

McHugh et al. identify Being with Reason (e.g., Ibid.:72). Reason leads to descriptions and analysis. These in turn give rise to the gross level of concrete phenomena. McHugh et al.'s method starts with the (1) concrete in order to generate (2) analysis that provides analysts with an intimation of (3) Reason or Being. These authors have no intrinsic interest in the concrete or in analysis. Analysis is necessary, however, in that it leads to the no-thing that McHugh and his associates believe lies behind analysis as its grounds. That is, analysis of the concrete leads to Being.

The ethnomethodology I have been developing in these pages seeks to celebrate the everyday, not to denigrate it. By contrast, McHugh et al. call everyday speech and writing "an inadequate activity" (Ibid.:11).

They speak of their method as a means of "elevating" the word from its common usage among "the tribe," and maintain that speech that participates in their program is "true speech." It:

> recognizes that it is not self-sufficient, that *it is not first but derivative*. True ·speech re-cognizes the difference between *time and eternity*. . . .
> Concrete speech . . . conceals from itself its dependency upon that which is beyond it. In Plato's language concrete speech (at its best) formulates its grounds as ideas, forgetting its grounds as ideas, forgetting *the ground of speech is that which surpasses idea* (Ibid.:151; italics added).

McHugh et al. opt for the eternal over time, for that which surpasses idea over ideas. As I said before, this is a commitment to Being as an entity preferable to both concrete phenomena and descriptions of those phenomena. I do not believe that these commitments are required by their method.

McHugh et al. praise Plato and embrace his theory of the real. They believe that Being is not merely coequal with being. Being is "deeper" than the grounds of analysis and the concrete. In the next four chapters, I argue that Being and being can be viewed as mutually constitutive. Each is dependent upon and independent of the other. Such a view tempers the dilemma that the reflexivity of reflexivity forces on ethnomethodologies. It reveals that this problem is a problem only if one assumes that X cannot both be a cause and an effect of Y. It treats eternity as an effect of time, and simultaneously claims that eternity is the cause of time.

By so altering McHugh et al.'s metaphysical commitments, one may use their method to search for grounds, while assuming that these grounds do in fact inform us about concrete phenomena. The relation between descriptive analysis and things described will always be essentially incomplete, but this need not be a reason for abandoning entirely the attempt to talk *about* things. Awareness of the essential incompleteness only changes our conception of how thoroughly talk captures phenomena—we will know that analysis does not depict phenomena impersonally. Such talk is not thereby shown to be worthless. It is revealed to be more mysterious than normally envisioned.

The analysis of grounds may still be used to produce intimations of Being. I intended this possibility when I used Wittgenstein's ladder metaphor at the close of Chapter 5. Such intimations, however, need not be taken to indicate a higher truth than everyday life. To embrace Being at the price of concrete existence parallels the dualistic sin that led positivism to embrace the concrete at the price of Being.

I can show some of my different commitments through McHugh et al.'s analysis of "travel," which offers a number of insights into what it means to be a traveler. As on reading their analysis of art, one feels at the end as if something significant has been said *about* a phenomenon familiar to us all. McHugh et al. would deny that their analysis so informs us. They claim that the analysis is only theirs and is incomplete. They maintain that it is not about any *thing* at all. Although this is a nihilistic position, the authors save themselves from being merely nihilistic by maintaining that their analysis of travel displays something about analysis itself. I would not shrink from making the ontological claim that descriptions are really about the things described. What they tell me about travel, as about art, snubs, evaluations, and so forth, often seems true to me. This is a feeling they identify with "the tribe." The common person does not know about reflexivity and thus does not recognize that phenomena are "only" there upon analysis. I think that one can simultaneously believe that phenomena are only there upon analysis and that they are really there independent of that analysis. The analysis creates them, but concrete phenomena at once create analysis.

I would not deny that analysts can use analysis as a means of transcending analysis. But this intimation of Being I would also treat as a phenomenon there upon analysis. It is no more or less real than concrete being.

Because of this alternative commitment, I disagree with much of McHugh et al.'s "travel" chapter. They say that to travel is to escape from the real problems of life. In travel, persons radically concretize themselves:

> The actor becomes a receptacle of what is there to be noticed, the self a collection of those pleasures and pains which mark the notice of something. To be alive comes to be the existence of states, to be dead to be incapable of notice, and self-expression the equivalent of cries of pleasure and pain. It is a sheer peopled world, an existential world, and in this sense the most factual of worlds, a world exclusively inhabited by words, people, and things (Ibid.:153).

Unlike McHugh et al., I would maintain that this analysis describes a concrete phenomenon, and describes it well. I further disagree with them in not finding this life repugnant. Because McHugh et al. are committed to the "mind" over the "eye" (see Ibid.:143), they find the traveler's life anathema. "A world exclusively inhabited by words, people and things" rather than language, communities, and analysis is to them a form of death. It is the most removed from Being and thus the form of life most to be avoided.

I do not think analysis need be so presumptuous. Analysis is different from traveling. Perhaps it does lead to Being. But it seems likely that traveling in the concrete draws one toward Being as well. Art seems to serve the same function as analysis, because it immerses the artist in the concrete.

GROUNDING COMMITMENTS

McHugh, Raffel, Foss, and Blum have created a method that discloses Plato and Heidegger's Being. It displays what, in a sense, Plato and Hiedegger were only able to talk about.

I agree with McHugh and his associates that one of the benefits of their method is that it leads to the exposure of commitments. It must be understood then that I have not been criticizing their work. I have been analyzing it, using it as a topic, an occasion for exploring my own grounds. In the next four chapters I further explicate these grounds. I would encourage the reader to treat those chapters as a first analysis upon which they will construct a dialogic second analysis. Using McHugh et al.'s method, you should seek my grounds. In so doing, you will find more clearly your own.

PART THREE

A
PROSPECTUS
FOR
ETHNOMETHODOLOGY

CHAPTER NINE

The
Structuring
of
Social
Action

All realities require reality work. Realities vary as they use different scenic practices. A variety of such structuring practices were reviewed in Chapters 4, 6, and 7. In this chapter, I offer some properties that all practices share. These properties of practices differ from the properties reviewed in Chapter 5. Unlike the features of "the model of the actor," the structuring properties of this chapter do not assume that reality is *created* by practices. The properties I offer are of the relation between an external reality of structures and scenic practices.

This difference will be clearer after I review the criteria I have established for the structuring theory. I examine these criteria by contrasting them with the general theory of social order that Parsons (especially [1937] 1949) has developed. Though Parsons's specific theorems are controversial, his general theoretic orientation articulates the implicit paradigm of contemporary social science (Gouldner, 1970; Mullins, 1973; Wilson, 1970; see Chapter 4 above). The structuring properties I offer in this chapter constitute an alternative approach to the problem of social order.

Like my theoretical goal, my method recalls Parsons's *The Structure of Social Action* (1949). Parsons builds his theory "with special reference to a group of recent European writers." I employ the work of Harold

Garfinkel much as Parsons used the work of Marshall, Pareto, Durkheim, and Weber. Such a method does not produce impartial exposition. Garfinkel is no more the author of my structuring theory than Durkheim[1] was the author of Parsons's theory.

THE MEANING OF A GENERAL THEORY OF SOCIAL ORDER

When Hobbes [(1651) 1962] formulated the problem of social order, he assumed that order existed independently of persons' actions. Social theorists who came after Hobbes retained this assumption. Social order was not regarded as intentional. Different theorists explained the origin of order differently, but all agreed that this order is external to and constraining on social beings. Persons could either act as the order dictated or be deviant. Because social order was a reality *sui generis,* persons could not influence or modify its fundamental constituents. If they could modify the constituents, it would imply that social order was a psychological phenomenon. This position was anathema to social science.

Parsons's work continues this view of the problem of social order. Parsons assumes that external order can be taken for granted (e.g., Ackerman and Parsons, 1966). His social theory attempts to describe the structures of that external order. Parsons then seeks the functional interrelations of these external structures.

Parsons also describes how these structures work at the level of individual action. Persons are called "actors." They see the relevance of certain norms in social situations. Both the situations and the norms come to them from without. The actor's job is to match the norms with the scene and then enact the proscribed action. I outlined this theory in Chapter 4.

Garfinkel (1967a: 66ff.) has said that this model of action treats the social actor as a "judgmental dope." The various studies reviewed in Part 2 of this book suggest an alternative model. This model still begins by accepting the reality of an external and constraining world. To this assumption is added an acceptance of the facticity of ceaseless reality work. The problem of a general theory of social order is thus determining the properties that relate structuring activities to structural "facts."

Garfinkel (Garfinkel and Sacks, 1970) has explored some requirements for such an ethnomethodological approach to the problem of order. He offers four criteria for ethnomethodological "formal structures." I will call these structures "structurings" to emphasize their departure from traditional theoretical concerns with structures. Garfinkel's first two criteria speak to the sui generis reality of structures. His third and fourth criteria recollect ethnomethodology's concern with structuring activities.

The first criterion for a structuring is that it "exhibit upon analysis the properties of uniformity, reproducibility, repetitiveness, standardization, typicality, and so on" (Ibid.: 346). This is a criterion of *invariance*. Garfinkel's second criterion insists that this invariance be "independent of particular production cohorts" (Ibid.). This criterion adds the requirement of *independence* to the invariance. The invariance of a structuring must not be accidental or controvertible by the will of the particular persons exhibiting the structuring. A structuring is independent of "transformations of context." It is "invariant to in and out migrations" (Ibid.:357).

These two criteria are more rigorous than those social scientists usually adopt. The structures of sociology are frequently "quasi-laws," implying a sense of conditional or probable invariance (Garfinkel, 1967a:2–3). Garfinkel's criteria exhort us to seek structurings that are essentially invariant.

While Garfinkel's first two criteria respect sociology's concern with social structures, his second two criteria introduce a new concern. The third criterion states that the first two criteria must be "a phenomenon for members' recognition" (Garfinkel and Sacks, 1970:345). Candidate structurings are not to be accepted unless lay persons recognize the essential invariance of that structuring. This does not mean that samples of persons should be polled about candidate structurings. Rather, this third criterion establishes that candidate structurings must themselves appear within substantive reality work. Members themselves must recognize candidate structurings in their everyday affairs.

Garfinkel's fourth criterion elaborates the third. It says that the first three criteria must be "every particular cohort's practical, situated accomplishment" (Ibid.:346). This criterion establishes that even though a structuring be invariant, independent, and a member's phenomenon, it is not therefore to be viewed as possessing a "prior" existence. Essential structures are "every particular cohort's" accomplishment. Structures appear and are recognized only within the stream of practical reality work.

With his first two criteria, then, Garfinkel makes the traditional sociological concern with structures more rigorous. Garfinkel's two additional criteria alter the ontology of these structures. They are said to appear only within substantive scenes among an empirical multitude of everyday realities. Such structurings are not causal. They are essential invariants in all meaningful action. They describe how structuring activities and external structures mutually constitute each other.

I offer a candidate list of seven structurings which meet these four criteria below.

ESTABLISHING THE WARRANT FOR A CORRESPONDENCE THEORY OF MEANING

Traditional treatments of the problem of social order have ignored the phenomenon of everyday structuring activity. A correspondence theory of meaning grounds this indifference to structuring.

Parsons's work is a prototype of the use of this theory. The correspondence theory of signs does triple duty in Parsons's work. First, the theory is assumed to provide for the relations between everyday actions and norms. Norms are assumed to be signs with finite meanings. They are treated as pictures of possible actions. They show people what to do, like a street sign flashing "walk" and "don't walk." Norms are asserted to exist independently of particular situations and of particular actors.

Second, the norms are assumed to be signs standing on behalf of structures. The norms face two ways. They correspond to concrete actions *and* they correspond to external structures that are "abstract." This correspondence explains how abstract structures make an appearance as external constraints within the everyday lives of persons.

Garfinkel (1952:93) argues this theory of signs assumes that "the cake of the universe may be cut in diverse ways, or that the objects of the outer world are indubitably there but may be variously invested with meaning." Parsons assumes that all persons share a common universe. They differ from one another in the norms they use to cut that common cake. Every society's substantive norms are a schema of categories which "render some sort of approximation of what is actually out there" (Ibid.).

Societies differ in the norms they develop as the one universe may be variously invested with corresponding meanings. But the constant cake of the universe sets some limits. Every system of norms must contend with these limits to survive. As a result, all substantive systems of norms can be searched for common properties. These properties are the functional requirements of structural-functionalist theorizing.

To organize these functional requirements, Parsons has offered several schemata, of which the best known is the pattern variables. Schemata like these exhibit a dependence on the correspondence theory of objects. Without the assumption that there is one real world setting constraints, there would be no warrant for seeking common properties among various particular societies and social scenes.

The assumption that norms evoke a sense of a constant cake beyond them is not peculiar to social theorists; it is a sense shared by all persons. Most people would quickly agree that there is an order to their action that lies beyond particular actions. Theorists such as Parsons accept this everyday belief and seek to refine it. The theory of structurings I offer seeks to make the belief in a constant cake itself a phenomenon.

The correspondence theory of signs plays a third part in Parsons's theory. Like other social theorists, Parsons uses that theory of signs to provide for the relation between his theory and the world. Parsons does not expect us to read his words as instances of typography, or as nonsense syllables, or as poetry. His books present themselves as signs depicting actual events and relations in *the* constant world beyond his writing. Just as Parsons assumes that actions correspond to norms, and norms to structures, he assumes that his theory corresponds to actual relations among actions, norms, and structures. Parsons,s theory claims to picture these relations (cf. Ackerman and Parsons, 1966).

Parsons claims that the one universe can be variously invested with meaning. Although Parsons's theory itself is but one more cutting, he assumes that his is a superior piece of cake. It is not merely any man's cutting, it is a scientific cutting.

Parsons's theory claims that the one universe may be variously invested with meanings; it does not maintain that some of these ways better represent that universe. A system of norms may more or less smoothly fulfill the functional requirements the universe imposes. But all normative systems are equally "accurate" cuttings. The idea that science meets these requirements better than any other social system is not an integral part of the theory. Faith, like Parsons's, in logico-empirical methods is an ad hoc addition, which requires a faith in a set of "universal and unchanging primary categories" and a faith that observers can view the world "independent of the historical [i.e., normative] conditions of the observer's circumstance" (Garfinkel, 1952:93–94). Parsons's theory does not justify either of these faiths. The theory does not explain how a group of persons can escape normative categories so as to view the one universe "objectively." Parson's theory does not provide for the possibility of itself.

The studies reviewed in Part 2 recommend an alternative theory that undercuts the correspondence theory of sign use. In Chapters 4 and 5 I argued that actors do not passively match norms with situations. Actions are symbolic indexes, not signs. They are a creative embodiment of one of the innumerable possibilities presented by any particular situation.

In Chapter 7, I emphasized that actions do not merely index the external world. Actions also reflexively alter situations. Parson's elements of actors, situations, and norms are removed from a correspondence relation and the three are made mutually constitutive. Situations are constituted by actors indexing norms. Actors are constituted by situations displaying normative possibilities. Norms themselves appear only within an ever-shifting series of particular situations.

Social order exists. But its existence always appears within interaction. The problem of social order is thus not a problem of constructing structures about the external world. It is instead a problem of understanding how the sense of a corresponding external world is accomplished by every interactional activity.

I described a variety of these structuring activities in Chapters 5, 6, and 7. As Garfinkel (see Chapter 7 above) emphasizes, such activities exist in empirical multitude. New ones are always being developed. No exhaustive list of structuring practices could ever be compiled. They will not provide us with a *general* theory of social ordering. In this they are like the empirical multitude of norms. No list of norms constitutes a general theory of structures. Parsons's solution was to seek common properties of substantive lists of norms, his functional requirements. A similar strategy can be adopted in examining lists of scenic structuring activities. I will offer seven common properties of such lists below.

The structurings of social action are quite unlike traditional social theories in another way. They cannot be, in their first appearance, *about* social action. I have abandoned the correspondence theory of objects. I cannot reclaim that theory until I have provided for its possibility. The structurings must provide a warrant for correspondence talk before they can be treated as signs that are theoretical descriptions of events in a world. There is a method by which this work can be done.

Each of the structurings that follow is itself a social action. As each structuring speaks about the properties of all reality work, it should be expected to speak about itself. The reader thus must take an active part in the construction of this theory. The reader must not read each of the structurings as if it were about something else besides itself. Each structuring must first "prove" itself. If a structuring does not apply to itself it reveals that it does not apply to all structuring activities. But if the structurings do both index and reflexively prove themselves, we will then be prepared to read them a second time. This reading will treat them as descriptive signs. The possibility of such correspondences will have been established.

My concept of "social action" thus collects various ideas that have been developed in this book. Social action may be read as collecting "scenic practices," "language practices," "reality work," "structuring activity," and so forth.

SOME STRUCTURINGS OF REALITY WORK

1. *The structuring of essential difference.*   An action is meaningful only if it displays something beyond itself. An action must expose both itself and a realm that is not itself. An action must testify to the existence of others in manifesting itself.

A gesture is a paradigmatic instance. A hand moving through the air shapes itself by shaping that which shapes it. If the movement is meaningful, the meaning depends on the hand uncovering space that is not hand movement.

Eventually we can ask if this structuring well describes some list of actions or practices. First, however, we must inquire if it "describes itself." These paragraphs themselves are a social action. They exhibit a species of reality work. The reader is invited to examine this and each of the structurings to see if it both indexes and reflexively provides for itself. In the present case, you must determine if you can understand the structuring of essential difference without simultaneously experiencing that it is exhibiting a realm that is not itself. The structuring seems to describe a property of all actions. It claims that these actions paint a world that is other than themselves. In understanding this claim, does not the reading of the structuring exhibit the essential difference as well? The structuring is not a valid description of action if it does not describe itself. We will be in no position to speak of the structurings as descriptions unless, as we go along, they establish a warrant for making such correspondence claims.

2. *The structuring of essential glossing.* The structuring of essential difference evidences that actions display other in presenting themselves. The structuring of essential glossing shows that this other is a *prior* other. Action illumines an other hitherto invisible. This other is simultaneously exposed to have been there all along. The practice does not create the other. It makes it manifest. Though this prior other is revealed to have preceded the particular action's appearance, its priorness is a constitutive part of the present action. The prior other is revealed by the present action and that action is constituted in the here and now by that priority.

Again, the reader must investigate the utility of this structuring by treating my statement of it as a phenomenon. In understanding the meaning of my written action, the meaning should turn upon itself. This structuring, which talks "about" a prior other, displays a prior other in accomplishing that talk.

3. *The structuring of essential indifference.* Any reality work displays an other and prior world in displaying itself. This other and prior world is simultaneously displayed to be indifferent to the social action that illumines it. By indifferent I mean that the other and prior realm is *independent* of particular social actions. Social action events may add to the other and prior realm but these actions are not displayed as the creator of that realm. The other and prior realm appears only in particular social action displays, but this realm is nonetheless displayed to be independent of such displays.

Social actions do not importantly change the world. They only report on it. This is true whether that new action is as novel as Newton's laws, or Beckett's plays, or the writing of this structuring. Such actions do not unveil a prior and other world of their creation. They display an other and prior and *independent* world. The independence of this world makes it seem indifferent to and essentially unaltered by novel (or repetitive) social actions.

4. *The structuring of essential openness.* A social action exhibits an other, prior, indifferent realm as the background to its foreground appearance. The immediate outlines of this other realm are quite distinct. They touch the borders of the action. It is easiest to think of this in space. A body gesture traces the outlines of its other realm on the penumbras of its movement. Thus it has a definite relation to that other

realm. Nonetheless, the action displays a structuring of vagueness as well. The relation of any particular action and the other, prior, indifferent world it evinces is an open relation. No single action exhausts that relation.

This structuring provides for an open horizon reaching beyond the definite border of action and other. One's arm moving through the air on the left side of one's body definitely defines the space that encloses this gesture. However, beyond this immediate proximity stretches the rest of the other world of space that is not the gesture. This horizon is opened by any social action but not exhausted by it. The structuring of essential openness points to the *more* than itself that lies beyond any particular social action. A social action marks a definite space, but this space is not ever exhausted by that single action.

5. *The structuring of essential pairing.* The first four structurings illumine how social actions manifest the world. Structurings five and six expose the special place social actions have as "parts" of that world.

Every social action attests to the possibility of *equivalent* social actions. Every social action testifies to the existence of other social actions that would mean the same as it. This is the structuring of essential pairing. The potentially equivalent action may be more inclusive than the initial action. In science, for example, a theory may be offered from which an initial utterance (social action) is said to be derived. The paired action may be of equal generality as well. Offering a synonym for a word illustrates such an instance. A similar kind of pairing occurs when a hand gesture is used to further illustrate the meaning of a facial grimace or an utterance.

A third analytical possibility of such pairings arises when equivalent actions are offered that are less general. In such instances, more specific actions are presented which, as a composite, are presumed to equal the first action. For example, I have now described three specific levels of pairings. These are presumed equivalent with my initial general statement as to what this structuring accomplishes.

This structuring demonstrates that actions are a special constituent of the world. The earlier structurings demonstrated that actions are not equivalent with the world they display. The structuring of essential pairing indicates that actions are equivalent to other actions. Although two actions occur at different times and places, through separate bodies and mediums, they may be the same. This equivalence possibility is displayed by every concrete action.

Parts of the world that are not actions never exhibit such a capacity for pairing. Actions may pair events that occur at different times and places. But it is the actions themselves that are counted equivalent. Events in the world are paired only indirectly through the actions that symbolize them (cf. Kaiman, 1969).

6. *The structuring of essential incompleteness.*   Although actions may be displayed as paired equivalents, no set of pairings is presumed exhaustive. The world that a set of actions manifests is never exhausted by the actions. Every action thus makes visible its own incompleteness. This occurs whether the action is the second, third or nth equivalent action display. There is always more that can be uttered or gestured or written or painted about the actions in the world that "says the same." Every action must expose this incompleteness in itself in order to be meaningfully complete in any here and now.

This structuring is an analogue of the structuring of essential openness. That structuring spoke to the incompleteness of any single action. The structuring of essential incompleteness indicates that this openness remains even when a set of equivalent actions has been compiled.

Recall that I am not telling you *about* something. The structuring of essential incompleteness must first stand as a self-referential statement. It should be read to see if it indexes what it seems to talk about, thereby reflexively proving its existence.

The structuring says that every set of actions displays that every set is incomplete. The world they together conjure is inexhaustible. As I presented this structuring I offered sentence after sentence. These can be viewed as equivalent actions. In finding sense in my utterances you have had to find that I was talking about something, and that that something could not ever be exhausted by this or any string of meaningful action.

7. *The structuring of essential irony.*   The structuring of essential irony points to the relationship that actions display between the world and themselves. The first four structurings uncover a world that is other, prior, independent, and more than the actions that make that world appear. These structurings testify to a world that is *definite, constant,* and *finite.* Structurings 5 and 6 manifest certain peculiar qualities of actions that expose this finite world. These two structurings exhibit that all actions may be replaced with equivalent actions and that such replacements can never exhaustively display the world they manifest. These

two structurings thus indicate that social actions are *indefinite, inconstant,* and potentially *infinite.*

The structuring of essential irony attests to every action displaying this relationship between actions and the world. It attests to every action's intrinsic modesty. Actions themselves may be merely accidental, but the world of which they speak is nonetheless displayed as essential. Rather than treat the indefiniteness of actions as a weakness, this structuring illumines how actions transform this indefiniteness into a virtue. The more often actions change and are added to, the more often the world they display appears as a definite realm beyond and independent of them.

The irony of the relationship between structures and structuring is evident. Meaningful actions display themselves as derived from the world. The world is there, yet our reality work constitutes the world.

Actions are like a subset of a set (World). The subset of actions reveals the set (World) to be finite and constant. Yet, how is it possible for an unequivocal world to generate an essentially equivocal subset? The structuring of essential irony asserts that every action both raises and answers this question, and that this accomplishment is an essential property of all meaningful activity (cf. Pollner, 1970).

Of course I am not talking about mathematical theories of sets or about scientific theories of the universe. For the purposes of a first reading, the structuring of essential irony is only a display of itself. Once and if a correspondence theory can be recovered, this structuring will still not be about mathematical and scientific theories. It will be about mathematicians' and scientists' actions, however. They can be expected to display this structuring in their meaningful actions, whether everyday or theoretic. I have already pointed to this structuring in the social theorizing of Parsons. His faith that the universe is "out there" but can be variously invested with meaning is an articulation of the structuring of essential irony. The irony manifests itself in Parsons's theory when he makes the claim that one of these cuttings of the universe is superior to the others.

RECOVERING THE CORRESPONDENCE THEORY

On first encountering the list of structurings, I exhorted you to suspend the correspondence conception of language to seek its grounds. I asked you to repress the sense that the structurings were talking about something. I asked you to treat each structuring as itself a social action, thus to see if it accounted for itself. I asked you to see that reality work *does things*. This required that you focus not on the things accomplished but rather on the accomplishing. Meaningful action illuminates a world it finds to have been there prior to its illumination. Meaningful action is thus like a flashlight turned on in the dark. I asked you to gaze at the action's light while ignoring the concrete things the light revealed. I asked you to look at light shining on light.

Once a list of structurings has been created, the correspondence theory of objects can be reintroduced. The list can be read a second time. Each structuring now stands as a theoretical proposition *about* essential properties of all reality practices. The first reading of the structurings has provided for the possibility of this second reading. It has established a warrant for correspondence talk. The reflexive reading of the theory has provided for a second, objective reading. The theory of structuring can now be treated like other social actions, as an independent accomplishment of the real and external world.

THE STRUCTURING OF SOCIAL ORDER

The theory informs us that every meaningful action displays a sense of social order beyond itself. This recurrent accomplishment led Hobbes to take the fact of order for granted. He was led to ask how order is possible. Contemporary theorists reject Hobbes's answer, but retain his question. I have chosen to ask not how order is possible, but rather to ask how a sense of order is possible.

This is not to reduce the problem of social order to psychology. The structurings are not psychological variables. The sense of social order is not in the head; it is displayed in every meaningful action. Social order appears *on* gestures and *in* utterances. The structurings are a theoretical description of what gestures and utterances do to accomplish this display of order. The structurings are thus a theory of social order. Order, however, might more accurately be understood as order*ing*. As meaningful action, social order is always becoming.

The theory of structuring is not a *constitutive* theory. Some ethnomethodologists have claimed that social structures are created by structuring activities (see Chapter 7). I review some philosophical grounds for this claim in Chapter 10. My theory of structuring rejects this belief. Just as the theory refuses to reify social structures, it refuses to reify structuring activities. The theory is not committed to the apostasy of either of these dialectical poles. The structurings illumine the relations between the poles. The theory of structuring is not dialectical. Structures and structuring practices *mutually contain* each other. Mutual containment grounds the very possibility of dialectical relations (see Chapter 10).

Unlike much previous ethnomethodology, then, my theory is not of the reality *constructor* (see Chapter 5). It envisions persons as reality *participants*.[2] The structurings describe how persons signal this participation to others and to themselves.

In the next chapter, I further review the image of man this theory encourages. In Chapter 11, I explore the morality of adopting this image as an incorrigible proposition in one's form of life. In Chapter 12, I review a conception of science engendered by this image of social being. I conclude with a manual of instructions to enable interested readers to begin immediately their own ethnomethodological investigations.

NOTES

1. Using Durkheim as a paradigm case, Pope (1973) criticizes Parsons qua historian. Such expositions leave Parsons's theory untouched. Similarly, my theory of structuring is a theory, not a historical exposition of Garfinkel's thought.

2. The term "reality participants" was suggested to me by Melvin Pollner.

CHAPTER TEN

Some Philosophical Grounds for Ethnomethodology

Sociology studies social structures, and at the empirical level, treats these structures as variables. Most social science studies seek to find relationships among these variables. Ethnomethodology claims that structures are constituted by social structuring activities. Ethnomethodology says social science ignores these structuring activities and reifies structures. In ethnomethodology, the concern for structuring activities (also called practices, methods, procedures, reality work, and so forth), has caused the pendulum of social theory to swing from an exclusive concern with structures to an equally exclusive concern with structuring. In this chapter, I relate ethnomethodology's prejudice to several philosophical theses. I offer an image of social being that alters ethnomethodology's early vision. I begin with this image of social being.

THE HERMENEUTIC SPIRAL

Heidegger (1962) has distinguished between an interpretive and an understanding phase in social being. I will adapt these concepts to create an image of social being that integrates several ethnomethodological insights. My purpose is not to summarize Heidegger's early philosophy. I have borrowed selectively, following several insights contained in Wallace's (1972, 1973, forthcoming) "theory of social being."[1]

Interpretation is symbolic activity. It includes the reality work, practices, methods, and procedures discussed throughout ethnomethodology. In the *understanding* phase, people find themselves within a primordially meaningful world. Understanding refers to the sense people have every moment that they occupy a particular here and now. This world is given to them with no effort on their part. A mood is an instance of an understood experience. Moods come to us from beyond. We may seek their "reasons," but we do not feel as if we create moods. They are not a concrete interpretive act.

A visual metaphor may be helpful. Understanding is like night. Interpretation is like day. People's meaningful lives spiral into the unknown like the cycle of nights and days. Any particular day has an existence independent of the previous night. But, at once, it is dependent upon the substance of that previous night, and upon the totality of nights and days before the most recent night. Just so, any interpretation has its independent meaning. It is an activity and stands apart from the stillness that preceded it. Simulataneously, however, it is dependent upon the understood horizon that provided it with the here and now upon which the activity arose. An understood horizon includes previous interpretations that have entered the understanding. It includes previous understandings as well.

In the spiral of night and day, there are two penumbras where they blend into each other. At dawn, understanding—our night—drifts into interpretation. At dusk, interpretation—our day—shades into understanding. These two passages provide the motor for the theory (see Merleau-Ponty, 1955, in 1970:141). They are the places of mystery for ethnomethodology. It is in these two areas that people make their quantum leaps to meaningfulness. Ethnomethodologists have called dawn "indexicality," and dusk "reflexivity."

Studies of indexicality seek to illuminate the relations of interpretations to prior understandings. The studies of the incompleteness of rules (see Chapter 4) are an example. Rules are interpretations. They arise from particular understandings. The prereflective night is brought into the symbolic light. But more can always be said; alternative rules can always be invoked.

Once any interpretive activity has occurred, it fades into understanding. This is the ethnomethodological penumbra of dusk, or reflexivity. People act and their actions alter the world. This altered world then appears before them as an autonomous reality. It is external and constraining. Past interpretations enter understanding and engender new possibilities. The next interpretation must contend with that previous interpretation, now integrated within understanding. The studies discussed in Chapter 7 explore this reflexivity.

This imagery places people within a spiral of meaningfulness. People create meaning, but the world comes to them independently of their interpretive activities. There are times when persons are aware of this creative force and others when they are not (see Schwartz, 1971; Shumsky and Mehan, 1974; and Chapter 7 above). I call this image of human being the "hermeneutic spiral."[2] In the remainder of this chapter I review some contrasting images of social being, including the image presented by earlier ethnomethodology.

THE CONSTITUTIVE TRADITION

There is a belief within the Western intellectual tradition that people create meanings out of meaninglessness to combat their own nothingness. For convenience, I label this belief the "constitutive faith." Malraux (1968:23) has expressed the faith succinctly:

> The greatest mystery is not that we have been flung at random among the profusion of the earth and the galaxy of the stars, but that in this prison we can fashion images of ourselves sufficiently powerful to deny our nothingness.

One mystery is that humans have "been flung at random" into a meaningless prison. A greater mystery, says Malraux, is that we can create meanings among ourselves that "deny our nothingness."

This faith has been most prominent since the ascendency of modern scientific theory. The constitutive faith undergirds the Hobbesian problem of order which fathered social science. With Hobbes [(1651) 1962], it has been assumed that order must be explained. Disorder and meaninglessness are more natural and so unproblematic. The nineteenth century founders of sociology tried to use science to avoid the specter of disorder that haunted Europe in the name of industrial progress. As Ernest Becker (1971:111) describes the nineteenth century experience that generated sociology, "Society was headed for the kind of chaos that Homo sapiens fear most: the chaos of undependable and immoral behavior in his fellow men, the chaos of unregulated, irresponsible social life."

Becker (1968, 1971) argues that sociology's historical task has been to help keep this feared chaos at bay. Becker assumes that belief in this primordial chaos is shared by sociologists and lay persons alike. In another passage, Becker says that people need "symbolically contrived meanings" as "much as the air" they breathe (1971:62). These symbols give people "an imagined sense" of their "own worth."

American social scientists frequently invoke the premiere American philosopher, William James, to support their version of the constitutive faith. In his early works, James maintained that "Whatever organization may be found in experience is *bestowed* upon it by the mind working on the 'primordial chaos of sensation' " (1890, quoted in Gurwitsch, 1964:28). The constitutive faith was not "mere" philosophy for James. It arose as an analysis of a personal experience which precipitated a crisis in his life. James wrote in his journal for 1870 that he had experienced "that pit of insecurity beneath the surface of life" (James, 1967b:4). James was so shaken that he wrote, "for months I was unable to go out into the dark alone" (1967b:6).

Ackerman and Parsons (1966) maintain that James's constitutive faith is a commonplace truth. They use James to argue that *"The 'facts of science are myths'* . . . We select from what William James called 'blooming, buzzing' reality; we establish boundaries, we ascribe limit":

> We exclude—and what we exclude haunts us at the walls we set up. We include—and what we include limps, wounded by amputation. And, most importantly, we must live with all this, we must live with our wounded and our ghosts. There can be no Bultmann of science, pleading that we 'de-mythologize': *analytic thought itself is mythologization* (Ibid.:25–26).

The constitutive faith is not merely a social science image of science. It is a social scientific image of social being. Novak (1971:23) justly refers to the social sciences to document the following facts:

> Experience rushes in upon us in such floods that we must break it down, select from it, abstract, shape and relate . . . . A culture is constituted by the meaning it imposes on human experience . . . even the most solid and powerful social institutions, though they may imprison us, impoverish us, or kill us, are fundamentally mythical structures designed to hold chaos and formlessness at bay . . . culture begins and ends in the void.

This faith engenders a fear of the natural world beyond people. That world is theorized to be void. People must cooperate to fend off the "blooming, buzzing" confusion. The constitutive faith is thus intimately connècted with runaway technology, alienation, and fear. It exhorts man to master the world. Earlier ethnomethodologies represented an apotheosis of this constitutive fear.[3]

BEYOND CONSTITUTIVE ETHNOMETHODOLOGY

When Garfinkel (1952) examined the Hobbesian problem of order, he argued that Hobbes had not taken the facticity of chaos seriously enough. Without humanity's unceasing work, Garfinkel claimed, there would not be a war of all against all, as Hobbes said. There would not even be a world within which such conflicts could occur. There would be instead a formless meaninglessness more frightening that any vision social science had conceived.

Early ethnomethodology arrived at this faith through the adoption of Schutz's (1962, 1964, 1966) and Gurwitsch's (1964, 1966) reading of Husserl. As Bauman (1973) indicates, there is nothing of interest to sociology in the early works of Husserl. But Schutz and Gurwitsch transformed that work. Ethnomethodology accepted the fecundity of the translation, building its theory on the base provided by Schutz and Gurwitsch. Schutz (e.g., 1962:11) spoke of the everyday world as constituted by "mental processes" and "operational steps." Gurwitsch (e.g., 1966:xvi) wrote that the world was made up of mental "acts of consciousness." Garfinkel transformed these acts into interactional activities, and ethnomethodology was born.

Garfinkel explained his transformation in the following passage:

> I shall exercise a theorist's preference and say that meaningful events are entirely and exclusively events in a person's behavioral environment, with this defined in accordance with Hallowell's usage. Hence there is no reason to look under the skull since nothing of interest is to be found there but brains. The "skin" of the person will be left intact. Instead questions will be confined to the operations that can be performed upon events that are "scenic" to the person (1963:190).

Garfinkel transformed Schutz's mental processes into public, scenic processes. He remains faithful to this policy in his later work (e.g., in Hill and Crittenden, 1968:47; Garfinkel and Sacks, 1970). The policy transformed a philosophy into a social science, but it did not alter the constitutive faith that Gurwitsch and Schutz shared. Bauman (1973) has reviewed the consequences of this faith in the works of many ethnomethodologists. It is well exhibited on the final page of Wieder's (1973:224) monograph:

> The problems encountered in describing and explaining social action hinge in part on the notion that on the one hand there is an event which is the description of that action and of the method of producing that description. This dualism—which is an instance of the subject-object dualism—generates the issue of the veridicality of the description and, in the context of science, the necessity of literal description.
>
> The abandonment of the dualism leads to the single phenomenon, an account-of-social-action, or an accounting-of-social-action.

Wieder recommends abandoning the dualism by making interpretative "accounts" or "accounting" phenomenal, and understanding epiphenomenal. Wieder's program is built upon the constitutive faith.[4] Interpretation is constitution. The "objective reality of social facts" is treated "as an ongoing accomplishment of the concerted activities of daily life" (Garfinkel, 1967a:vii). Activities constitute facts. The facts do not exist except through constituting practices.

This image led to a conceptual confusion within ethnomethodology. Indexicality was usually represented as a phenomenon derived from reflexivity. The indexed was conceived to be constituted by previous reflexive activities. Without prior interpretation, there were no facts "there" to be interpreted.

By placing interpretation and understanding in a spiral, I hope to have removed this constitutive bias. The facticity of an objective world is now an explicit feature of the theory. The objective world is returned to the lives of the people. This does not mean that reflexive interpretations cannot dominate so completely that people find themselves in a world almost entirely of their own construction. This can and does happen, for example, in conversation, or theorizing, or lecturing, or meditating. But interpretations are not made *the* foundation of the social world. They share this ground with understandings.

Joining ethnomethodology with the hermeneutic spiral changes ethnomethodology. The hermeneutic spiral encourages an end to the fear of chaos. Most ethnomethodology assumes that without man's work there would be nothingness. Ethnomethodology thus implicitly exhorts its readers to stay busy working, lest the void overwhelm them. The hermeneutic spiral suggests an alternative faith. It indicates that we need not fear to cease our busy work. We need not fear to cease wresting meaning from nothingness. We can gaze upon the earth's wonders. We are in a spiral of our own making, but it is at once beyond our making.

The hermeneutic spiral contrasts with several other images of humanity as well.

THE DETERMINIST TRADITION

The constitutive faith speaks to the origins of the meaningful world. As Novak (1971:23) says, these meanings may become so institutionalized that they "imprison us, impoverish us, or kill us." In such a rigidified form, meanings are treated as "facts." This is a faith undergirding empirical social science. Though humanity may have ultimately created the world's meaning, for all practical purposes the world can be viewed as the *cause* of humanity's meaningful behavior. Understanding becomes the primordial phase of human being. Interpretation is seen as an effect of the world's variables and structure. People are presumed to share a common intersubjective world. This is a Lockean faith, well stated by d'Alembert ([1751] 1963:31) when he proclaims that "all our knowledge is ultimately reduced to sensations that are approximately the same in all men."

In this view, persons become unimportant. Their interpretive actions are nothing more than emanations of their place in the social structures. The world speaks through the person. This is a faith reified in vulgar Marxism, behaviorism, and positivist social science. Researchers of these schools maintain that, like mirrors, social beings only reflect. Mirrors may have quirks. Some distort more than others. But no mirror plays a creative role in the images it displays. People live the life their social facts dictate.

Of course, ideas and attitudes are accorded importance within this faith. Social beings' interpretations are given a place. What is denied is that these actions constantly alter the world. "Ideas" and "attitudes" are treated as *things*. They are placed in the external world. They do not pass through humanity's interpretation *every time* (see Merleau-Ponty, 1955, in 1970:141). Instead, social beings are visualized as being forced along a path separate from them. Little changes as humanity steps.

In the hermeneutical spiral image of humanity, the understood world is altered fundamentally every time it enters social beings. The understood world and the interpreting person are mutually determinative (cf Wieder, 1974:216). The world swings through social beings, social beings swing through the world. Together they constitute a spiral, together they form a life.

FAITHS IN BEING

When I speak of these affairs of faith, I am speaking philosophically. Philosophy is an interpretation one person offers about the fact of understood horizons. The particulars of a horizon are interpreted when one does everyday acts, or science, or art. In philosophy the facticity of the understood horizon itself is spoken about.

In offering the image of humanity that is the hermeneutic spiral, I am speaking from my understood horizon. It is true for my horizon. It is not Truth. I equate Being with Truth.

There have been two important faiths in Being. Each approaches Being from a different direction. One can be seen as an extension of the constitutive faith. The other can be seen similarly as an extension of the determinist faith. I will describe the faiths of constitutive Being and of deterministic Being, and then describe the Being of the hermeneutic spiral.

Constitutive Being

It is unsettling to hold the constitutive faith. If humanity is *the* source of meaning, meaning must be frighteningly fragile. A faith in constitutive Being has frequently been added to the constitutive faith to give humanity's meanings a firmer foundation.

Plato offered the most influential theory of constitutive Being. Within this faith, phenomena are arranged hierarchically. The lowest realm is the understood world. Above that realm is one's interpretations. This is the arrangement of the constitutive faith. Constitutive Being adds a yet higher realm. The meaning one finds in one's interpretations is said to participate in the Truth of Being. In this way, a person's meanings are made less fragile. They are not arbitrary or merely human. They more or less recall Being. They are gifts from the Godhead of Ideas.

Lovejoy ([1936] 1960) traces the history of this idea. Descartes provided a formulation of constitutive Being that reconciled it with science. As I mentioned in Chapter 8, Blum and McHugh and their associates have revived the faith and offered it to social science. A faith in constitutive Being strengthens humanity's faith in meanings, but at a price. It further denigrates the natural world. It increases humanity's fear of that world. The flesh is made unholy. The world is the enemy. Sin is identified with "worldliness." Truth is identified with a path away from the world.

Deterministic Being

Einstein could not believe that God would play dice with the universe. This expresses the deterministic faith that the world is a God-given order. Most contemporary scientists are content to search for that order. They do not seek a God behind it. This was not so for the pioneers of natural science. Galileo, Kepler, Newton, Boyle, and others, were like medieval alchemists. They inquired of nature's wonders not to know nature, but to commune with God. Plato's hierarchy was reversed. The world was elevated to a status superior to humanity. Beyond this natural world was Being. This Being was the Great Watchmaker, who set the universe in motion and then retired. To know God, it was necessary to search the world for the signs God had left. These signs were designated "natural laws."

It is difficult for us to imagine science as such an enterprise. Today, science has no interest in Being. The world was once the means for science; now it is the end. Science's original faith in deterministic Being has deteriorated into merely a deterministic tradition. Faith in deterministic Being is still alive, however. It is most noticeable in Oriental religions (see Jung, 1963).

Rather than search the material world for Being, the religions of the Orient counsel searching one's own body and life. For example, a Buddhist manual of meditation says that spiritual practices lead people to eliminate "the smoke screen of preferences and associated thoughts through which we see not what *is*, but what we think *about* it" (Mangalo, n.d.: "Foreword"). This exhibits a faith in deterministic Being. Rational thinking is denigrated. Spiritual practices rid the person of this rational "smoke screen" so that the real may be seen. This real is the understood world. Rational processes are an illusion. If one can escape these processes and see only "what is," one will know that deterministic Being appears as "what is."

The faith in constitutive Being sets up a hierarchy that runs from the world, to humanity, to Being. Faith in deterministic Being rearranges the order. The social being, as thinking creature, is the lowest form of being. The path to Being lies through a loss of self in the understood world. The tradition of Plato, of constitutive Being, treats the *sense* that there is a world beyond one's self as a mystery. Problems of solipsism and intersubjectivity are perennial. Alternatively, the alchemical tradition of deterministic Being finds the sense of an interpreting ego separate from the world a mystery. Problems of the "illusion" of egos have thus been perennial.

Faiths in constitutive Being have explained away the world as a function of interpretive actions. Their world is constituted by persons.

Faiths in deterministic Being have explained away individual persons as a function of the world worlding. Their persons are constituted by the world.

Mutually Determinative Being

These two faiths in Being share a common prejudice. They elevate Being beyond being. They explain being as a function of Being. Both of these views of Being assume a dialectical relation.

A faith in constitutive Being claims that interpretation is real to the extent that it participates in a relation with Rational Being. The external world is thought to be real to the extent that it, too, recalls this Being. A faith in deterministic Being claims that the understood world is real to the extent that it participates in a relation with Natural Being. Interpretations are thought less real as they are one step further removed from this unsullied Reality. The hermeneutic spiral suggests that Being exhibits different relations. Unlike the relations of constitutive and deterministic Being, hermeneutic Being is not dialectical.

By dialectical I mean a form of thought which imagines one entity or concept to emanate from another. There are many other dialectical theories besides the two I have outlined here. Traditions differ in terms of which entity is seen as emanation, and which as source. These differences are complicated by another dimension about which the traditions vary. Different traditions assume different concepts. They speak about dialectical relations among different species of entities. For example, some traditions begin with spatial entities and concepts, while others begin with temporal entities and concepts. Some traditions explain Being by Becoming, others explain Becoming by Being.

I believe that all metaphysics could be found to be dialectical philosophies in the above sense. Their similarity is obscured by the dissimilarity of their concepts. The dialectical base of these philosophies has been further obscured in modern philosophy by the ascendency of epistemological concerns. Wiess (in Kiley, 1969:ix) has suggested how epistemology and ontology are dialectically related: "God's creation is the insistence on the dependence of "epistemology" on ontology; man's acknowledgement of creation is an insistence on the epistemological recovery of ontology." Wiess thus suggests that epistemology emanates from ontology. Constructing epistemologies is an attempt to sketch the face of its source. The preoccupation of modern philosophies with epistemology is thus transformed into another instance of dialectical metaphysics.

When I described understanding and interpretation, I called them phases. I invoked the image of time. First an understanding occurs, then an interpretation, then an understanding, and so forth. The passing from one of the other was indexicality and reflexivity. The image of time is felicitous but incorrect. Time does not exist independently of the spiral. The spiral creates time. The experience of time is the experience of the rhythm of the spiral. Like the speed of the spiral, time is not uniform. Time and the spiral are mutually determinative.

It is thus incorrect to think of the spiral as containing two dialectically related parts. Understanding and interpretation do not relate to one another as source and emanation. Their relations are nondialectical. The spiral creates the possibility of dialectics, just as it creates time.

A metaphysics drawn from the hermeneutic spiral identifies constitutive Being with Interpretation, and identifies deterministic Being with Understanding. Interpretation and Understanding are related to each other as are understanding and interpretation. The latter exhibit in the everyday epistemological microcosm what Understanding and Interpretation exhibit in the Empyrean ontological macrocosm. Like interpretation and understanding, then, the two Beings are related as are night and day. Neither is said to be the source, and the other the emanation. Each is at once source and emanation. Each is independent of and dependent upon the other. Neither is denigrated. Neither is elevated. As constitutive Becoming and deterministic Becoming, the two are mutually constitutive. As constitutive Being and deterministic Being, the two are mutually contained.

Indexicality and reflexivity generate these relations. Constitutive Being indexes deterministic Being. By so indexing, constitutive Being both emanates from and becomes a source for deterministic Being (See Escher's "Drawing Hands," frontispiece). The former relation is established by constitutive Being's dependence upon deterministic Being's horizon of possibility. The latter relation is established by constitutive Being's reflexive disappearance into deterministic Being, thereby recasting that Being. Consititutive and deterministic Being are, therefore, One and Many.

THE IMAGE OF HUMANITY

In the preceding sections, I explored the metaphysics of the hermeneutic spiral by comparing it with some alternative metaphysical conceptions. This metaphysics is not essential to the spiral. The hermeneutic spiral itself is a more concrete image. It is suggested by the empirical studies of ethnomethodology. One need not be committed to speculations about Being to embrace the image of humanity that the spiral suggests.

As an image of humanity, the hermeneutic spiral makes everyone an artist, every act creative, every moment mysterious. Every moment is mysterious, as the understood horizon of the moment is inexhaustible. Every interpretive act indexes this mystery in an unpredictable way. A person's every action is thus creative; it reflexively alters the world. The person begins with certain materials that set limits, and then acts and in acting alters those limits. These new limits form the material of another creative act, ad infinitum.

This is the image of humanity undergirding my understanding of realities (see Chapter 2). Realities are forms of life, I said. And forms of life are always forms of life forming. Realities are always realities becoming.

NOTES

1. This chapter is an interpretation of Wallace's pioneering studies. Wallace offered suggestions on several earlier drafts. Since I have ignored many of these, the reader should

not suppose that all thoughts in the chapter are Wallace's own. Sam Edward Combs's and Marshall Shumsky's gentle devastation of an earlier draft was also invaluable.

2. The hermeneutic spiral should be contrasted with Dilthey's (see Hodges (1944) pioneering studies of hermeneutics (see Palmer, 1968), and with what Heidegger (1962) calls the "hermeneutic situation."

3. Much of what is called "phenomenological sociology" also exhibits the constitutive faith. Psathas (1973) provides an excellent introduction to this approach (see especially Psathas and Waksler, 1973; and Manning and Fabrega, 1973). Heap and Roth (1973) provide a critique of some earlier attempts to apply phenomenological insights to sociology. See also Wieder (1973), who claims to have used a modified form of the phenomenological reduction to generate his findings. Manning (1973) treats phenomenological sociology within a larger movement that he labels "existential sociology." Manning suggests that ethnomethodology is one variant of this tradition. I provide an alternative version of ethnomethodology's origins in Chapter 11.

4. Schwartz (1971), Bauman (1973), Goldthorpe (1973), and Bittner (1973) have previously complained about ethnomethodology's constitutive bias. I reviewed Schwartz's alternative program in Chapter 7. Pollner (1970) anticipated these criticisms in his dissertation. However, Pollner's use of Merleau-Ponty occasionally led him to the opposite extreme: Pollner (1970:32ff., 46n) sometimes suggests that understanding is primordial, and interpretation but an epiphenomenon of the world worlding. The separate modifications of ethnomethodology offered in W. Handel (1972) and in Jennings (1972) may also be understood as spawned by early ethnomethodology's constitutive faith.

CHAPTER ELEVEN

The
Morality
of
Ethnomethodology

Why do ethnomethodology? Academics and scientists frequently invoke two justifications. One is that knowledge is for knowledge's sake. This defense assumes that experts develop knowledge superior to laypersons. I have attempted to undercut this belief throughout this book. I have argued that all persons have elegant knowledge of their own reality. That knowledge is absolute within realities. I cannot justify my ethnomethodology as a pursuit of privileged knowledge. Every farmer, freak, witch, and alchemist has such knowledge.   .

The second justification relies on variants of the claim that "knowledge is power." This claim is intimately related to the first. It assumes that knowledge leads to prediction and control that most people do not possess. Theoretical rebuttals to this belief are scattered throughout this book. For example, there is my claim that the "power" of scientific knowledge is only proven reflexively. Belief in the predictive efficacy of scientific knowledge is an incorrigible propostion. Like other incorrigibles, it does not permit objective test. Failures prove its truth (see Chapter 2).

This argument turns upon itself. Scientists reflexively experience the absolute truth of their methods and theories every day. We who live within scientific societies experience similarly. We feel absolutely that science really is power. Science's child, technology, oppresses us. It has moved beyond the Western nations to begin paving the world. Theoretical arguments that science is just one more way of knowing are like sermons preached to a condemned man reminding him that execution is just one more way of dying.

Ethnomethodology can be an act of rebellion against the scientific monolith. Of course the contemporary scene is already overpopulated with such rebellions. But these rebellions share a common weakness: they are nonscientific. Manifestos, philosophies, and poems abound attacking science [see Roszak's (1973) bibliography]. But as they do not speak in the scientific idiom they little alter science's course. "Objectivity" is the modern language of power. A Homer or an Aquinas may rise who speaks elegantly against that power, but he will not be heard. Ethnomethodology speaks from within the scientific idiom. It is an objective study of objectivity. Ethnomethodology is not a theoretical rebuttal to science. It adopts the scientific vision to produce a transcendence of that vision.

Ethnomethodology is not, therefore, antiscientific. It exhibits a great faith in science. Ethnomethodology treats science as an activity of liberation. For centuries the method has been turned on the world, and humanity has not benefited. Perhaps by turning the scientific method upon itself, science will begin to repay humanity in more humane coin.

This is a naively optimistic idea. But ethnomethodology has had this effect on a few of its practitioners. In this chapter, I try to show how it can do the same for others.[1]

THE DIALECTICAL TRADITION

Ethnomethodology may be viewed as a synthesis of two traditions that are commonly considered mutually exclusive. One of these traditions is scientism. This tradition assumes that the scientific method produces knowledge that is superior to that produced by any of the other methods. As Habermas (1971:4) writes: " 'Scientism' means science's belief in itself: that is, the conviction that we can no longer understand science as *one* form of possible knowledge, but rather must identify knowledge with science." Bacon and Descartes were early spokesmen for this tradition. Newton is commonly supposed to have justified this faith.

This is the tradition that created sociology in the nineteenth century. The task of Comte, Spencer, Pareto, Durkheim, Weber, and the others was to show how the method was applicable to human phenomena (see Becker, 1968, 1971). Scientism flowered in the early decades of this century and culminated in Wittgenstein's *Tractatus Logico-Philosophicus* [(1921) 1961], in logical atomism and logical positivism. This tradition is known today as *logico-empiricism*.[2] It finds its voice in the works of Quine, Hempel, Brodbeck, Nagel, Reichenbach, and other contemporary philosophers. It is a common theme among all the quarreling schools of standard American sociology.

The hermeneutic-dialectical tradition, logico-empiricism's antithesis, arose as a cry of alarm at first sight of science's face. Blake is this tradition's classic poet. Kierkegaard was a spokesman early in the nineteenth century, Nietszche at the century's end. In the twentieth century, it has been represented by some phenomenologists and existentialists (see Manning, 1973), by the Frankfurt School, and by the philosophies of the later Wittgenstein, Feyerabend, and others (see note 4, Chapter 3). Feyerabend (1972:206, in Radnitzsky, 1973:417) summarizes the hermeneutic-dialectic doctrine as follows:

> science is only one of the many monsters which have been created by man, and I am not at all sure that it is the best. There may be better ways of finding the "truth." And there may be better ways of being a man than trying to find the truth.

These two traditions feed off each other. Each defines itself in part by attacking the other. In this sense they are both dialectical. Ethnomethodology is a child of the two. It is an *activity* that transcends them. Ethnomethodology has borrowed its *methodology* from its logico-empiricist father. Ethnomethodology's *theory* has been derived from its hermeneutic-dialectic mother. Ethnomethodology does not choose sides in the war between its parents. As a result, both traditions find ethnomethodology anathema.[3]

THE LOGICO-EMPIRICIST RESPONSE

Many followers of the logico-empiricist tradition acknowledge that scientific consciousness has spawned the earth's current malaise. This feeling haunted both Weber and Durkheim. They saw science as a means to counter chaos. Today even many natural scientists feel similarly. But *within* the scientistic tradition there seems to be but one solution: more hair of the dog, more science to solve the problems science has created. Government grants are requested to decrease populations that other government grants nourished to explosion. Similarly, scientific agencies that once developed techniques of fouling the air request more monies to develop devices for freshening it. Social scientists spend millions studying "social problems" that earlier sociologists in part created.

These proposals exhibit science's incorrigible faith in empiricism as a privileged way of knowing. Like Azande oracle use, science's failures are used reflexively to prove once more the faith that generated the failures (see Chapter 2).

As the hermeneutic-dialectic tradition grew more strident in the 1960s, the scientist's defenses grew more frenetic. Leach's (1974) defense is prototypical. Reviewing a book (Hymes, 1973) that attempts to "reinvent" anthropology within the hermeneutic-dialectic tradition, Leach says "I fully sympathize with the frustrated exasperation of . . . [the] contributors" concerning the negative consequences of science in the modern age. Leach then characterizes the hermeneutic-dialectic theory as the understanding "that the observer is part of the scene that he observes" (1974:34). This indexes the theory I have developed in this book: The observer always in part *constitutes* the scenes he observes. Leach's summary seems fair, but he follows with this polemic, "But God forbid that we should propose the search for mystical experience as a proper substitute for the pretensions of objectivity. I have no wish to muddle up my scholarly concerns with the ethics of a Franciscan friar" (Ibid.).

Leach later complains that "None of this would be subject to any sort of empirical verification. If this is anthropology reinvented, give me cross-cousin marriage every time" (Ibid.:35).

Leach replies angrily to an angry book, because he is ultimately committed to "empirical verification." He rejects the radical implications of the theory that the observer reflexively constitutes the scenes he enters because it has been presented to him as a theory dialectically opposing "objectivity." Ethnomethodology accepts the incorrigibles of both traditions. It maintains that one can do objective inquiries using the incorrigible theory of observer constitution.

Of course this joining of long-opposed incorrigibles changes the face of social science. Ethnomethodology is led to phenomena that social science ignores.

Ethnomethodology investigates everyday life. Social science colleagues sometimes ask me to tell them about ethnomethodology. I have developed presentations using videotapes of everyday scenes. I find that sociologists have had little experience at such observation. They have little competence to analyze concrete interactions. This incompetence is remarkable, since social order must occur in everyday interactions if we are to claim it is real, and not just the social scientist's ideal invention. My audience typically protests that I am not doing social science. They ask for my indicators and measurements. They want to talk about these. They have no interest in the scenes themselves. It is only when they are discussing abstracted concepts that they feel secure. I am often made to feel as if I have breached some deep taboo by even suggesting that the problem of social order is related to everyday interactions.

The differences between us are not difference of methods. I try to speak objectively about the scenes I display. I record them on videotape in an effort to validate my observations. The taboo such work breaches is a theoretical taboo. By demanding that my objective analysis be closely tied to actually recorded scenes, I explicitly turn objectivity itself into a phenomenon. One cannot repeatedly view a concrete social scene without raising questions concerning the place of the observer in constructing those observations. This makes sociologists angry, just as Leach expressed anger in his book review. I have had sociologists walk out in the middle of my presentations. One called out, "That's not sociology!" as she fled the room.[4]

The hermeneutic-dialectic theory as refined within ethnomethodology commits me to the study of concrete scenes and to the recognition that I am always a part of those scenes. Social science is committed to avoiding both of these involvements. Social science journals and monographs that contain arguments about concepts and methods, all of which assume that there is *one* real world out there and that this world is independent of social science's concepts and methods, starkly reveal the differences in our forms of life. As Garfinkel (1964, in 1967a:35) writes, the world for these scholars is only a "technical mystery" for which their work offers only technical solutions.

Social scientists rarely risk disruption of their own everyday routines. Theirs are fundamentally talking disciplines. The research they do beyond their dissertations is mostly completed through graduate students. It is these students who get their hands dirty in the field. Even what little contact these students make with the everyday world is usually made only through technical instruments—experiments, interviews, and surveys—that assure that contact will not become "messy." They feel that the "real work" begins only when they are back in their offices talking about these materials.

The ethnomethodology I am outlining in this book is not primarily a talking discipline. It is a way of working. It is an activity that forces the practitioner to take risks. Although it adopts an empirical stance, empiricism itself is part of the phenomenon. This phenomenon is not to be found merely by writing about it. It must be experienced firsthand. Leach is able to transform the idea "that the observer is part of the scene that he observes" (1974:34) into a bromide because for him it is simply an idea. He has not used it as a principle to organize research of which he himself was a part. If he had, he would see that it is a theory that turns upon itself, as it turns upon the scene studied and the observer observing it. Ethnomethodology as I see it is an activity of doing just this kind of reflexive research.

THE HERMENEUTIC-DIALECTIC RESPONSE

Ethnomethodologists share a common theoretical perspective with thinkers of the hermeneutic-dialectic tradition. Ethnomethodologists diverge from these thinkers in what they do with that theory. They agree with these thinkers when they argue that science is not a superior method of knowing. Ethnomethodologists differ from these thinkers in arguing that this insight itself must be treated as "only" a reflexive accomplishment.

Thinkers in the hermeneutic-dialectic tradition argue *ex cathedra* against the doctrine of scientism. They offer carefully reasoned proofs challenging the logico-empiricist philosophy. However, these arguments have little chance of deflecting the scientific monolith. The hermeneutic theories themselves explain why this is so. They inform us that science is a form of life (Blum, 1970a, 1970b; McHugh et al., 1974). Logico-empiricist philosophy arose only as an ad hoc justification for the scientific reality. Scientists will not be convinced by opposing philosophies that demand abandoning a form of life that demonstrates its power daily. To tell scientists that their proofs are "only" reflexive accomplishments does not alter the experiential validity of those accomplishments. Science as an activity does not rise and fall on the consistency of its "reconstructed logics" (see Kaplan, 1964).

The hopelessness of attempting to alter science by reasonable persuasion can be illustrated in another way. Although the hermeneutic-dialectic theorists typically disparage science's absolute validity, they continue to embrace science's accomplishments in their daily lives. They reject science's philosophy but continue to turn to physicians when they become ill, to machines when they wish to travel, to telephones when they want to communicate. Few hermeneutic-dialectic thinkers have attempted to build alternative societies. They continue to embrace the accoutrements of science while disparaging science's absolute intellectual warrant.

This is not to call such theorists hypocritical. They must work within the circumstances of their life. I am questioning whether their way of working is efficacious. It is one thing to *argue* that rain dances and prayers are as valid as soil chemistry. It is quite another thing to work one's garden eschewing scientific principles. The hermeneutic theorists' arguments do not alter the experience of their daily lives. The style of life of these thinkers is quite like the style of life of those who embrace the logico-empiricist tradition. However their philosophies may differ, they both experience realities in a manner more similar to each other's manner than to that of persons who live in nonscientific realities.

I am trying to create a discipline that does more than construct theories that denigrate science. I believe that we need not deny the scientific method. It can be used to investigate the theories associated with the hermeneutic-dialectic perspective. We will no longer speak against science *ex cathedra*. We can present our discoveries in a scientific idiom. These discoveries will be about the possibility of such an idiom. And, as importantly, these discoveries will be about the possibility of ourselves making discoveries.

Many theorists within the hermeneutic-dialectical tradition have called for similar work (e.g., Gouldner, 1970). From my point of view, however, these theorists are not reflexive enough. They typically grant themselves a privileged position. Reflexive theory is presented as the only means for approaching the truth.

These exhortations for a reflexive theory perpetuate the dialectical tradition I mentioned above. The world is rigidly bifurcated. Lines are drawn and guns are pointed. These claims are equivocated by invocations of the idea of "dialectical relations." But these dialectics assume that entities have mutually exclusive properties. They dialectically inform one another, but their absolute separateness is still assumed.

In the previous chapter, I offered an outline of a postdialectical perspective. It hinges on the idea that A and B are mutually constitutive. A is *at once* dependent upon and independent of B. B is similarly related to A. A and B here stand for *all* things, events, persons, relations, and so forth.

Dialectical theories maintain that some A's turn into some B's. They assume the existence of time; the theory of mutual containment is atemporal. It speaks to the possibility of time. It is not claimed that *some A*'s turn into *some B*'s over time. Rather, it asserts that *all A*'s are simultaneously both B and not B. These relations create the possibility of time and of dialectics.

Of course, one should not choose between the hermeneutic-dialectic theorists and ethnomethodology on the basis of such abstractions. My deeper criticism of the so-called reflexive theorists is that they are not sensuous. They do not alter the everyday experience of either the theorist or the theorist's audience. And, as importantly, there are theories that talk about worlds the theorist has never entered. Ethnomethodology is committed to avoiding such "promiscuous discussions of theory" (Garfinkel, 1967a:viii).

Radical Theorists

The most strident spokesmen of the hermeneutic-dialectic tradition are the "radicals." These persons embrace a theoretical perspective much like ethnomethodology. Hansen's (1967) "Dialectical Critique of Empiricism" is paradigmatic. Hansen offers a program for a new social science, where:

> What must be remembered is the dialectician's insistence upon the historical and subjective (understood as inter-subjective) nature of all inquiry. Man is the agent of theorizing and "fact-collecting," and without man's *intent* there would be no "scientific facts" at all, let alone theories (Ibid.:15).

This is a position I tried to display in actual materials in Part 2 (especially Chapter 3). Hansen uses this theory both to interpret texts and to interpret others' empirical work. He attacks empiricism. He claims that logico-empiricists ignore the "historical and subjective . . . nature of all inquiry" and thus are foolish and possibly evil. But Hansen argues that his own theory is more than one more historically situated theory. He assumes a privileged position. Hansen has not adopted the dialectical theory to relativize science. He maintains instead that it provides a deeper ground for doing science. He writes, for example:

> Lest it be thought the dialectical viewpoint parallels the idealist view which would allow for all sorts of hair-brained theories to account for man's experienced world, it should be pointed out that the dialectician (*qua* scientist) requires empirical evidence for *any* theory put forth, including his own properly scientific theories (Ibid.:14).

In the course of his paper, Hansen argues for his beliefs that the phlogiston theory is really inferior to the oxygen theory, and that such disciplines as witchcraft and alchemy are really "factually" incorrect. Hansen thus accepts the absolutist stance of scientism. He has merely given that position a different theoretical frame.

Much radical theorizing is like this. The hermeneutic-dialectic theories are not used to relativize all theories. Instead, they are invoked to provide the theorist with a weapon for attacking scientism while retaining the findings science has unearthed. The truth of "the historical and subjective . . . nature of all inquiry" is represented as an empirical truth beyond interpretation. And yet, the basis for knowledge is claimed to reside ultimately in the external world.

My approach treats the hermeneutic-dialectic theories as themselves interpretive accomplishments. All theories may be reflexively proved in dialogue with the "external world." But no theory is really there more than any other. If I choose to undertake scientific inquiries it is not because I think other prescientific theories are "hair-brained," as Hansen claims. It is rather because I think that such inquiries can accomplish something valuable for me, given my present historical circumstances. Merleau-Ponty (1955, in 1970:140) complained that Weber's sociology "does not carry the relativization of relativism to its ultimate conclusion." The same may be said of most radical theorists. Merleau-Ponty also summarized my alternative position when he asked, "But would not a more radical criticism . . . lead us to recover the absolute in the relative?" (1970:140).

Critical Theorists

Mullins (1973:270–293) argues that "radical" theorists must be distinguished from "critical" theorists.[5] Critical theorists are more theoretical and historical. Radical theorists are more action-oriented and tend to work outside the academy. There is overlap between the two groups. Both share the hermeneutic-dialectic tradition.

The work of Habermas (1970a, 1970b, 1971) provides an example of the critical theory in the tradition of "German idealism." Habermas argues for the kernel of truth in German idealism in an effort to demonstrate that it "is not quite obsolete" (1971:314). Because ethnomethodology's theory derives from this tradition as well, in its broader appearance as the hermeneutic-dialectic perspective, much of Habermas's theorizing is compatible with my program. I agree with most of what Habermas *writes*. I disagree, however, with what Habermas proposes that social scientists *do*.

In one of Habermas's (1971:301–317) most important essays, he distinguishes between the "empirical-analytic" and the "historical-hermeneutic" modes of cognition. Having analyzed these, he offers a synthesizing alternative, which he calls "critical." The three roughly correspond to the three traditions I have called in this chapter "logico-empiricism," "hermeneutic-dialectic," and "ethnomethodology." Like my view of ethnomethodology, Habermas calls his third alternative "emancipatory" (Ibid.:308–311). But his method of emancipation must be distinguished from the method I recommend.

Habermas's (Ibid.:304) "conception of theory as a process of cultivation of the person" leads to a call for self-reflection. Habermas believes in the power of individual reason. He argues that persons can think their way to emancipation. I argue that persons must work their way to this experience through contact with concrete empirical materials.

In my interpretation of the hermeneutic-dialectic theory, there is "no time out" (see Garfinkel and Sacks, 1970:361). Habermas, on the other hand, believes that self-reflection "releases the subject from dependence on hypostatized powers," (1971:310). This "emancipatory cognitive interest" can "determine when theoretical statements grasp invariant regularities of social action as such and when they express ideologically frozen relations of dependence" (Ibid.:310). Habermas is thus led to distinguish between "ideological" or "justifying" motives, and "real" motives (Ibid.: 311). In my use of the theory, all motives are equal phenomena. All are real accounts.

Habermas agrues that science is ideological. As a result, he rejects science's method. He offers instead a "discipline of trained thought" that aims to "outwit its innate human interest" (Ibid.:311). As a result,

Habermas writes scholarly papers about ideas. These provide the raw materials for his use of the method of self-reflection. Habermas argues, "The mind can become aware of this natural basis reflexively," (Ibid.: 312). Habermas believes that persons can think their way to this emancipatory truth.

Habermas's critical approach is being widely adopted in the United States of America. For example, Schroyer (1971:301) adopts Habermas's thesis "that the scientistic image of science is the fundamental false consciousness of our epoch. If the technocratic ideology is to lose its hold on our consciousness, a critical theory of science must lay bare the theoretical reifications of the scientistic image of science." Schroyer's "critical theory of science" is not an empirical theory, however. "The interest of a critical science is the emancipation of all self-conscious agents" (Ibid.:313). For Schroyer, as for Habermas, the method of achieving such self-consciousness is identified with reading and writing philosophy.

I trust that such mental exercises work. However, I do not think that the method of these theorists is generally applicable. In order to use Habermas's method as he and his followers do, one must first study many recondite texts. Kant, Hegel, Marx, and Husserl are preliminary requirements for the "discipline of trained thought." My method requires the gathering and analysis of materials which are "objective" in their first appearance and which include the researcher as a constituent part. Perhaps in the tradition from which Habermas speaks, his method is more efficacious than mine. Within the English-speaking world, I believe that a method based on "data" will prove more useful.

THE POLITICS OF EVERYDAY LIFE

Radical and critical theorizing are abstract disciplines, much like the rest of social science. These theorists spend most of their time writing and talking about a truth they feel is absolute. Much of this talk is about "politics."

Politics is a concept. It is conceived only in the form of objects of perception, not as "sensuous human activity." But, as Marx goes on to write in his *Theses on Fuerbach* (1947), "All social life is essentially *practical*." It consists of "an ensemble of social relationships." Radical theorists use these words as a weapon with which to attack opponents. And they use the weapon as a philosophical theory and maintain that it is a superior insight. For ethnomethodologists, Marx's words are an exhortation to do practical studies of the essentially practical human world.

If all social life is "essentially practical," Marx's theory itself must have been an outgrowth of his particular "ensemble of social relationships." To turn it into a theory about the world seems a mockery. A better use seems to be to seek to experience its truth in the every day. Politics are thus not claimed to be something people *have*. They are actions people *do*. There are no things in the sensuous world like "bourgeois consciousness" or "class" or "the capitalist system." There are only people doing their lives in a succession of here and nows. To treat people as abstract categories illustrates the alienation of the theorist, not the alienation of those the theorist talks about.

I am not maintaining that ethnomethodology is apolitical. I am arguing that ethnomethodology has a commitment to Marx's dictum that philosophers have only interpreted the world, while the point is to change it. Ethnomethodology is a way of changing oneself. But it is not merely that. It is also a way of sharing this change with others. It is a discipline that has a chance of changing the way some people live their lives.

Consider once more the concept of politics. Power relationships do occur, but they show themselves only in particular social scenes. People do not unfold conceptual categories. They are reality participants and construct their lives in concert with others. Examination of concrete scenes reveals extraordinary power differentials. Politics are always the politics of everyday life. Where else could political forces be found? Abstract categories—"alienation," "capitalism," and so on—must be tied to everyday events.

Pollner (1973) has employed the concept of politics in his ethnomethodological researches. Borrowing from Laing (1967), he calls these the "politics of experience." They are not to be confused with the concept of politics enunciated in critical theories. Pollner does not merely talk about power differentials. He displays the operations of these differentials in transcripts compiled from everyday events.

The bulk of Pollner's (1970, 1973) published materials are drawn from the encounters between alleged traffic violators and judges. With Emerson (Emerson and Pollner, in preparation), he has begun to refine this analysis by joining psychiatric emergency teams. These teams are an arm of a municipal agency which enters the home of persons alleged

by relatives, neighbors, police, or others to be either a danger to themselves or to others. Pollner's approach to the reality of politics is illustrated by Laing and Esterson's (1970) work. Pollner (1973) analyzes the
following report that Laing and Esterson (1970:40) offer concerning
the relations of a "schizophrenic" girl and her parents:

> When they were all interviewed together, her mother and father kept ex-
> changing with each other a constant series of nods, winks, gestures, knowing
> smiles, so obvious to the observer that he commented on them after twenty
> minutes of the first such interview. They continued, however, unabated
> and denied.
>
> The consequence, so it seems to us, of this failure by her parents to
> acknowledge the validity of similar comments by Maya, was that Maya could
> not know when she was perceiving or when she was imagining things to
> be going on between her parents. These open yet unavowed non-verbal
> exchanges between father and mother were in fact quite public and perfect-
> ly obvious. Much of what could be taken to be paranoid about Maya arose
> because she mistrusted her own mistrust. She could not really believe that
> what she thought she saw going on was going on. Another consequence
> was that she could not easily discriminate between actions not usually in-
> tended or regarded as communications, e.g., taking off spectacles, blinking,
> rubbing nose, frowning, and so on, and those that are—another aspect
> of her paranoia. It was just those actions, however, that were used as signals
> between her parents, as "tests" to see if Maya would pick them up, but
> an essential part of this game the parents played was that, if commented
> on, the rejoinder would be an amused, "What do you mean?" "What wink?"
> and so on.

Pollner (1973:4) argues that Laing's and his own materials illustrate
that in everyday life persons encounter "endless equivocalities." In concert with others, persons must establish some unequivocal foundation
beneath these equivocalities. Because people experience differently, "the
achievement of a consensual resolution requires that one or another
of the protagonists relinquish their experience of the world as the certain
grounds of further inference" (Ibid.:21). All persons are "versed in the
rhetoric of reality" (Ibid.:18). But some persons force their versions on
others. It is here and only here that power differentials exert their politics. The procedures by which parents force their reality on their children's experience are the same procedures by which any more powerful
groups subdue the less powerful. This is the way alienation is created.
This is the way "The essential intersubjectivity of the world is preserved
at the expense of a particular subjectivity" (Ibid.: note 6).

By treating politics as relations among concrete persons, ethnomethodologists provide a means of linking the abstract to the concrete experience of all human beings. So doing illustrates a faith that "the political struggle in America today does not concern power and interests merely, but new perspectives on what is real" (Novak, 1971:98).

Critical theorists argue that the great mass of people are forced to live in worlds they did not create. Ethnomethodology displays the everyday practices of this alienation.

MARX AS ETHNOMETHODOLOGIST

Borges (1964:201) writes that "every writer *creates* his own precursors." For example, if we know Marx's work we read Hegel and Fuerbach in a new way. We see in Marx's predecessors the potential Marx exploited. Similarly, after absorbing the insights of ethnomethodology one can return to Marx and read him as a crypto-ethnomethodologist. Adapting the method of Blum and McHugh (McHugh et al., 1974; see Chapter 8 above), such a reading of Marx has been offered in a series of essays by Filmer, Phillipson, Roche, Sandywell, and Silverman (1973). They use Marx not to illumine Marx but rather to reveal their own practices of alienation. I discuss their work not to describe Marx or them, but rather to illumine my own understanding of alienation.

Stratifying Practices

The image of language that the hermeneutic-dialectic tradition has spun sees language as "the house of being" (cf. Heidegger's later works). As Roche (1973:79–80) says, it is theorized that "the world does not form speech, but speech forms the world, or gives form to the world." Marx can be viewed as a progenitor of such a theory, but obviously it will not be the Marx of the "vulgar Marxists." Nonetheless, this interpretation retains the claim that "class" is a fundamental phenomenon.

However, class is now seen as something persons do with their speaking practices. "Speakers enact class—show, display, illuminate or manifest it—in their speaking it. Class is what is shown in their class speech" (Ibid.:81). Grounds for this conception can be found in Marx. In the

1844 manuscripts, Marx (1959:129; see Sandywell, 1973:36) claimed that in alienating capitalist societies, language is "the agent of divorce." In his *Grundrisse* (1971:71), Marx compared this fetish of language with the fetish of money:

> It is no less false to compare money with language. It is not the case that ideas are transmuted in language in such a way that their particular nature disappears and their social character exists alongside them in language, as prices exist alongside goods. Ideas do not exist apart from language (see Sandywell, 1973:34).

Ideas do not exist apart from language, Marx avers, just as the value of goods does not exist apart from the labor of those who produce goods. But in certain times language is reified. It is treated as a thing divorced from the practical circumstances of its speaking. Language becomes a commodity. It is bought and sold as if it had a value apart from the speaking labor of those who produce it during their "essentially practical" "ensemble of social relationships" (*Theses on Fuerbach*; see above). There came an evil time, Marx (in *The Poverty of Philosophy*, 1963:32) writes,

> when everything men had considered an inalienable became an object of exchange, or traffic, and could be alienated. This is the time when the very things which till then had *been communicated, but never sold; acquired, but never bought*—virtue, love, conviction, knowledge, conscience, etc.—when everything, in short, passed into commerce. It is the time of general corruption, of universal venality . . .

This describes our present age. Love, conviction, and knowledge are today treated as things. We exchange them as commodities through our language use. We classify each other according to the commodities that issue from our mouths. Pollner's work illustrates this process in everyday talk. Filmer et al (1973) display the alienation of scholarly and scientific speech, where the process of alienating speech appears in apotheosis.

The warrant for scholarly talk is always attributed to the things themselves. Scholarly speakers present themselves as messengers of nature. They are but vehicles for things that are beyond them. Reports are written on behalf of the "facts," not on behalf of human beings. Scholars invoke such phrases as "it can be maintained," "the data suggest," "the facts indicate." Within science, literal measurement is the ideal because it is presumed that nature alone produces the numerals. Operational definitions are another favored device. They are like price fixing (see Silverman, 1973:65). These and similar rhetorical devices are invoked to pretend that ideas exist apart from language. Scholars and sceintists display their alienation by treating their ideas as fodder that they sell for their livelihood.

Because ideas are presented as objects and not as "sensuous human activity," they may be classified. They are offered as ways of stratifying self and others. This is true of all speaking that forgets that "Ideas do not exist apart from language." Filmer et al. treat sociology as a paradign case. They argue that social scientists assume stratifying speech practices in order to construct analyses of "class" and "stratification." Social scientists create "class" as a thing in the world only by simultaneously treating their talk and themselves as things.

Such authors distinguish their analysis from the analyses of those they speak about. They claim that their own speech is deauthored, and thus objective. Those they speak about are claimed to be subjective. Such analysts stratify themselves hierarchically above the person in the street.

They next distinguish themselves from other sociologists. They claim that the speech-things they are offering are superior to the speech-things others have offered. They rate themselves as superior because they have better removed their practical circumstances from their analyses. The best analysts are claimed to be those who speak nature's truth with no "distoring" personal participation whatsoever.[6]

Stratifying speech also occurs in naturally occurring conversations. All speech is alienating when it ignores its origins and treats world and speaker as things, rather than as essentially practical activities.

Practices that classify are not necessarily alienating. They are only alienating when the categories employed in these practices have been broken "from their concrete human foundations, whence they originally arise and in which they might have been once valid" (Piccone, 1970:340). As the editor of *Telos* (Ibid.) further remarks, "Thus alienated from their only proper habitat . . . these categories become abstract, and, in the form of institutions, concepts or rules, they come to bound the very subjects that initially created them." Individuals who are not alienated can *labor*. To labor is to recognize one's creativity. It is to be a reality participant. "The worker, in producing the object, also produces himself and the categories needed to grasp his reality in the process" (Anonymous, 1970:298).[7]

Marx as a Reflexive Theorist

We are now ready to understand Marx's theory is a new way. His interpretation was not *about* the world. He was attempting to change himself and the world.

Marx was working with the same two traditions I named as ethnomethodology's progenitors. He was a student of Hegel, and so the hermeneutic-dialectic tradition. He was also a student of Fuerbach and the "scientific socialists," and so of the logico-empiricist tradition. His commitment to this latter tradition is evidenced in his first "Introduction" to the German edition of *Das Kapital*. Marx (1967:8ff.) compares his work with chemistry and physics, praises the use of statistics, and maintains he has discovered society's "natural laws of movement" (Ibid.:10). His *method* is empirical. But his *theory* is drawn from the antithetical tradition. His "natural laws" are not an alienated listing of nature's things. He offered empirical findings as a creative, reflexive act. As we have seen, Marx was attempting to display (not report) that "ideas do not exist apart from language."

Marx employs the scientific mode of stratifying. He opposes his theories to other theories and to the ideas of the masses. But his theory was simultaneously a reflexive saying. I assume that Marx had not forgotten his claim in *The Poverty of Philosophy* (1963:105) that *scientific* theories are "only the theoretical expressions, the abstractions of the social relations of production." In Marx's *Grundrisse* (1971:16–17), he has asked his readers to see the work of classical economists as "only the aesthetic fiction of the small and great adventure stories." Marx expected his readers to understand that his theories were not being offered as commodities. They were authored fictions arising from his own practical circumstances. To use Merleau-Ponty's (1970:140) phrase, their absolutism is found only in this relativity.

In other words, "Marx's analysis of class presents itself as a class analysis of class; it is the theorizing of the proletariat. . . . Marx's analysis of class is presented as being ground in, made intelligible by, reflexive upon, and a further instance of that which it theorizes about, i.e., class" (Roche, 1973:93).

Marx's theory is thus not competitive with other theories of history. When Marxist scholars argue with their bourgeois counterparts from a Marxist perspective they betray Marx. Marx's theory is not a:

truth, hidden behind empirical history, as much as it presents empirical history as the geneology of truth. *It is superficial to say that Marxism reveals the meaning of history.* This "philosophy of history" does not give us the keys to history so much as restore it as a permanent question. It only makes us aware of our time and its partialities (Merleau-Ponty, 1970:160; italics added).

Marx's theory is thus not *about* stratifying. It is an attempt to end stratifying speech by raising that speech to a scream. Marx was attempting to create a new mode of being. His "scientific laws" were reflexive laws. They were to prove themselves in use. If the proletariat could be exhorted to speak as Marx proposed, after a cataclysm of class speaking stratification would end. By speaking the theory, people would create a world in which the theory was nonsense. In socialism people would know the origins and power of speech. People would once more be self-conscious reality participants (see Roche, 1973:94–95).

Ethnomethodology as De-stratifying Practice

Marx's theory has failed in the Western world. People have not been freed by it. His "laws" have not been treated as reflexive scientific laws. Their logico-empiricist origins have repressed their reflexive sense. The Marx I present was not talking about truth. He was offering laws about stratifying practices that would raise the consciousness of people so that they would end such practices. Instead, Marx's formulations have been treated as things. Scholars read and write books *about* praxis.

Such exegesis may have its use, but ethnomethodology has different commitments. Filmer et al. (1973) offer their analysis of Marx not because they are interested in what Marx really meant, but because they wish to end their own stratifying practices. They suggest that the "proletariat" be read more as a metaphor than as a description of things. Anyone is a member of the proletariat who produces alienated speech. As scholars, Filmer and associates thus suggest that they are proletarians. They have attempted to transcend this mode of being. They do research and write papers together, but not in an effort to describe the world. Instead their work represents a "commitment to another community. A community in which speech is no longer a commodity bought (read) and sold (written) for instrumental purposes . . . the mode of existence which is enslaved by what it seeks to enslave" (Silverman, 1973:75).

The purpose of this community is to tutor one another in the experience that all praxis is sensuous human activity. Reading and writing are not to be excluded from this conception. Theirs is a method by which they hope to experience Marx's reflexive truths.

The method Filmer, Phillipson, Roche, Sandywell, and Silverman have adopted is but one of the possibly dealienating activities that ethnomethodology has spawned. It alone has been tied closely to Marxist conceptions, but I believe that the other studies this book has described could be similarly tied to Marxist conceptions. It is the Marxists who most often accuse ethnomethodology of being reactionary and amoral. That is why I have chosen Marx as a vehicle for detailing the moral implications of ethnomethodology as a form of life.

From an ethnomethodological point of view, today's radical and critical theorists are not radical or critical enough. They treat Marxist thought as an object. They stratify themselves. They claim a privileged position. They interpret Marx's truth, but they have not experienced it. Ethnomethodology can be seen as an activity of destratification. Because ethnomethodologists do this among others and attempt to share their procedures with others, ethnomethodology is a radical discipline. It may be able to change the perspective of many who will not be convinced by polemic or philosophy.

MY HYPOCRISY

I have argued that ethnomethodology takes no sides in the polemical war between the two traditions that give it birth. Yet I presented this neutrality polemically. I argued that both of ethnomethodology's forebearers were guilty of thinking their reality absolute. Yet I have spoken of ethnomethodology as if it, too, were absolute. I argued that both the hermeneutic-dialectic and the logico-empiricist traditions commit the sin of abstraction. Essentially talking and writing disciplines, they thus perpetuate rather than diminish alienation. Yet most of this book has been talk.

My hypocrisy is justified only if it has encouraged readers to put aside this book and begin ethnomethodological practices of their own. Numerous research programs have been reviewed in these chapters. Any of them can be profitably repeated and refined.

In addition to the procedures I have already described, there is another array of activities which are equally efficacious. I close the book by listing some of them. To do ethnomethodology, one must pursue some of these activities. Further reading will not make one an ethnomethodologist. It is only because ethnomethodology is essentially a way of working that it may liberate us from what Blake called "single vision and Newton's sleep."

NOTES

1. This chapter profited from the encouragement and suggestions of Harvey Molotch. Molotch (e.g., Molotch and Lester, 1974) and some of his students: Mark Fishman, Pam Fishman, Marilyn Lester, and David Leon are working to relate ethnomethodology with critical concerns.

2. I borrow the labels "logico-empiricism" and "hermeneutic-dialectic" from Radnitzky (1973). Interested readers will find there reviews of the literature of each tradition. Radnitzky's call for a "theory of research which is neither logical reconstruction nor psychology or sociology of science" (see especially his Volume 3) contrasts with the program developed in the present book. Gouldner (1970:488ff.) and Habermas (1971; especially 301ff.) also discuss these two traditions and a reflexive alternative.

3. Insiders to both the logico-empiricist and the hermeneutic-dialectic traditions will find my caricatures of these traditions disturbingly glib. They must realize that I do not wish to describe these traditions, but rather to use them in order to illuminate the very possibility of descriptions. They may find comfort in the knowledge that my treatment of ethnomethodology has been similarly glib.

4. For a hint of the kinds of reactions I am speaking of, see Hill and Crittenden (1968) and the edited discussion at the end of Mehan (1973:335ff.)

5. Mullins provides short bibliographies of these traditions (1973:287–293). Jay (1973:42–44) provides references to the most important recent works of the "critical theorists," most of which remain untranslated.

6. Filmer (in Filmer et al., 1973) reviews this stratifying work in Parsons's theory of classes. Silverman (1973) discusses its appearance in Davis and Moore and their critics. The strident stratifying practices of Marxist writers themselves should be obvious.

7. The journal *Telos* is a valuable resource for *theoretical* examinations of the concept of praxis I have adopted. Kosok's (1970a, 1970b, 1970c) papers there are especially valuable. Piconne's articles are also important, although as Dallmayr (1973) points out, Piconne remains committed to the possibility of transcendental truths, a faith I do not share. Dallmayr's (1973) review of Paci provides an introduction to the history of phenomenological Marxism. The articles in Israel and Tajfel (1973), especially Janousek's "On the Marxian Concept of *Praxis*," should also be consulted. Merleau-Ponty's (e.g., 1964, 1969, 1970) work has been a resource not only for this chapter but for the entire book. Pollner (1970) first illumined Merleau-Ponty's relevance for ethnomethodology.

CHAPTER TWELVE

Becoming
the
Phenomenon

This book has pointed to various phenomena that warp when passed through the grid of scientific description. The undistorting study of realities requires a new methodology that is more becoming to the phenomena realities display. One such methodology dictates that researchers themselves become the phenomena they investigate. Such an inquiry implies a relativist view of scientific procedure.

ABSOLUTIST AND RELATIVIST VIEWS OF SCIENCE

There are at least two ways of looking at science as a way of knowing. One view treats scientific propositions as direct reflections of the universe. Facts are in nature to be discovered. Truth is out there. Laws are a direct reflection of the truth in the universe. This version makes science an absolute and certain source of knowledge. It is a privileged way of knowing. The scientific method is impartial. Correctly applied, it ensures objective findings.

This "absolutist" view of science (Phillips, 1974) contrasts with a view that sees science as a human activity. In this view, scientific theories occupy no privileged epistemological status. No one belief system is superior to another, for no absolute criteria exist to make comparisons. This "relativist" view (Feyerabend, 1965a, 1965b, 1970a, 1970b, 1972; Kauffman, 1944; Phillips, 1974) treats science as a construction of human communities. All theories and facts are the result of human activities. Nature never speaks. Scientists speak about nature. There are no facts independent of a theoretical paradign (Kuhn, 1970; Polanyi, 1958, 1969). Observations always occur within a shifting web of practical circumstances.

The absolutist view of science treats the scientific method as the ultimate authority for knowledge. The relativist view says that authority for knowledge rests in the scientific community. The community of scholars constructs findings by comparing them to the standards that exist at that time. Propositions are moves in a scientific game; they are not direct reflections of nature. As Kauffman (1944:48) writes, "the idea of immediate apprehension of truth by acts of perception can not bear close examination." Scholars do not merely *match* observations with propositions. They *decide* truth through discussions, arguments, and other practical human activities. An organized consensus decides what is and what is not warranted as knowledge. Within the game of science, this is done in accordance with the established procedural rules. Scientists decide whether phenomena, propositions, or findings are part of the scientific corpus of knowledge. The truths of science are argued, not revealed.

"Good reasons" may be offered about why any particular observations validate or invalidate particular propositions. Decisions are always based on the scientific situation, including the propositions and procedural rules in effect at any particular time. "That the scientific situation changes in the course of time suggests that there can be no timeless logic of scientific procedure" (Ibid.:52-53).

I view science as a human activity no more absolute or relative than any other. I will now offer some new procedural rules for playing the social science game. I think they will make our studies more valuable both to ourselves and to others.

BECOMING THE PHENOMENON

Conventional social science investigations progress through the following stages. First, the researcher selects a phenomenon, and then applies certain methods (e.g., participant observation, experiment, the survey) to the problem. The researcher is cautioned to retain distance from the phenomenon so that "objective" findings can be obtained. After materials are gathered, the researcher leaves the field to conduct a *propositional analysis*.

This analysis separates the phenomenon into parts, and seeks relations among them. The relations have an "if . . . then" or causal quality. Propositional analysis implies that matters of fact, truth, and correctness are at stake (Schwartz, 1971). A propositional analysis seeks clarification through description (Ten Houten and Kaplan, 1973:104).

Propositional analysis demands that the findings of an investigation be compatible with the corpus of knowledge, rules, and propositions that compose "scientific knowledge" (Garfinkel, 1967:185–206) at the time of the findings. "The incumbent [is] to harmonize his sense of the situation with the external body of knowledge known as 'the literature' " (Ten Houten and Kaplan, 1973:135).

The goal of propositional analysis is the corroboration of findings. Their reliability and validity is checked against the community of scholars who make up "the discipline." "In science . . . the telling, the formalizing, to others is primary" (Ibid).

In social science, such descriptions are produced by methods not employed in the production of the phenomenon. Researchers do not report the reality work they employed in the production of findings (see Chapter 3).

If the purpose of the research is to know the reality work of a phenomenon, then the researcher must begin by first becoming the phenomenon. The researcher must become a full-time member of the reality to be studied. As I made clear in Chapter 2, my concept of reality is flexible. It collects what have been variously called "scenes," "subcultures," "cultures," "societies," and "social systems." To become the phenomenon means to do a reality as its members do.

Membership cannot be simulated. The researcher must not hold back. The researcher who holds back in the name of objectivity never comes to respect that reality or be respected by its practitioners.

Traditional field work techniques counsel researchers to withhold a part of themselves to remain "objective." As Bittner (1973) remarks, this assures that researchers will not experience as their subjects experience. The practical circumstances of the reality they are studying will not be their circumstances. As a result, they will only be able to infer the meanings events have for bona fide members. While this methodological aloofness protects researchers from becoming "merely one of them," it also effectively prohibits knowing any of them.

There is a danger. As Turnbull (1973) says, such researchers will never return the same persons they were when they began. There is the risk that they will not return at all. Analysis may be abandoned in favor of the adopted form of life.

It is time social scientists took such risks. For too long they have been speaking on behalf of others as if they were superior to them. For too long sociologists have offered policy for altering lives they have never lived. Social scientists have fed like parasites off the realities of others. We must begin to feed from our own lives or starve.

In becoming the phenomenon, the researcher does not enter a reality for the purpose of describing it. Rather than analyze an activity for its truth value, the researcher learns to do it. This implies a social science methodology where "the notion of success replaces truth as criteria for validity" (Schwartz, 1971:270). The validity of an inquiry is not tested against the corpus of scientific knowledge. It is tested against the everyday experience of a community of people. Researchers must be able to demonstrate to the natives that they can talk as they talk, see as they see, feel as they feel, do as they do. When members' "moral facts" become their moral facts, researchers will know that they have become members (cf. Schneebaum, 1969; and Chapter 2 above).

Ten Houten and Kaplan (1973) describe inquiries that are the "mirror image" of science. Where science seeks clarity, "appositional inquiries" seek opacity. Where science employs formal logic, appositional studies employ structured perception to guide investigation. Where science requires a formalized report of findings, appositional studies have no such requirement. As Ten Houten and Kaplan say:

> a practitioner reaches an understanding of his subject and knows the practices and sensual components of a situation. That one has a perception of a situation and is free to remain silent about it is a choice open in synthetic inquiries. That one senses is sufficient; telling and formalizing are of secondary importance (Ibid.:135).

Having become the phenomenon, the researcher has attained a personal knowledge. The researcher can choose to remain silent. This choice is consistent with those who compare ethnomethodology with the occult (Eglin, 1973; cf. Pollner, 1970).

If researchers wish to avoid the occult and tell of their work, there are various ways this can be done. Some of these valuable alternatives were described in the earlier chapters of this book. Kauffman (1944) recommends another. A community of scholars who have experienced a phenomenon corpus and decorpus propositions about it.

Another alternative is for researchers to display the phenomenon they have become. "A display revolves around the issue of faithfulness rather than correctness" (Schwartz 1971:263) The display is not offered as a report or description of the phenomenon. It presents a phenomenon. (Schwartz (1971) recommends various dramaturgical techniques for this purpose.

These recommendations underscore my belief that ethnomethodology is not a reading and writing discipline. It is a form of life. One must do some work before the studies mentioned in this book and listed in its bibliography will have any deep meaning.

The program outlined to this point in the chapter is an idealized program. It requires disengagement from family, job, friends. Perhaps the risks are so great that it will never be undertaken in its entirety. Few will be willing to give up their present lives so completely. A shorter entry into becoming the phenomenon is also possible. I end the book with a manual of practices that will enable people to begin their own studies in ethnomethodology. Instead of reporting about a phenomenon, they enable phenomena to be displayed. After a researcher has conducted a study using the procedures recommended here, and another asks "What *is* Ethnomethodology?" or "Tell me about ———" (an ethnomethodological concept), the researcher will be able to engage that person in one of these procedures. Doing that procedure will display the phenomenon.

A MANUAL OF PROCEDURES

The following techniques provide a means for persons to become the phenomenon. Some require more than one researcher; some require technical aids. Others can be done alone, without equipment. All require daring and perseverance. Each encourages an experience of the mutual constitution of observer and observed.

Some of these techniques have been associated with particular analyses, which I briefly mention after describing each technique. These formulations are only suggestive. Each technique is amenable to analysis drawn from ethnomethodological studies of situated rule use (see Chapter 4), or of the model of the actor (Chapter 5), or of language (Chapter 6) or scenic (Chapter 7) practices, or of dialectical dialog (Chapter 8), or of structurings (Chapter 9), or of the hermeneutic spiral (Chapter 10), or of some combination of the above, like the five features of reality (Chapter 2). The particular ethnomethodological analysis that is used is irrelevant. Others will wish to create their own (cf., e.g., Wieder, Zimmerman and Wilson, and Schwartz [Chapter 7]; Wallace [Chapter 8]; and Pollner [Chapter 11]). The *raison d'etre* of each procedure is the experience it provides its user, not the formulations that are created to index these experiences.

Occasioned Maps

"Occasioned maps" are documents drawn by persons directing others to places unknown to the map user. Researchers should encourage others to draw such documents for them when opportunity arises in their daily lives. They should study these maps prior to embarking. If possible, a tape recorder should be employed. When ready to follow the instructions, the researcher should begin by recording the meaning of the map as it appears at the point of departure. As the trip progresses, the researcher should speak into the recorder detailing the connections that are made between the symbols and the world that is encountered along the way. If and when the destination is reached, the researcher should once more talk into the tape recorder while reviewing the map, again indicating the meaning that the symbols have assumed.

Transcripts of several such trips should be assembled. Some of the maps should be used twice or more than twice. Some should be followed to the point of origin after the destination has been reached.

This procedure was developed by Garfinkel. One frequent analysis offered about this procedure elaborates Merleau-Ponty's claim (in Dreyfus and Dreyfus, 1964) that life is an unfolding wherein the "hitherto meaningless becomes meaningful." One can also search the transcripts for the documenting practices (see Chapter 7) that occasioned maps require. The procedure provides a vehicle for experiencing the mutual determinations of signs, persons, and world.

Zatocoding

Garfinkel (in Hill and Crittenden, 1968:205, 240) has adapted the system of Zatocoding developed by Mooers (1951, 1956) into another solo technique. Researchers are directed to create a collection of thoughts, references, quotes, and so forth, one to an index card. Once a collection of a hundred or more has been assembled, the researcher begins to construct a list of "descriptors." These are words or phrases that the researcher believes will index the corpus of data the cards represent. Researchers then code each of the cards with one or more descriptors. New descriptors are created as the researcher's sense of the corpus grows. New items of information are added as new thoughts, references, quotes, and so on appear.

The procedure is like entering a library that has no card catalog. Researchers construct an indexing system while simultaneously adding new items to the "library" shelves.

Once several hundred items have been indexed, researchers are directed to converse with their deck of cards. One chooses a descriptor and examines all the items that have been indexed under that title. Researchers are directed to inspect the cards to see what they share. The meaning of any inspection is presaged by the descriptor. Any similarly coded collection of çards presages the meaning of the descriptor they share as well. Descriptors that are close in meaning may be compared. The separate corpus of items they collect can be contrasted. Similarly, descriptors that seem to have no similar meanings can be compared. The more researchers converse with their decks, the more they learn about their creation. This "created" information bank comes to the researcher from without. It is external and constraining.

This procedure illumines coding and documenting practices. It has been used as well to search for properties of those practices (cf. Kaiman, 1969). Numerous analyses are possible. More importantly, the procedure enables the researcher to experience firsthand various ethno-methodological phenomena.

This procedure is arduous. Many researchers abandon it because it seems dull. Little "accountable" happens until a large deck is constructed. Perseverance furthers, however. The following are a few diary entries made by one researcher about his experiences in constructing descriptors and coding items:

> It suddenly hits me as an impossible task. I am in a flow and the task demands stability of descriptors, library, and coder/me.

> Things are getting so bad I just began marking some things off a card I had written but a few minutes before (making a correction on an example

there) and just about stopped thinking I could not "correct" anything: It had to have been correct when I wrote it. . . . If I did not make myself cease thinking as I do . . . I think I would become immobilized.

. . . the horror of becoming self-conscious of your coding-self . . . is feeling that the world does not stand still. That there is no *the* world but a swarm. And the time will be past quitting or saving one's sanity when I begin to feel that that insight too is not "something" but a temporally unfolding and evanescent creation . . . (Wood, 1969a:12).

Wood says that these entries hint at indescribable experiences. He speaks of feeling the "swarm" engulf him. He was physically ill from vertigo. In these experiences the sense of objects and self were dissolved. These diary entries preceded these dissolutions. When the vertigo was relatively mild, Wood reports "saving" his reality by escaping from his desk and, in a daze, walking the streets. An hour of "mindless" walking would bring him "back" once more to his old world. Stronger experiences passed through and "destroyed" him before he could so escape.

Similar experiences are engendered by conversing with the deck. Whatever analysis is built upon such experiences must be determined by the researcher, according to the scientific community to which the researcher wishes to speak.

Breaching with Equipment

Garfinkel has developed several techniques that require special equipment. One requires the use of inverted lenses.

These lenses are worn like glasses. They are prisms that turn the visual field upside down. Researchers are directed to wear such lenses for a specified period each day, increasing the time until they are worn for all of one waking period. Researchers are asked to attempt to continue with their ordinary routines. At first, sight-dependent tasks are very difficult or impossible. Researchers describe their activities by speaking into tape recorders. With practice, most normal tasks can once more be done. Researchers learn to conform to the old social order in a new way that preserves the old order. The transcripts and memory provide a record of this new work.

Once researchers are able to pass with inverted sight, the lenses are removed. The world is returned to its "normal" pattern. Researchers find that they are almost as incompetent as they were when they first donned the inverted lenses. They must learn once more to do the world as others do. This procedure provides experience of the taken for granted practices "normals" do "out of awareness." The technique especially reveals the embodied locus of these activities. The inverted and "normal" worlds are not in the head behind the eyes. They are worlds within which our bodies participate.

A comparable procedure Garfinkel (in Hill and Crittenden, 1968:161–168) has developed requires a recording apparatus with a side-tone delay mechanism. The researcher wears earphones connected to the machine. Sounds come to him more slowly than normal. Researchers attempt to read, or talk, or play musical instruments. Without the normal interval of reflexive sound input, these activities are at first impossible. But researchers learn to compensate. Researchers can describe the practices they use to recover speech. The experience provides an indication of the practices normals use to "compensate" for the normal delay all persons experience "out of awareness."

A related procedure Garfinkel has developed requires researchers to wear masks that leave them totally blind (see Ima, 1971). Researchers are directed not to focus on the blindness. They are told to concentrate on the practices they develop for producing an ordered world through the blindness.

Another Garfinkel procedure requires researchers to develop facility with mechanical arms, hands, and other devices for the handicapped. They learn to do the normal world with seemingly abnormal methods. This procedure, like the others, can be analyzed variously. Its prime function, however, is to make the researchers aware of the way they normally do the world by requiring them to learn to do it otherwise.

Doing Instructions

Mehan has devised a procedure for two or more researchers. One researcher devises a simple geometric shape, such as:

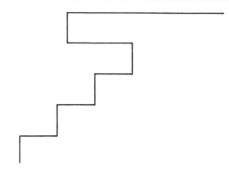

A second researcher stands at a blackboard. The first researcher talks to the second, telling him or her what to draw. Neither researcher looks at the other. Some self-correcting mechanisms of ordinary conversation are thus suspended.

The first researcher usually gives instructions like: "Draw a vertical line. Then draw a horizontal line off one end." When the instruction giver is satisfied that a full description has been given, the drawings are compared.

The discrepancies are always enormous. Researchers experience the complexity of descriptions. If they continue to practice with new figures, they learn to produce similar drawings. They learn to do new descriptive practices within a new language game. These new games compare with the descriptive practices they first employed much as scientific description does with everyday description.

Mehan has developed another instruction-following procedure that can be done by solitary researchers. Researchers are instructed to learn a new activity from a set of written rules. Hoyle's book of games, cookbooks, and sewing manuals provide a large set of possible activities. Researchers are directed to do only what the instructions say. They are neither to improvise nor to make allowances. They are to approach the document as "strict constructionists."

Researchers discover that the activities cannot be done. In following a recipe, for example, instructions are given for preparing the food, and for preheating the oven. There are seldom explicit instructions to put the food in the oven. Sometimes the instructions indicate that eggs still in their shells are to be placed in mixing bowls, or beaten with a stick, or whipped with a belt. Cookies sometimes must be dropped on the floor, not on cookie sheets. Researchers search in vain for behavioral representations of "cook until tender," "saute," "blanch," "fold."

Card games and sewing rarely even begin. Interested researchers must discover the reason for this themselves.

These procedures are obversely related to occasioned map following. Contrastive analyses of such similar procedures may be constructed, according to the experiences of the researcher.

Coordinating Practices

Schelling (1960) provides several coordination problems. Two people are asked to imagine a month, date, day of the week, place, and time they would meet each other. Mehan directs researchers to do the problems one at a time. After each person does the problem, two researchers compare predictions and discuss their reasons for choosing as they did. Researchers then do the next problem, compare answers and strategy, and then begin the next.

Researchers find that their strategies alter over the course of the exercise. As their knowledge of the other changes, their attributions to that other differ. In the beginning, strategies such as "choosing the most obvious number" are often employed. These seldom result in a coordinated choice. What is obvious for one researcher is obscure for the other. Previous familiarity with a coresearcher often impedes coordination. One researcher may choose the other's birthday; the other may choose the first's birthday. In such cases, different numbers result from a commonly adopted strategy.

This procedure is especially susceptible to analysis through the concepts of indexicality and reflexivity.

Enjambing

Jennings and Mehan (1969) have developed a procedure that requires an "enjambed conversation." An enjambed conversation is a transcript of talk stripped of all social markings. The number and social identity of speakers, turns, utterances, punctuation, and setting are omitted. One such transcript follows:

> hi come on in how are you today fine good Lillian I want you to look at some pictures with me get them in the right order what were you doing when you came playing what were you playing I was seeing books did

you do a picture today yeah what did you draw a picture of of flowers and then are you going to write a story about it um hmm what are you going to tell about in your story I don't know you haven't decided yet are you going to take a trip this summer or are you going to be here I'm going to take a trip where are you going to go to Mexico to see you grand ma yes

This material must be provided to a researcher by another party. Researchers are then given these instructions:

> Your first order of analysis is to "punctuate the conversation," then assign the words spoken to the speakers in the conversation.
>
> After you have broken the conversation into utterances and assigned turns to speakers, then answer the following questions:
>
> 1. What is the age, sex, name of each speaker?
> 2. How many people are involved?
> 3. What is the location of the encounter?
> 4. What is the relationship between the speakers (e.g., friends, members of the same family, business associates)?
> 5. What is being talked about?
>
> For each answer you give, also include the reason that you answered as you did. That is, for every answer you give, supply a justification, a "because." It is possible that you will not be able to answer each question. If you can't, say so, but also say why you can't answer the question. For example, the first question is: "What is the age of each speaker?" You might answer: "I don't know the answer to this question because there is no reference to the age of the speakers in the transcript."
>
> It is also possible that you will have more than one answer for each question. Include all the answers you have and the reasons why you think they are possible.

Researchers are required to provide reasons for their punctuation, determination of speakers, identification of speakers, and so on.

Once this first stage is complete, the researchers are provided with successive layers of additional information. Next they are allowed to hear an audio tape of the talk. They are then to answer the same set of questions in light of this knowledge. Researchers again are encouraged to provide reasons for their new analysis. A videotape of the scene is then presented and the same series of questions answered again. A new analysis is constructed on the basis of this experience.

At the end of the first stage of the analysis, analysts report difficulty in assigning utterances and turns to speakers. The number and names of speakers is not clear. Many possible places of the conversation are reported. Yet, directed to find a sense of meaning in the available information, the analysts are able to do so.

When the analysts hear the audiotape, many of the decisions made previously are called into question. Many changes in the analysis occur, while other information, such as the number, age, and sex of speakers now becomes "perfectly clear." But many questions remain unanswered.

The videotape provides visual information that supplements the auditory information presented previously. The addition of this information once again changes the interpretations made earlier. And some questions cannot be answered at all.

Each stage of the procedure produces an analysis of what the conversation "really is." Though the analysis changes as new information is acquired, the sense that the conversation is one real event remains throughout. Researchers are able to experience over the course of the procedure the various practices they have for participating in the construction of stable events. Once the videotape has been studied and a "final" analysis constructed, further information can be introduced. Researchers can once more pursue the questions considering that the display is a play, or the result of the splicing together of random events which had occurred at different times.

The Auditory Illusion

Warren (1968; Warren and Warren, 1970) have developed an "auditory illusion" effect. An audiotape is constructed that repeats a single sound. No pause occurs at the end of each utterance. People hear the voice on the tape alter, even though the same utterance occurs again and again.

Wallace has developed a procedure based on such tapes. He advises two or more researchers to listen together. At the end of one minute, the sound is discontinued. One researcher tells the other about the utterances heard. The recording is begun again. The second researcher writes the different utterances heard on a piece of paper and holds it before the first researcher, who then concentrates on this written word until it is spoken from the tape. The first researcher then presents the second with each of the other utterances heard, waiting each time until the other researcher indicates having heard them on the tape.

Once the first researcher exhausts the list, the two researchers exchange tasks. The second researcher now presents the first with any additional hearings that have not yet been shared between them.

The sound on the tape is stable. Researchers know this and yet they hear extreme changes in intonation, syllabification, and vowel sounds. These changes come from without. They are experienced as objective and constraining events in the world. A researcher looks at a printed word and shortly thereafter the voice on the tape "alters" its sound and plainly says the word. The sound may be thought of as a "stimulus." The written words are a part of the context of that stimulus. Changes in context lead to dramatic shifts in the stimulus. The procedure encourages a direct confrontation with the mutual constitution of persons, objects, and signs.

MY REALITY OF ETHNOMETHODOLOGY

In Part 3, I have indicated the form of life ethnomethodology has become for me. Unlike social science and much earlier ethnomethodology, my ethnomethodology is a form of life. It is not a body of theory nor of method. I envision ethnomethodology as a collection of practices similar in purpose to the practices artists and craftsmen teach and use. That my understanding is radically unlike contemporary social science seems a virtue to me. In committing itself above all to reporting, social science has shown itself to be a form of life that denigrates the integrity of non-Western, nonmale, nonliberal, nontechnological realities.

My vision of ethnomethodology undermines this practice. I do not suggest that social scientists cease studying human phenomena, only that they begin to use methods that are more becoming to the mysterious phenomena ethnomethodology has unearthed. To become one's own phenomenon is such a method.

Bibliography

Ackerman, Charles, and Talcott Parsons
   1966   The Concept of "Social System" as a Theoretical Device. In Gordon J. DiRenzo (ed.), *Concepts, Theory and Explanation in the Behavioral Sciences.* New York: Random House.

Anderson, Alan Ross, and Omar K. Moore
   1966   Models and Explanations in the Behavioral Sciences. In Gordon J. DiRenzo (ed.), *Concepts, Theory and Explanation in the Behavioral Sciences.* New York: Random House.

Anderson, P. W.
   1972   More Is Different. Science **177**:393–396.

Anonymous
   1970   The First *Telos* International Conference: The New Marxism. *Telos* **6**:294–317.

Austin, J. L.
   1961   *Philosophical Papers.* London: Oxford University Press.

Bar-Hillel, Yehoshua
   1954   Indexical Expressions. *Mind* **63**:359–379.

Barth, John
   1966   *Giles Goat-Boy.* Garden City, N.Y.: Doubleday & Company.

Bauman, Zygmunt
   1973   On the Philosophical Status of Ethnomethodology. *The Sociological Review* **21**: 5–23.

Becker, Ernest
   1968   *The Structure of Evil: An Essay on the Unification of the Science of Man.* New York: George Braziller.
   1971   *The Lost Science of Man.* New York: George Braziller.

Becker, Howard
   1953   *Outsiders—Studies in the Sociology of Deviance.* New York: The Free Press.
   1968   History, Culture and Subjective Experience: An Exploration of the Social Bases of Drug-Induced Experiences. *Journal of Health and Human Behavior* **8**:961–968.

Bittner, Egon

   1963   Radicalism and the Organization of Social Movements. *American Sociological Review* **28**:928–940.

   1965   The Concept of Organization. *Social Research* **32**:239–258.

   1967a The Police on Skid Row. *American Sociological Review* **32**:699–715.

   1967b Police Discretion in Emergency Apprehension of Mentally Ill Persons. *Social Problems* **14**:278–292.

   1973   Objectivity and Realism in Sociology. In Psathas, 1973.

Blake, Judith

   1961   *Family Structures in Jamaica.* New York: The Free Press.

Blum, Alan

   1970a The Corpus of Knowledge as a Normative Order: Intellectual Critiques of the Social Order of Knowledge and the Commonsense Features of Bodies of Knowledge. In John C. McKinney and Edward A. Tiryakian (eds.), *Theoretical Sociology.* New York: Appleton-Century-Crofts.

   1970b Theorizing. In Douglas, 1970.

Blum, Alan, and Peter McHugh

   1971   The Social Ascription of Motives. *American Sociological Review* **36**:1:98–109.

Blumer, Herbert

   1971   *Symbolic Interactionism.* Englewood Cliffs, N.J.: Prentice-Hall.

Borges, Luis Jorge

   1964   *Labyrinths.* New York: New Directions Publishing Corporation.

Boulding, Kenneth

 [1956] General Systems Theory—The Skeleton of Science.

   1968   In Buckley, 1968.

Brown, Roger

   1965   *Social Psychology.* New York: The Free Press.

Buckley, Walter

   1967   *Sociology and Modern Systems Theory.* Englewood Cliffs, N.J.: Prentice-Hall.

   1968   (ed.) *Modern Systems Research for the Behavioral Scientist.* Chicago: Aldine Publishing Company.

Burke, Kenneth

 [1931] *Counter-Statement.* Los Altos, Calif.: Hermes
   1953   Publications.

Campbell, Norman Robert

 [1920] *Foundations of Science: The Philosophy of Theory and Experiment.* New York: Dover Publications.

 [1921]

 [1952] *What is Science?* New York: Dover Publications.

Castaneda, Carlos

  1968   *The Teachings of Don Juan*. Berkeley: University of California Press.

  1971   *A Separate Reality*. New York: Simon & Schuster.

  1972   *A Journey to Iztlan*. New York: Simon & Schuster.

Chomsky, Noam

  1959   *Syntactic Structures*. The Hague: Mouton & Co.

  1965   *Aspects of the Theory of Syntax*. Cambridge: The M.I.T. Press.

Churchill, Lindsay

  n.d.   On Everyday Quantification Practices. Unpublished manuscript.

  1971   Ethnomethodology and Measurement. *Social Forces* **50**:182–191.

  1972   The Grammar of Questioning. Paper distributed at 23rd Annual Sociolinguistics
           Roundtable: Language and Linguistics, Georgetown University, March 16–18,
           1972.

Cicourel, Aaron V.

  1964   *Method and Measurement in Sociology*. New York: The Free Press.

  1968   *The Social Organization of Juvenile Justice*. New York: John Wiley & Sons.

  1970   Language as a Variable in Social Research. *Sociological Focus* 3:2.

  1972   Cross Modal Communication. Paper presented at the 23rd Annual
           Sociolinguistics Roundtable: Language and Linguistics, Georgetown University,
           March 16–18, 1972. In Roger Shuy (ed.), *Monograph 25, Linguistics and Language
           Science*. Washington, D.C.: Georgetown University Press, 1973.

  1973a   *Cognitive Sociology*. London: Macmillan & Co.

  1973b   *Theory and Method in a Study of Argentine Fertility*. New York: John Wiley & Sons.

  1973c   Ethnomethodology and Cognitive Theory. Paper presented at American Sociol-
           ogical Association Annual Meeting, New York, September 1, 1973.

  1973d   Memory and Interviewing. In Colin Cherry (ed.), *Theory and Decision*. Dordrecht:
           Reidel.

Cicourel, Aaron V., and John I. Kitsuse

  1963   The Educational Decision Makers. Indianapolis: The Bobbs-Merrill Co.

Cicourel, Aaron V., et al.

  1974   *Language Use and School Performance*. New York: Academic Press.

Coleman, James S.

  1968   Review: Studies in Ethnomethodology. *American Sociological Review* **33**:122–130.

Comte, Auguste

  1853   *The Positive Philosophy of Auguste Comte*. Translated and condensed by H. Martin-
  [1953] eau. London: J. Chapman.

Crowle, Anthony

  1971   Post Experimental Interviews: An Experiment and a Sociolinguistic Analysis.
           Unpublished Ph.D. dissertation. University of California, Santa Barbara.

d'Alembert, Jean Le Rond
[1751]
    1963   Preliminary Discourse to the Encyclopedia of *Diderot*. Indianapolis: The
            Bobbs-Merrill Co.

Dallmayr, Fred R.
    1973   Phenomenology and Marxism: A Salute to Enzo Paci. In Psathas, 1973.

Douglas, Jack D.
    1967   *The Social Meaning of Suicide*. Princeton; N.J.: Princeton University Press.
    1970   (ed.) *Understanding Everyday Life*. Chicago: Aldine Publishing Company.

Dreyfus, Hubert L., and Patricia Allen Dreyfus
    1964   Translators' Introduction. In Merleau-Ponty, 1964.

Durkheim, Emile
    1938   *The Rules of Sociological Method*. Chicago: University of Chicago Press.

Eglin, Trent
    1973   Introduction to a Hermeneutics of the Occult: Alchemy. Unpublished manu-
            script, UCLA.

Emerson, Robert M.
    1969   *Judging Delinquents*. Chicago: Aldine Publishing Company.
    1972   Notes on Discretion as a Reflexive Feature of the Criminal Process: Shoplifting
            Materials. Unpublished working draft, UCLA.

Emerson, Robert, and Melvin Pollner
    in preparation
            Studies of Psychiatric Emergency Teams. Department of Sociology, UCLA.

Ervin-Tripp, Susan
    1973   *Language Acquisition and Communicative Choice*. Stanford: Stanford University
            Press.

Evans-Pritchard, E. E.
    1937   *Witchcraft, Oracles and Magic Among the Azande*. London: Oxford University Press.

Feyerabend, Paul F.
    1965a   On the "Meaning" of Scientific Terms. *Journal of Philosophy* **62**:266–274.
    1965b   Problems of Empiricism. In Robert G. Colodny (ed.), *Beyond the Edge of Certainty*.
            Englewood Cliffs, N.J.: Prentice-Hall.
    1970a   Problems of Empiricism, Part II. In Robert G. Colodny (ed.), *The Nature and
            Function of Scientific Theories*. Pittsburgh: University of Pittsburgh Press.
    1970b   Consolations for the Specialist. In I. Lakatos and A. Musgrave (eds.), *Criticism
            and the Growth of Knowledge*. New York: Cambridge University Press.
    1972   *Against Method*. London: New Left Books.

Filmer, Paul, M.
    1973   Sociology and Social Stratification in Filmer, et al. 1973.

Filmer, Paul, M. Phillipson, M. Roche, B. Sandywell, and D. Silverman

    1973   Stratifying Practices. Unpublished manuscript. Goldsmith's College, London.

Friedman, Maurice S.

    1967   *To Deny Our Nothingness: Contemporary Images of Man.* New York: Delacorte Press.

Garfinkel, Harold

    1952   Perception of the Other. Unpublished Ph.D. dissertation. Harvard University.

    1956a Conditions of Successful Degradation Ceremonies. *American Journal of Sociology* **61**:420–424.

    1956b Some Sociological Concepts of Methods for Psychiatrists. *Psychiatric Research Reports* **6**:181–195.

    1959   Aspects of the Problem of Common Sense Knowledge of Social Structures. *Transactions of the Fourth World Congress of Sociology,* **4**:51–65. Milan: Stressa.

    1960   The Rational Properties of Scientific and Common Sense Activities. *Behavioral Science* **5**:72–83. (Chapter 8 in Garfinkel, 1967a.)

    1962   Common Sense Knowledge of Social Structures: The Documentary Method of Interpretation. In Jordan M. Scher (ed.), *Theories of the Mind.* New York: The Free Press.

    1963   A Conception of and Experiments with "Trust" as a Condition of Concerted Stable Actions. In O. J. Harvey (ed.), *Motivation and Social Interaction.* New York: The Ronald Press Company.

    1964   Studies of the Routine Grounds of Everyday Activities. *Social Problems* **11**:225–250 (Chapter 2 in Garfinkel, 1967a.)

    1967a *Studies in Ethnomethodology.* New York: Prentice-Hall.

    1967b Practical Sociological Reasoning. In Edwin S. Schneidman (ed.), *Essays in Self Destruction.* New York: International Science Press.

Garfinkel, Harold, and Harvey Sacks

    1970   The Formal Properties of Practical Actions. In John C. McKinney and Edward A. Tiryakian (eds.), *Theoretical Sociology.* New York: Appleton-Century-Crofts.

Gasking, Douglas

    1955   Mathematics and the World. In Anthony Flew (ed.), *Logic and Language.* Garden City, N.Y.: Doubleday & Company; Anchor Books.

Goffman, Erving

    1959   *The Presentation of Self in Everyday Life.* Garden City; N.Y.: Doubleday & Company; Anchor Books.

    1961   *Encounters.* Indianapolis: The Bobbs-Merrill Co.

    1969   *Strategic Interaction.* Philadelphia: University of Pennsylvania Press.

Goldthorpe, John H.

    1973   A Revolution in Sociology? (Review article.) *Sociology* **7**, 3:449–462.

Gouldner, Alvin W.

    1970   *The Coming Crisis of Western Sociology.* New York: Basic Books.

Gurwitsch, Aron
    1964   *The Field of Consciousness.* Pittsburgh: Duquesne University Press.
    1966   *Studies in Phenomenology and Psychology.* Evanston, Ill.: Northwestern University Press.

Habermas, Jurgen
    1970a Toward a Theory of Communicative Competence. In Hans Peter Dreitzel (ed.), *Recent Sociology No. 2.* New York: Macmillan.
    1970b *Toward a Rational Society: Student Protest, Science and Politics.* Boston: Beacon Press.
    1971   *Knowledge and Human Interests.* Boston: Beacon Press.

Handel, Judith
    1972   Learning to Categorize. Unpublished Ph.D. dissertation. University of California, Santa Barbara.

Handel, Warren
    1972   Perception as a Constructive Process. Unpublished Ph.D. dissertation. University of California, Santa Barbara.

Hansen, James E.
    1967   Dialectical Critique of Empiricism. *Catalyst* **3**:1–19.

Heap, James L., and Phillip A. Roth
    1973   On Phenomenological Sociology. *American Sociological Review* **38**:354–367.

Heidegger, Martin
    1962   *Being and Time.* New York: Harper & Row.

Herrnstein, James
    1971   IQ. *The Atlantic Monthly,* September:43–64.

Hill, R. C., and K. S. Crittenden (eds.)
    1968   *The Purdue Symposium on Ethnomethodology.* Monograph No. 1, Institute for the Study of Social Change. Purdue University.

Hobbes, Thomas
[1651]
    1962   *Leviathan.* New York: Macmillan.

Hodges, H. A.
    1944   *Wilhelm Dilthey.* London: Routledge & Kegan Paul.

Holt, John
    1964   *How Children Fail.* New York: Pittman Publishing Corporation.

Husserl, Edmond
    1913   *Ideas.* London: George Allen & Unwin.

Hymes, Dell (ed.)
    1973   *Re-Inventing Anthropology.* New York: Basic Books.

Ima, Kenji
   1971   Unpublished Lectures, Illinois Institute of Technology.

Israel, Joachim and Henri Tajfel (eds.)
   1972   *The Context of Social Psychology: A Critical Assessment.* New York: Academic Press

James, William
   [1890]
   1950   *The Principles of Psychology.* New York: Dover Publications.
   [1909-
   1912]
   1967a *Essays in Radical Empiricism* [*and*] *A Pluralistic Universe.* Gloucester, Mass.:
          Peter Smith.
   1967b *The Writings of William James.* John J. McDermott (ed.) New York: Random
          House.

Janoušek, Jaromir, On the Marxian Concept of Praxis. In Israel and Tajfel, 1972

Jay, Martin
   1973   Recent Developments in Critical Theory. *Berekley Journal of Sociology,* **18**:27–44.

Jennings, Kenneth L.
   1968   Notes On a Theory of Experiments. Presented in partial fulfillment of M.A.
          program. University of California, Santa Barbara. Presented at Language, Society
          and the Child: Summer workshops in Sociolinguistics, University of California,
          Berkeley.
   1972   Language Acquisition: The Development of Rational and Rationalizable Skills.
          Ph.D. dissertation. University of California, Santa Barbara.

Jennings, Kenneth L., and Sybillyn Jennings
   1974   Tests and Experiments. In Cicourel et al., 1974.

Jennings, Kenneth L., and Hugh Mehan
   1969   Enjambing: A Mechanical Method to Make Interpretive Procedures Visible.
          Unpublished manuscript. University of California, Santa Barbara.

Jensen, Arthur
   1969   How Much Can We Boost IQ and Scholastic Achievement? *Harvard Educational
          Review* **39**:1–123.

Jules-Rosette, Bennetta
   forth-
   coming Song and Spirit: Their Use in the Management of Ritual Context. *Africa.*

   1973   Ritual Context and Social Action. Unpublished Ph.D. dissertation. Harvard Uni-
          versity.

Jung, C. G.
   1963   Psychological Commentary. In Walter Y. Evans-Wentz (ed.), *The Tibetan Book
          of the Great Liberation.* London and New York: Oxford University Press.

Kaiman, Ron

   1969   A Companion to Wood's Zato Coding as a Model for Ethnomethodology. Unpublished paper presented to a seminar led by Don H. Zimmerman. University of California, Santa Barbara, April 9, 1969.

Kalish, Donald, and Richard Montague

   1959   *Principles of Logic*. Los Angeles: University of California Student's Store.

Kaplan, Abraham

   1964   *The Conduct of Inquiry*. San Francisco: Chandler Publishing Company.

Kauffman, Felix

   1944   *Methodology of the Social Sciences*. New York: Humanities Press.

Kiley, John F.

   1969   *Einstein and Aquinas: A Reapproachment*. The Hague: Martinus Nijhoff.

Kinch, John W.

   1963   A Formalized Theory of the Self Concept. *American Journal of Sociology* **68**:481–486.

Kitsuse, John I., and Aaron V. Cicourel

   1963   The Use of Official Statistics. *Social Problems* **11**, 2:131–139.

Kosok, Michael

   1970a The Dynamics of Paradox: Phenomenological Dialectics of Science. *Telos* **5**:31–43.

   1970b The Dialectical Matrix: Towards Phenomenology as a Science.*Telos* **5**:115–159.

   1970c The Dialectics of Nature: A Unified Field Theory of the Sciences. *Telos* **6**:47–103.

   1971   A Proposal for A Symposium in Nonlinear Research in Sciences and Humanities. Unpublished Paper, Department of Physics, Fairleigh Dickinson University, Rutherford, New Jersey.

Kroeber, Theodora

   1961   *Ishi in Two Worlds*. Berekley: University of California Press.

Kuhn, Thomas S.

   1970   *The Structure of Scientific Revolutions*. Chicago: University of Chicago Press.

Labov, William

   1969   *The Logic of Nonstandard English*. Urbana, Ill.: National Council of Teachers of English.

Laing, R. D.

   1967   *The Politics of Experience*. New York: Basic Books.

Laing, R. D., and A. Esterson

   1970   *Sanity, Madness and the Family*. London: Penguin Books.

Lazarsfeld, Paul F.

   1958   Evidence and Inference in Social Research. *Daedalus* **87**:99–130.

   1966   Concept Formation and Measurement in the Behavioral Sciences: Some Historical Observations. In Gordon J. DiRenzo (ed.), *Concepts, Theory and Explanation in the Behavioral Sciences.* New York: Random House.

Leach, Edmund

1974   Anthropology Upside Down. *New York Review of Books* **21**:33–35.

Leiter, Kenneth

1969   Getting It Done. Unpublished M.A. thesis. University of California, Santa Barbara.

1971   Telling It Like It Is: A Study of Teachers' Accounts. Unpublished Ph.D. dissertation. University of California, Santa Barbara.

1974   Ad Hocing in the Schools. In Cicourel et al., 1974.

Lewis, C. I.

1918   *A Survey of Symbolic Logic.* Berkeley: University of California Press.

Lovejoy, Arthur O.

[1936]
1960   *The Great Chain of Being.* New York: Harper Torchbooks.

MacKay, Robert

1973   Conceptions òf Children and Models of Socialization. In Hans P. Dreitzel (ed.), *Childhood and Socialization.* New York: Macmillan.

1974   Standardized Tests: Objective and Objectivized Measures. In Cicourel et al., 1974.

Malraux, Andre

[1967]
1968   *Antimemoirs.* New York: Holt, Rinehart and Winston.

Mangalo, B. K.

n.d.   *A Manual of Recognition.* London: The Buddhist Society.

Manis, Jerome G., and Bernard N. Meltzer

1967   *Symbolic Interaction.* Boston: Allyn & Bacon.

Mannheim, Karl

1952   *Essays in the Sociology of Knowledge.* Paul Kecskemeti (ed.). New York: Oxford University Press.

Manning, Peter K.

1973   Existential Sociology. *Sociological Quarterly* **12**, 2:200–225.

Manning, Peter K., and Horacio Fabrega, Jr.

1973   The Experience of Self and Body: Health and Illness in the Chiapas Highlands. In Psathas, 1973.

Marx, Karl

1947   *Theses on Feuerbach. The German Ideology, Parts I and III.* New York: International Publishers Co.

1959   *Economic and Philosophic Manuscripts of 1844.* Moscow: Progress Publishers.

[1867]   *The Poverty of Philosophy.* New York: International Publishers Co.
1963

1967   *Capital. Vol. I: A Critical Analysis of Capitalist Production.* New York: International Publishers Co.

1971   *Marx's Grundrisse.* O. McLellan (ed.). London: Macmillan & Co.

McHugh, Peter

1968   *Defining the Situation.* Indianapolis: The Bobbs-Merrill Co.

1970   On the Failure of Positivism. In Douglas, 1970.

McHugh, Peter, Stanley Raffel, Daniel C. Foss, and Alan F. Blum

1974   *On the Beginning of Social Inquiry.* London: Routledge & Kegan Paul.

Mead, George Herbert

1934   *Mind, Self, and Society.* Chicago: University of Chicago Press.

1959   *The Philosophy of the Present.* La Salle, Ill.: Open Court Publishing Company.

Mehan, Hugh

1972   Language Using Abilities. *Language Sciences* **22**:1–10.

1973   Assessing Children's Language Using Abilities. In J. Michael Armer and Allen D. Grimshaw (eds.), *Methodological Issues in Comparative Sociological Research.* New York: John Wiley & Sons.

1974   Accomplishing Classroom Lessons. In Cicourel et al., 1974.

Mehan, Hugh, and Houston Wood

1969   A Proposal for a Theory of Talk. Unpublished paper presented to a seminar led by Don H. Zimmerman. University of California, Santa Barbara, January 21, 1969.

Merleau-Ponty, Maurice

1962   *Phenomenology of Perception.* London: Routledge & Kegan Paul.

1964   *Sense and Non-Sense.* Evanston, Ill.: Northwestern University Press.

1969   *Humanism and Terror.* Boston: Beacon Press.

1970   Western Marxism. *Telos* **6**:140–161.

Moerman, Michael

1972   Analysis of Lue Conversation. In David Sudnow (ed.), 1972.

Molotch, Harvey, and Marilyn Lester

1974   News as Purposive Behavior. American Sociological Review **39**; 101–12.

Mooers, Calvin

1951   Zatocoding Applied to the Mechanical Organization of Knowledge. *American Documentation* **2**, 1:20–32.

1956   Zatocoding and Developments in Information Retrieval. *ASCITS Proceedings,* vol. 8.

Mullins, Nicholas J.

1973   *Theories and Theory Groups in Contemporary American Sociology.* New York: Harper & Row

Nagel, Ernest

1961   *The Structure of Science.* New York: Harcourt Brace Jovanovich.

Norman, Donald A.
  1969 *Memory and Attention.* New York: John Wiley & Sons.

Novak, Michael
  1971 *The Experience of Nothingness.* New York: Harper Colophon Books.

Palmer, E. R.
  1968 *Hermeneutics.* Evanston, Ill.: Northwestern University Press.

Parsons, Talcott
  [1937]
  1949 *The Structure of Social Action.* New York: The Free Press.

Parsons, Talcott, and Edward Shils (eds.)
  1951 *Towards a General Theory of Action.* New York: The Free Press.

Peirce, Charles Saunders
  1933 *Collected Papers.* Cambridge: Harvard University Press.
  1957 *Essays in the Philosophy of Science.* New York: Liberal Arts Press.

Pepper, Stephen
  1942 *World Hypotheses.* Berkeley: University of California Press.

Phillips, Derek
  1971 *Knowledge from What?* Chicago: Rand McNally & Company.
  1974 Epistemology and the Sociology of Knowledge. *Theory and Society* **1**:59–88.

Phillipson, Michael
  1973 In Filmer et al 1973.

Piccone, Paul
  1970 What Is the Crisis? Unpublished manuscript. Quoted in *Telos* **6**:340.

Polanyi, Michael
  1958 *Personal Knowledge.* Chicago: University of Chicago Press.
  1966 *The Tacit Dimension.* Garden City, N.Y.: Doubleday & Company.
  1969 *Knowing and Being.* Chicago: University of Chicago Press.

Pollner, Melvin
  1970 On the Foundations of Mundane Reason. Unpublished Ph.D. dissertation. University of California, Santa Barbara.
  1973 The Very Coinage of Your Brain: The Resolution of Reality Disjunctures.
  1974 Mundane Reasoning. *Philosophy of Social Sciences,* vol 4, 1:35–54.
  forth-
  coming Notes on Self Explicating Fields of Action. In Roy Turner (ed.), *Socialization: The Acquisition of Membership.* New York: Basic Books.

Pope, Whitney
  1973 Classic on Classic: Parsons' Interpretation of Durkheim. *American Sociological Review* **38**:399–415.

Prosch, Harry

   1973   Polanyi's Tacit Knowing in the "Classic" Philosophers. *Journal of the British Society for Phenomenology* **4**:201–216.

Psathas, George (ed.)

   1973   *Phenomenological Sociology*. New York: John Wiley & Sons.

Psathas, George, and Frances C. Waksler

   1973   Essential Features of Face-to-Face Interaction. In Psathas, 1973.

Radnitzky, Gerard

   1973   *Contemporary Schools of Metascience*. Chicago: Henry Regnery Company.

Ramos, Reyes

   1973a   The Production of Social Reality. Unpublished Ph.D. dissertation. University of Colorado, Boulder.

   1973b   A Case in Point. *Social Science Quarterly* **53**:905–919.

Reich, Charles A.

   1970   *The Greening of America*. New York: Random House.

Riel, Margaret M.

   1972   The Interpretive Process. Unpublished paper presented to a seminar led by Paul Filmer, University of California, San Diego.

Roche, Maurice

   1973   Class Analysis and the Showing of Dichotomy. In: Filmer et al., 1973.

Rosen, Stanley

   1969   *Nihilism: A Philosophical Essay*. New Haven: Yale University Press.

Roszak, Theodore

   1969   *The Making of a Counter Culture*. Garden City, N.Y.: Doubleday & Company.

   1973   *Where the Wasteland Ends*. Garden City, N.Y.: Doubleday & Company, Anchor Books.

Roth, David R.

   1972   Children's Linguistic Performance as a Factor in School Achievement. Unpublished Ph.D. dissertation. University of California, Santa Barbara.

Russell, Bertrand

   1940   *Inquiry into Meaning and Truth*. New York: W. W. Norton & Company.

Sacks, Harvey

   1963   Sociological Description. *Berkeley Journal of Sociology* **8**:1–17.

   1965–
   1968   Unpublished lectures at University of California, Los Angeles and Irvine.

   1966   The Search for Help: No One to Turn to. Unpublished Ph.D. dissertation. University of California, Berkeley.

1972a An Initial Investigation of the Usability of Conversational Data for Doing Sociology. In Sudnow, 1972.

1972b Notes on Police Assessment of Moral Character. In Sudnow, 1972.

1972c On the Analyzability of Stories by Children. In J. J. Gumperz and Dell Hymes (eds.), *Directions in Sociolinguistics*. New York: Holt, Rinehart and Winston.

1973 On Some Puns with Some Imitations. In Roger Shuy (ed.), *Monograph 25, Linguistics and Language Science*. Washington, D.C.: Georgetown University Press.

Sacks, Harvey, Emmanuel Schegloff, and Gail Jefferson

1974 A Simplest Systematics for the Analysis of Turn Taking in Conversation. *Language*. **50**:696–735.

Sandywell, Barry

1973 Introduction; and Marx, Alienation and Speech. In Filmer et al., 1973.

Schegloff, Emmanuel A.

1967 The First Five Seconds. Unpublished Ph.D. dissertation. University of California, Berkeley.

1968 Sequencing in Conversational Openings. *American Anthropologist* **70**:1075–1095.

1972 Notes on a Conversational Practice: Formulating Place. In Sudnow, 1972.

Schegloff, Emmanuel A., and Harvey Sacks

1973 Opening Up Closings. *Semiotica* **8**:289–327.

Schelling, Thomas A.

1960 *The Strategy of Conflict*. New York: Oxford University Press.

Schenkein, Jim

1972 Towards an Analysis of Natural Conversation and the Sense of Heheh. *Semiotica* **6**:344–377.

Schneebaum, Tobias

1969 *Keep the River On Your Right*. New York: Grove Press, Inc.

Schroyer, Trent

1971 The Critical Theory of Late Capitalism. George Fischer (ed.), *The Revival of American Socialism*. New York: Oxford University Press.

Schutz, Alfred

1962 *Collected Papers I: The Problem of Social Reality*. The Hague: Martinus Nijhoff.

1964 *Collected Papers II: Studies in Social Theory*. The Hague: Martinus Nijhoff.

1966 *Collected Papers III: Studies in Phenomenological Philosophy*. The Hague: Martinus Nijhoff.

1967 *The Phenomenology of the Social World*. Evanston, Ill.: Northwestern University Press.

1970a *On Phenomenology and Social Relations*. Chicago: University of Chicago Press.

1970b *Reflections on the Problem of Relevance*. New Haven: Yale University Press.

Schwartz, Howard
  1971   Mental Disorder and the Study of Subjective Experience: Some Uses of Each
          to Elucidate the Other. Unpublished Ph.D. dissertation. UCLA.
  n.d.   Towards a Phenomenology of Projection Errors. Unpublished paper. Depart-
          ment of Sociology, Harvard University.

Shumsky, Marshall
  1972   Encounter Groups: A Forensic Science. Unpublished Ph.D. dissertation. Univer-
          sity of California, Santa Barbara.

Shumsky, Marshall, and Hugh Mehan
  1974   The Comparability Practice of Description in Two Evaluative Contexts. Paper
          prepared for presentation at 8th World Congress of Sociology, Toronto,
          Canada, August 18–23, 1974.

Silverman, Charles E.
  1970   *Crisis in the Classroom.* New York: Random House.

Silverman, David
  1973   Davis and Moore, Market Speech and Community. In Filmer et al.,.1973.

Speier, Mathew
  1973   *How to Observe Face to Face Communication.* Pacific Palisades, Calif.: Goodyear Pub-
          lishing Co.

Stycos, J. Mayone
  1955   *Family and Fertility in Puerto Rico.* New York: Columbia University Press.

Sudnow, David
  1965   Normal Crimes. *Social Problems* **12**:255–276.
  1969   *Passing On: The Social Organization of Dying.* Englewood Cliffs, N.J.: Prentice-Hall.
  1972   (ed.) *Studies in Interaction.* New York: The Free Press.

Ten Houten, Warren, and Charles Kaplan
  1973   *Science and Its Mirror Image.* New York: Harper & Row.

Trow, Martin A.
  1963   Notes on Sociological Research. In Leonard Brown and Philip Selznick (eds.),
          Sociology. New York: Harper & Row.

Turnbull, Colin M.
  1973   Human Nature and Primal Man. *Social Research* **40**:511–30.

Turner, Roy
  1970   Words, Utterances and Activities. In Douglas, 1970.
  1972   Some Formal Properties of Therapy Talk. In Sudnow, 1972.

Wallace, H. Thomas
  1972   Culture and Social Being. Unpublished M.A. thesis. University of California,
          Santa Barbara.
  1973   Untitled, unpublished papers.

forth-
coming Culture and Social Being: An Ethnography of an Ethnography of Freaks. Unpublished Ph.D. dissertation. University of California, Santa Barbara.

Warren, Richard M.
1968 Verbal Transformation Effect of Auditory Perceptual Mechanisms. *Psychological Bulletin* **70**:261–270.

Warren, Richard M., and Roslyn P. Warren
1970 Auditory Illusions and Confusions. *Scientific American* **223**:30–43

Weber, Max
1947 *The Theory of Social and Economic Organization.* New York: The Free Press.

Wedow, Susan
1973 From the Zodiac to Everyday Life. Unpublished Ph.D. dissertation. University of California, Santa Barbara.

Whyte, W. H.
1955 *Street Corner Society.* Chicago: University of Chicago Press.

Wieder, D. Lawrence
1970 Meaning by Rule. In Douglas, 1970.
1973 *Language and Social Reality.* The Hague: Mouton.

Wieder, D. Lawrence, and Don H. Zimmerman
1973 On Explaining by Rule. Unpublished manuscript. University of California, Santa Barbara.

Wilson, Thomas P.
1970 Conceptions of Interaction and Forms of Sociological Explanation. *American Sociological Review* **35**:697–709.
1971 The Regress Problem and the Problem of Evidence in Ethnomethodology. Paper presented at American Sociological Association Annual Meeting, Denver, August 31, 1971.

Wittgenstein, Ludwig
[1921]
1961 *Tractatus Logico-Philosphicus.* London: Basil Blackwell, & Mott.
1953 *Philosophical Investigations.* London: Basil Blackwell & Mott.

Wood, Houston
1968 The Labelling Process on a Mental Hospital Ward. Unpublished M.A. thesis. University of California, Santa Barbara.
1969a Zato-Coding as a Model for Ethnomethodology. Revision of a paper presented to a seminar led by Harold Garfinkel. University of California, Los Angeles, February 14, 1969.
1969b Notes on Some Criteria for Doing Science. Unpublished paper. Department of Sociology, University of California, Santa Barbara.

Zimmerman, Don H.

   1966   Paper Work and People Work. Unpublished Ph.D. dissertation. University of California, Los Angeles.

   1969   Tasks and Troubles. In Donald A. Hansen (ed.), *Explorations in Sociology and Counseling.* Boston: Houghton Mifflin Company.

   1970a Record Keeping and the Intake Process in a Public Welfare Agency. In Stanton Wheeler (ed.), *On Record.* New York: Basic Books.

   1970b The Practicalities of Rule Use. In Douglas, 1970.

   1973   Preface to Wieder, 1973.

Zimmerman, Don H., and Melvin Pollner

   1970   The Everyday World as a Phenomenon. In Douglas, 1970.

Zimmerman, Don H., and D. Lawrence Wieder

   1970   Reply to Denzin. In Douglas 1970.

   n.d.   *The Social Bases for Illegal Behavior in the Student Community: First Year Report.* San Francisco and Santa Barbara: Scientific Analysis Corporation.

Zimmerman, Don H., and Thomas P. Wilson

   1973   Prospects for Experimental Studies of Meaning-Structures. Paper presented at American Sociological Association Annual Meeting, New York, August, 1973.

Subject Index